Tending the Flock

Congregations and Family Ministry

K. Brynolf Lyon
Archie Smith, Jr.
editors

Westminster John Knox Press
Louisville, Kentucky

Book and cover design by Jennifer K. Cox

First Edition

Published by Westminster John Knox Press
Louisville, Kentucky

This book is printed on acid-free paper that meets the American National Standards Institute Z39.48 standard. ∞

PRINTED IN THE UNITED STATES OF AMERICA

98 99 00 01 02 03 04 05 06 07 — 10 9 8 7 6 5 4 3 2 1

Library of Congress Catologing-in-Publication Data
Tending the flock : congregations and family ministry / K. Brynolf
    Lyon and Archie Smith, editors.
        p.   cm. — (The family, religion, and culture)
    Includes bibliographical references.
    ISBN 0-664-25627-9
    1. Family—Religious aspects—Case studies.   2. United States—Religion—1960–
—Case studies.   3.Family—Religious aspects—Christianity—Case studies.   4. Church
work with families—United States—Case studies.   I. Lyon, K. Brynolf, 1953– .
II. Smith, Archie, 1939– .   III. Series.
BL2525.T46   1998
259′.1′0973—dc21   98-7434

Contents

Series Foreword

There is an important debate going on today over the present health and future well-being of families in American society. Although some people on the political right and left use concern about the state of the family primarily to further their respective partisan causes, the debate is real, and it is over genuine issues. The discussion, however, is not well informed and is riddled with historical, theological, and social-scientific ignorance.

This is not unusual as political debates go. The American family debate, however, is especially uninformed and dogmatic. This is understandable, for all people have experienced a family in some way, feel themselves to be experts, and believe that they are entitled to their strong opinions.

The books in this series, The Family, Religion, and Culture, discuss these issues in ways that will place the American debate about the family on more solid ground. The series is the result of the Religion, Culture, and Family project, which was funded by a generous grant from the Division of Religion of the Lilly Endowment, and took place in the Institute for Advanced Study in the University of Chicago Divinity School. Part of the project proceeded while Don Browning, the project director, was in residence at the Center of Theological Inquiry in Princeton, New Jersey.

The series advances no single point of view on the American family debate and gives no one solution to the problems concerning families today. The authors and editors contributing to the volumes represent both genders as well as a variety of religious and ethnic perspectives and denominational backgrounds—liberal and conservative; Protestant, Catholic, and Jewish; evangelical and mainline; and black, white, and Asian. A number of the authors and editors met annually for a seminar and discussed—often with considerable intensity—their outlines, papers, and chapters pertaining to the various books. The careful reader will notice that many of the seminar members did influence one another; but, it is safe to say, each of them in the end took his or her counsel and spoke out of his or her own convictions.

The series is comprehensive, with studies on the family in ancient Israel and early Christianity; economics and the family; law, feminism, and reproductive technology and the family; the family and American faith traditions; and congregations and families; as well as two summary books—one a handbook and one a critical overview of the American family debate.

The stories in *Tending the Flock* are fascinating reading. Fifteen years ago when Professor James Hopewell, with the support of the Lilly Endowment, Inc., introduced congregational studies to theological education, we learned how riveting the stories and histories of congregations actually can be. Add the account of their work with families, and the narrative gets even richer.

But there is more than a good read in the case studies that Professors Bernie Lyon and Archie Smith have assembled in this book. Churches, both conservative and liberal, are profoundly disturbed, if not confused, about how to address the changing American family. Should churches try to stop these changes? If so, in the name of what—some nineteenth century model of the industrial family or some deeper truths to be found in the Christian faith? Or should churches attempt to adapt to these new family trends? If so, will they lose their souls to the cultural and social forces disrupting families so profoundly?

The congregational ministries to families found in this book will expand your imagination about the meaning of family ministry. We do not present them as ideal ministries, although many are quite effective. We offer them as suggestive, enriching, and thought provoking. We guarantee that you will learn something relevant to your ministry with families from each of these congregations, even if in the end you disagree with their basic direction. Your sympathies will be enlarged, your insights deepened, and your strategies sharpened by reading this book.

Don S. Browning
Ian S. Evison

Contributors

BRITA L. GILL-AUSTERN, PH.D., is associate professor of pastoral care and practical theology at Andover Newton School of Theology in Newton Centre, Massachusetts. She is the author of numerous articles focusing on the spirituality and psychology of women, pastoral theology, and congregational studies.

SANDRA SMITH BLAIR, M.A., is a doctoral candidate in historical studies at the Graduate Theological Union in Berkeley, California, and an adjunct faculty member at Pacific School of Religion. She also serves as associate minister at St.Paul's African Methodist Episcopal Church in Berkeley. Her research interests include the African American church, social reform movements, and women's history.

LOIS GEHR LIVEZEY, PH.D., is professor of Christian ethics at McCormick Theological Seminary in Chicago. She previously taught at Princeton Theological Seminary and is the author of numerous articles on justice, sexuality, and gender. Her current research focuses on sexual and domestic violence.

LOWELL LIVEZEY, D.MIN., is director of the Religion in Urban America Program at the University of Illinois at Chicago. He is author of *Non-Governmental Organizations and the Ideas of Human Rights*. His current research concerns the ways Chicago-area religious organizations serve urban people and address the issues of a rapidly restructuring metropolis.

K. BRYNOLF LYON, PH.D., is associate professor of practical theology and pastoral care at Christian Theological Seminary in Indianapolis. He is author of *Toward a Practical Theology of Aging* and a co-author of *From Culture Wars to Common Ground: Religion and the American Family Debate*. His current resarch focuses on the role of group dynamics in practical reasoning.

MICHAEL J. MCGINNIS, F.S.C., PH.D., is president of Christian Brothers University in Memphis. He previously served as professor and chair of the religion department at La Salle University in Philadelphia. His research addresses the theology of local congregations, spirituality, and the mission of independent, religiously affiliated universities in U.S. higher education.

BARBARA MCGINNIS-GILLISPIE, M.DIV., is a doctoral candidate in practical theology at the University of Chicago Divinity School. She most recently served as minister of Christian development at University Church in Chicago. Her research focuses on ministry with families in a manner drawing on the resources of the faith.

PAUL D. NUMRICH, PH.D., is research associate in the Religion in Urban America Program at the University of Illinois at Chicago. He is author of *Old Wisdom in the New World*. His research focuses on new immigrant religion in the United States and the growth of religion in "edge city" metropolitan regions.

DENISE SENTER, M.A., is a psychotherapist in private practice in Indianapolis and a consultant to mental health professionals. Her research addresses issues concerning antisocial children and the relationship of families, communities, and children's needs.

MAUREEN KELLY SIMONE, M.A., is pastoral associate at Saint Gabriel Catholic Church in Marlboro, New Jersey. Her research interests address youth in Christian communities and the changing roles of women in the Roman Catholic community.

ARCHIE SMITH, JR., PH.D., is the James and Clarice Foster Professor of Pastoral Psychology and Counseling at the Pacific School of Religion and Graduate Theological Union in Berkeley, California. He is author of *The Relational Self: Ethics and Therapy from a Black Church Perspective* and *Navigating the Deep River: Spirituality in African-American Families*.

D. MARK WILSON, M.DIV., is a doctoral candidate in sociology at the University of Michigan. He is senior pastor of McGee Avenue Baptist Church in Berkeley, California. His research interests focus on religion and social inequality and the challenges of multiculturalism.

Introduction

K. BRYNOLF LYON
ARCHIE SMITH, JR.

> The family as an institution has been declining since the beginning of history. It has lost functions to other institutions, and the nuclear family has become "isolated" or detached from the larger kinship group. Much of this decline is associated with human progress, especially individual freedom and personal and social achievement. . . . In recent decades the family has declined still further, not just changed as some scholars would have it. . . . Unlike previous family decline, this decline has led not to individual and social progress but to rising individual and social pathology—delinquency and crime, drug and alcohol abuse, suicide, depression, and eating disorders.
>
> —David Popenoe

> As we become increasingly a nation of wanderers, our lack of steady and sustained social connections—and consequent lack of competence in relationship skills—provokes even higher rates of depression. Our ethos of extreme individuality and personal rights over collective responsibility and social accommodation increases the likelihood that we will be lonely and depressed without the deep ties to family and friends that can immunize us against alienation and despair.
>
> —Michael Yapko

What is happening to Western families in general and American families in particular? At least since the Industrial Revolution, technological innovations, demographic shifts, cultural revolutions, social structural changes, and alterations in the political economies of Western liberal democracies have caused rapid—perhaps unprecedented—changes in families. How to understand what is happening in and to families in the midst of these broad movements has become a matter of great debate. The argument as to whether, for example,

American families are simply "changing" or are "disintegrating" has reached the forefront of the cultural wars ravaging American society. The mass media present us almost daily with a litany of the issues that have become the coinage of this debate: teenage pregnancy, divorce, abuse, gender roles, gangs, sexual orientation, and the effects of consumerism and the media itself on family life.

Whatever one's leanings in the larger debate, it is clear that the rapid changes in family life in the United States confront religious communities with large, complex problems. These problems offer new challenges to the life of congregations even as they present new needs for ministry both within and beyond congregations. What are the possibilities and limits for how congregations might respond? The answers to this question are momentous for congregations and for the broader society. For decades congregations were presumed to occupy a decreasing portion of life in an increasingly secularized society. Now in an era of growing fiscal and governmental austerity, civil society—and especially religious congregations—are expected to fill roles once taken by government, the market, or families themselves. Can they do it? Should they do it? The answers to these questions are important for the whole society.

While the essays in this volume do not answer these questions in full, they provide first signposts leading toward such answers. They provide markers that give us some idea of the possibilities and limitations of how congregations can aid families. Each of the authors in this volume has conducted a critical, practical theological case study of a congregation and has shown how the convictions and practices of that congregation can be a resource for family stability and renewal. In order to approach that concern, each case study addresses two general questions. First, what are the convictions and practices of the congregation as it relates to families? What is the "family theology" of this congregation? Each study shows—in whole or in part—what is communicated to congregational members about the nature and importance of families and the meanings and values that ought to govern various aspects of family life, such as marriage, divorce, raising of children, gender roles in family life, sexuality, and caring for elderly parents. Further, how does each congregation express its family theology in the strategies and programs that the congregation has developed to address the situation of families in its particular place?

The purpose of these case studies is not simply descriptive. They invite us to reflect on the appropriateness and adequacy of the responses of these congregations to families. Therefore, the second general question the case studies address, either directly or by implication, is this: What ought to be said evaluatively about the convictions and practices of these congregations as they relate to families? Each case study develops and/or invites a critical, practical theological perspective on the family ministry of the congregation with regard to such issues as the appropriateness of the congregation's family theology to Christian or Jewish witness, the moral fruitfulness of these ministries, and the adequacy of the congregation's response to the social contexts, psychological dynamics, and spiritual quests of the persons addressed by those ministries.

The case studies that have been chosen for inclusion in this volume cover diverse congregations, including family ministries that have been developed in African American, Jewish, mainline, and evangelical congregations. It should be noted, however, that these congregations were not chosen because they are a representative sample of the broad religious landscape in American society. Nor are they necessarily the most innovative or provocative strategies of family ministry today. Rather, these congregations were chosen more simply because they provide compelling pictures of the struggle to understand and enact the meaning of faith in response to the large social and cultural issues of our time as these issues have come to shape the situations of families in their particular locations—the tensions between individualism and community, pluralism and fragmentation, tradition and innovation, the marginalized and the powerful, and the reproduction of a moral community and the fate of those who fail in regard to its demands. These case studies are truly markers of the kinds of struggles, possibilities, and limitations facing family ministry today.

Lowell W. Livezey, for example, studies a predominately middle-class African American congregation in a large Midwestern urban center. The congregation understands itself as family, for its own members and for the surrounding community. This idea of the church as extended family, or suprafamily, incorporates all other family units within itself and is at the heart of the church's self-understanding. Livezey shows us how the congregation engages in the practical theological elaboration of this image through drawing on certain symbols and narratives of African culture and biblical Christianity and developing practices in its life that address the social and economic changes of its neighborhood and the strains in African American family life. In this, Livezey helps us see how this congregation struggles against, and seeks to provide an alternative to, two issues significantly affecting families today: the cultural individualism of much of American society and the effects of urban restructuring in corroding a sense of community.

These latter two issues arise in somewhat different form in the Roman Catholic congregation in the eastern United States studied by Michael McGinnis and Maureen Kelly Simone. The authors show how the parish's convictions and practices have evolved over time and become a resource for family and neighborhood stability and renewal amid urban change. Ministry with families is clearly at the heart of parish life. Indeed, the idea of the parish as family can be seen again here as an organizing image of congregational life. Yet, this case study demonstrates the tension between what "family" means and how that meaning seeks to form as well as support congregational members, as the congregation develops its identity out of its own traditions in response to the situations of its members. Thus, the authors demonstrate how the parish's commitment to diversity and inclusiveness (particularly with regard to gender and race) in the context of its Roman Catholic heritage has built a particular sense of family that seeks to undergird its social justice ministries and its efforts to support the variety of family forms in its midst.

Brita Gill-Austern, in her description of a Reform Jewish synagogue in New England, carries forward the question of how religious communities extend their religious heritage to the contemporary dilemmas of family life. Gill-Austern enables us to see how congregational culture shapes and is shaped by family culture. Familial, individual, and communal expressions of piety are woven together. This synagogue holds an inclusive vision of family life: one that recognizes Jewish and non-Jewish unions, mixed-race unions, gay and lesbian partnerships, and blended family forms. Gill-Austern identifies an egalitarian ethic and theology of family within the congregation that gives rise to this vision. Through a richly detailed, evocative study of this synagogue's life, the author shows how family ministries deepen the awareness of cultural and religious resources for family stability and renewal and strengthen Jewish identity in an increasingly secularized world.

The effort to develop and maintain a community that is an alternative to secular individualism, on the one hand, and a morally and theologically pluralistic religious community, on the other, is the focus of Paul Numrich's study of comprehensive family life ministries within an Assemblies of God Pentecostal megachurch in urban America. This church is challenged to be on the cutting edge of family ministries while maintaining (and transforming) its Pentecostal heritage and avoiding an accommodation to secularism. Can this congregation minister to the world without losing its soul? Despite the gap between its own beliefs about family life (particularly with regard to sexuality and divorce) and the beliefs of many of those in its surrounding community, Numrich provides a compelling portrait of a congregation at the symbolic margins of its neighborhood, one that nonetheless offers powerful resources for the families that find their way into its ministries.

Sandra Blair describes a newly formed United Church of Christ congregation with African American Pentecostal roots that directly confronts key cultural questions regarding the meaning of "family" and "family ministry." The congregation ministers to a predominately gay and lesbian population in a large West Coast city. It derives its sense of direction from a passage of scripture in Romans: "Him that is weak in faith receive ye, but not to doubtful dispositions" (Rom. 14:1, KJV). This view undergirds an inclusive theology and biblical hermeneutics that are embodied in the ministry and belief system of the church. The author carefully demonstrates how a congregation with such an inclusive theology seeks to be thoughtful about the meaning of "family" and the ministries that can reach out in care and support to families understood in this extended sense. It highlights an African American liberation theology of the family, as the congregation assumes a prophetic role among its members and in the community.

Lois Livezey's study of an affluent mainline Presbyterian church in a large Midwestern urban center shows the issues of inclusiveness in a different light. This congregation represents its historic identity as a public church that reaches out to the surrounding community. As such, the church proclaims the grace of God and the call to discipleship as inseparable from responsible democratic citizenship and public advocacy. The author demonstrates the important linkage that is made within the congregation between its theological beliefs, civic-mindedness, and its understanding of family life. In particular, the case study illustrates the tensions and possibilities the congregation faces as it supports and promotes the "democratization" of family relationships. This case study also shows that many of the ministries that are not explicitly identified as oriented to the support and nurture of families in fact play important roles in the church's relations to families.

The complexity of issues surrounding sexual orientation in theology and ministry arise again in D. Mark Wilson's case study of an African American Baptist congregation on the West Coast. The black church has historically been viewed as the backbone of the black family, and the congregation Wilson studies supports a wide variety of ministries directed toward nuclear families. Through compelling interviews with several gay members of the congregation, however, the author asks: How will the historic convictions and practices of the black church enable it to respond to an emerging minority within its own body? Thus, this case study presents a powerful portrait of the inner struggles and dilemmas faced by churches and gay men as they seek to articulate their identities in relation to one another in complex, changing times. Wilson raises compelling questions about black churches, black theology, and the meaning of "family."

Diversity and pluralism in the practical theology of the family in congregations is seen in a different light in Barbara McGinnis-Gillispie's study of an urban Midwestern Baptist congregation comprised of families from diverse cultural and language groups. Twenty-six nationalities as well as a variety of religious backgrounds have been identified within the congregation. With such cultural diversity and different understandings of family, tensions and misunderstandings are bound to arise. What convictions and practices help to unite such a congregation? How do they navigate potential conflict and avoid schism? McGinnis-Gillispie shows how Japanese congregants, Koreans, Filipinos, Euro-Americans, Africans, and African Americans—to name a few—nurture a deeply egalitarian spirit as American Baptists. They form a radically inclusive congregation, or family of God, that—true to American Baptist tradition—seeks to balance individual conscience and religious freedom with rights and obligations toward one another and to God. The strong emphasis upon the idea that *the Church is family* challenges each congregant and group within the congregation to be inclusive in their use of resources, planning, worship, education, and fellowship. Their shared affirmation of unity underlies their range of theological views and family ministries, and provides coherence and stability to this culturally diverse American Baptist congregation.

Finally, Denise Senter provides a portrait of family ministries in a African American AME congregation in the Midwest that seeks to deal forthrightly with the challenges of urban life. While issues of cultural individualism are important, this congregation also seeks to deal with the realities of urban violence and social justice as these affect the families within their membership and the broader community. Through the metaphor of the church as sanctuary, the author shows how the congregation seeks to be a place of hope and renewal for the strengthening and support of families in crisis, transition, and challenge. Senter also clearly documents the role of the charismatic female pastor in helping the congregation shape its direction and focus in relation to families.

As we stated above, these case studies provide markers for us about the struggles, possibilities, and limitations that face religious communities as they articulate and practice their faith in the face of difficult changes, disruptions, and crises in family life. Four general markers should be highlighted. First, we think it is important that all of the congregations studied here seek to provide ways for families, *as* families and not simply as a collection of individuals, to locate themselves within a broader moral and religious community. Whether through the imagery of the congregation as a suprafamily, a village, a public arena, a prophetic agent to the wider community, or a sanctuary, these congregations help protect families from collapsing in the face of cultural or market individualism. As suggested by the variety of images used, clearly there is a great deal of diversity in the rhetorical appeal used: whether through the resonances of intimacy and interpersonal solidarity of the church as family or village, the soothing and protecting nuances of the church as sanctuary, or the political imagery of a democratizing public arena. Yet, despite this diversity, all the congregations invite families to see themselves as embedded within a wider community of loyalty, justice, and responsibility.

A second marker concerns the ways that many of these congregations help provide the emotional skills and symbolic resources to sustain intimate relationships and to restore the self when intimate relationships fail. Expectations regarding intimacy in family life are rapidly changing. For increasing numbers of families today, the primary, if not sole, source of an intense (albeit historically peculiar) emotional intimacy and personal identity is expected to be the family. This expectation causes strains and ruptures that many of the congregations studied here attempt to heal. Three kinds of responses seem important to note. First, these congregations situate intimacy itself within a moral and religious framework where responsibility, grace, and love help structure an otherwise ambiguous expression of a popularized "therapeutic" ethos. Thus, the congregations provide a more or less implicit critique of certain understandings of intimacy. Second, many of these congregations have developed specific ministries to help persons develop the emotional skills needed to sustain and renew intimate relationships. Third, various of these congregations have also developed specific ministries to help persons deal with the emotional, moral, and financial realities of their lives when intimate relationships fail. While there is a great deal of diversity in the ways these three things are done, these congregations nonetheless articulate morally and religiously rich understandings of intimacy in family life and help persons live out the practicalities and consequences of those understandings.

A third marker revealed by many of these congregations concerns the emphasis on the socialization of children and adolescents, which brings up two important points. On the one hand, many congregations engage in significant ministries of socialization or resocialization for children and adolescents. Whether concerned with gender roles (what it means to become a man or woman), developing more general moral orientations and principles in the light of the complex dilemmas faced by today's youth, or inculcating a sense of citizenship along with discipleship, many of these congregations successfully supplement the socialization processes offered by schools and families themselves. On the other hand, most of these congregations do not understand themselves as simply taking over family functions. Indeed, they often offer parenting classes to strengthen the work of the more primary parenting persons. What these congregations seem to recognize is that those who bear the heaviest cost of the changes and failures in family life are children, who must, therefore, be a primary focus of attention.

A final marker revealed by these case studies is the ways in which these congregations, again in a variety of ways, help families mediate between the forces of contemporary life and the historic traditions of the faith. Each congregation provides a compelling language of conviction and practice, suited to its context and attentive to the religious traditions that it seeks to extend. While we might agree or disagree with the substance of certain of the faith claims some of these congregations make, they all take seriously their practical theological task. In doing so, they assist families in the process of symbolic reorganization that is needed to promote their sense of the kind of just and nourishing family life necessary to human flourishing.

From another angle, of course, these case studies demonstrate just how deep is the rift in this country between more conservative and more liberal perspectives on the family and how difficult it is for congregations to overcome the issues of the cultural war. These studies reveal quite clear differences regarding the nature and distribution of authority in family life, sexuality and sexual orientation, and understandings of what counts as "family." While we do not want to overstate these differences, the case studies demonstrate just how hard congregations must work to deal with differences in values regarding family life and, yet, how compelling is the success when they are able to accomplish this, in however modest a way.

What is happening to Western families in general and American families in particular? There is a growing awareness that families are both changing and in crisis. Mainline Protestantism and the moderate center of Judaism and Catholicism have failed to address this phenomenon articulately. Yet church and family need each other. Both have proven to be extraordinarily resilient institutions. In various ways, the authors show how the life of faith and family life are woven together and move toward a common future. The congregations described here mediate between family life and the wider society. By attending to people suffering, the congregations address the problems created by broad social change. At the same time, the church needs strong, committed families in order to survive. The faith communities studied here nurture the inner resources for renewal and seek to meet the social, spiritual, and emotional needs of their members. We believe that these congregations prove that the convictions and practices of various faith communities can contribute to innovative responses and renew hope for American families, communities, and culture.

1

Family Ministries at Carter Temple CME Church

LOWELL LIVEZEY

It is Spring Revival Week 1995 at Carter Temple CME Church in the Chatham neighborhood of Chicago's South Side. We enter the large sanctuary and find perhaps three hundred people comfortably spaced in the front half of the pews. This is "youth night" and the Christian Youth Fellowship (CYF) meeting has been folded into the revival. Those in attendance range in age from grade school children to the elderly. At least forty are teenagers, some seated together, others with parents, grandparents, or other adults. The youth choir of twenty-eight, about equally male and female, look immaculate in their robes of black, red, and green—the African national colors. There is Bible study, some questions and answers about the lesson, and a time of prayer led by Pastor Williamson, who seizes the moment to remind parents to read the Bible and pray with their kids. "Pray for them, yes, of course, but also pray with them."

The pastor introduces the evangelist by speaking directly to the youth, telling them that he knows their situation, that he knows "what it means to be dissed, to be knocked to the curb, again and again." And tonight's evangelist knows, too. The Rev. Paris Lester was "a child of this church, one of the worst cut-ups in CYF, who passed notes during prayer, grew up in pain, never knew his parents." A very human guy, just like the audience. Then he went off to "one of our fine CME colleges and it is a blessing to have him here tonight." The young man gives a

Note: My colleagues in the Religion in Urban America Program at the University of Illinois at Chicago, Joy Bostic, Shalanda Dexter, Larry Murphy, April Payton, Matthew Price, and Elfriede Wedam, did much of the field research for this essay. I also thank Joy Bostic and Larry Murphy for their overall analysis of the field data, David Daniels for his assistance with the discussion of black middle-class religion, and Janise Hurtig, Elfriede Wedam, and Lois Gehr Livezey for their insightful critiques of earlier drafts.

powerful sermon on the image of the "boomerang effect," from Galatians 6, "Whatsoever a man soweth, that shall he reap," and he goes through real-life examples, many from his own life, of doing wrong and suffering the results of sin. Not much about heaven and hell, but lots about drinking, drugs, and sex, and about compassion for brothers and sisters and respect for elders. He "hoops" and the organ accompanies him as he builds to a climax.

The pastor then gives the altar call, clearly the central event in the service. But it is not, at least not explicitly, an appeal to individuals to accept Christ as personal Lord and Savior. It is an invitation to the young people (ages 12–18) to accept the prayers and the loving surround of the church. First, he asks the girls to come kneel at the altar, to pray and be prayed for. About twenty-five of them do. Then he asks the women of the church who are willing to pray and care for these girls to come forward to stand behind the girls, put their hands on them and pray. More than forty women do, and the pastor assures the girls, "These women are your mothers. Even if you have a mother at home, or even if you do not, it makes no difference in this church because we are all your mothers and fathers. We love you. We care for you. You can count on us."[1] Then he asks the girls to stand up and hug the women behind them, and they do. "Hugging is healing," he says.

Next the pastor calls for the boys and then the men, and they come forward in about the same numbers. His call for prayer is more specific this time—to be spared of temptations and wrongdoings. "If you are drinking, cursing, stealing, dealing, on drugs, misusing and abusing young girls— ask God to help you stop. Men, ask God to help them stop. Boys, that man behind you, that's your father." He continues, as with the girls, but more passionately. He asks the boys to hug the men, and they do.

Then he speaks to all the youth, very intensely. "Always remember, this church is your family, we are your mothers and fathers. Mrs. Williamson and I are your mother and father. We love you. Call us any time, day or night. No matter how bad your trouble, no matter how much wrong you've done. We won't love you any less! We'll love you all the more, we'll love . . . you . . . all . . . the . . . more!"

Change Is the Only Constant: Neighborhood, Church, and Family

Carter Temple CME Church is in many respects a conventional church, but it draws on its deep roots to make innovations in ministry and possibly in theology. Carter Temple is engaged in a quest for a new kind of family ministry, one that is intricately intertwined with the evolution of ministry for the whole church. This includes defining the church as a family for its members and for others in the community. While this is not unprecedented,[2] it is important to examine just how the church develops the concept of itself as a family, articulates a theological and cultural rationale for that concept (partly by using symbols and images attributed to the people and cultures of Africa), and trains members to accept the consequent responsibilities. Moreover, as was evident at the revival services reported above, the church is adopting a perspective on the nuclear family—that even an intact family with parents at home is not sufficient. With or without a mother, a girl needs the church family.

This essay's central claim is that through its family ministries Carter Temple is rethinking what a good family is, how good families can be supported, and how to articulate a theological rationale for ministries to them. This is an exercise in "practical theology,"[3] in that the fundamental beliefs of the church are both reaffirmed and redefined in order to address individual and communal needs as circumstances change for members and their social systems. Church members do not present themselves as involved in theological innovation. The pastor emphasizes the "overarching Biblical concepts" such as "abundant life in Christ," not theological arguments. But Carter Temple's practice and explanation of the Christian life involve symbols, images, and rhetoric that are new to the congregation, and which redefine its understanding of the black church tradition and the Christian community.

The innovative family ministries of Carter Temple may be instructive for other churches, but they emerge from the particular circumstances of this church. Carter Temple's peculiar genius is constantly to refashion a ministry that reflects the actual circumstances of those who attend. The first part of this essay, therefore, describes Carter Temple and three dimensions of its environment most salient to these ministries—the local neighborhood as part of a restructuring metropolis, the wider black church and middle-class black religion, and the black family and the crisis of the American family. Each of these requires change and presents opportunities for innovation in Carter Temple's ministries.

Carter Temple and Its Neighborhood.

Carter Temple CME Church is a rapidly growing African American congregation in Chicago's South Side Chatham neighborhood, which is generally considered a "bastion of Chicago's black middle class." In the words of *Chicago Sun-Times* columnist William Braden, Chatham may have "the largest concentration of middle-class blacks in America outside of Harlem and Atlanta."[4] Chatham was sparsely settled (by whites) during the late nineteenth century, annexed by the city of Chicago in 1889, and grew moderately with the growth of employment opportunities in meat packing a few blocks north and in the steel mills and the Chicago port and rail freight centers not far to the east. These centers of employment were the economic lifeline of the Chatham neighborhood as it grew through the 1960s, and the loss of industrial employment is the underlying threat to the neighborhood's well-being today.

Yet it was a part of what Arnold Hirsch has described in *The Making of the Second Ghetto*[5] in the years 1940–60 that Chatham's distinctively black middle-class character was established. In those years Chicago's first ghetto, a narrow strip of land extending forty blocks south from Chicago's central business area, gave way to a much larger ghetto that was differentiated by class. The "first ghetto," known locally as Bronzeville, had received and retained black migrants from the South during the Great Migration before World War I and through the 1920s. These migrants brought or founded their own organizations and institutions, including churches, located within the geographic boundaries of Bronzeville.

With a second major wave of black migration to Chicago during and immediately after World War II, Bronzeville burst at the seams. Bronzeville's housing stock deteriorated with age, and the land it occupied became increasingly valuable with the growth of Chicago's overall population and industry. Bronzeville was a target for "urban renewal," meaning much of the original black population would be required to move elsewhere. Chatham and its northern neighbor, Greater Grand Crossing, gained from Bronzeville's loss as the destination of Bronzeville's most prosperous residents—the doctors, lawyers, teachers, and the more numerous unionized blue-collar workers. These members of Chicago's black middle class either bought homes from the white residents, who were now eager to move to suburbs, built homes on the many lots still available after the war, or rented the spacious apartments available near the still-prosperous neighborhood commercial centers.

However charming and desirable the neighborhood that was to be Carter Temple's home, it was still a part of the black ghetto. Black people with enough money could choose to live in this part of the ghetto, but with precious few exceptions they had to live within racially defined boundaries. The poorer blacks moved or were relocated to other, less pleasant, parts of the expanding ghetto, some to public housing, and some to other neighborhoods on the south and west sides of the city.

Like many of the older congregations of the historic black denominations like the CME, Carter Temple was founded in the first Chicago ghetto and moved with its members. A few of its older members came to Chicago as part of the Great Migration and helped found the church in 1921. The church prospered with a membership benefiting from the expanding industrial economy that offered opportunities to skilled laborers and a small but rising number of black professionals. As a member who attended Carter Temple with her parents and grandparents in the 1950s put it, "We didn't think of ourselves as middle class, and people had a wide variety of jobs and different levels of income. But we had what we now call middle-class values—the work ethic, honesty, integrity, get a job, get a house, get a car, standards of excellence."

In 1964 Carter Temple moved to its present location in Chatham and erected an edifice that seats over one thousand people for worship and provides space for extensive educational and social programs. By 1995 the church had over twenty-five hundred members, an increase of one thousand since Pastor Henry M. Williamson, Sr., was appointed in 1986. The year 1995 also saw the first annual budget over $1 million, and the addition of a third weekly worship service.

Pastor Williamson has an assistant pastor, two assistant ministers, and a paid staff of seventeen. Yet the ministries of the church far exceed the capacities of the staff, and the voluntary tradition is alive and well. The fifty-four-member Board of Stewards is active as a governing body and as a ministry of care, which provides a great deal of the connective tissue that enables the church to withstand—and to help its families withstand—corrosive social and economic forces. Under the pastor and the stewards, various ministries, activities, and programs are enacted, providing for prayer, nurture, education, and social action touching members, friends and neighbors of members, and residents of the surrounding neighborhood.

Yet powerful structural changes challenge Carter Temple and its neighborhood. The nearby stockyards and meat packing and steel industries that drove the development of South Side neighborhoods and employed their residents are now "rusted dreams."[6] Chatham residents who are not retired or unemployed now commute much farther to work. Indeed, workers of Chatham have a longer commute, on average, than workers in most Chicago neighborhoods and significantly longer than the workers of most Chicago suburbs. Moreover, except for churches, few of the institutions and activities available in the neighborhood meet the standards of the residents. On the commercial streets, marginal businesses have replaced prosperous ones. For quality public schools, children commute to magnet schools and academies in other parts of the city.

Not surprisingly, the population of Chatham has declined gradually but steadily since the 1970 census. People need to move for access to jobs and better schools, and they have more choice of residence as a result of gains made by the civil rights movement of the 1960s. So there are both push and pull factors leading to outmigration from Chatham, especially by younger generations. For those who remain, Chatham is becoming more of a bedroom community. Both outmigration and commuting undercut the networks of friendship and kinship that once characterized the neighborhood and sustained both families and churches.

Carter Temple is growing and prospering despite these changes, but it is changed. While some members of black middle-class urban churches have long traveled considerable distances to church, the extent of commuting is new. Less than a quarter of Carter Temple's members live in its zip code area. An equal number now live in suburbs and in racially integrated parts of the city. Most of the rest live elsewhere in Chicago's South Side, and commute five or more miles to church. What is important is not just the travel time, but the fact that the members do not live near each other, send their kids to the same schools, join the same civic organizations, shop in the same stores, nor work in the same plants. The more dispersed the congregation, the less likely are its members to be together in other settings. This situation reduces the ability of the church to be a community of care, to make up for the loss of neighborhood-based community experienced by its members. But this gets us ahead of our story.

Carter Temple and the Black Church in America

Carter Temple is significantly a part of the black church in America. Its members are all African American; it is part of one of the historic black denominations, the Christian (originally "Colored") Methodist Episcopal Church; and in the black church tradition, it anchors its neighborhood. Although the CME denomination was founded after the

Civil War, in 1870, its roots were in local churches that had been affiliated during slavery with the Methodist Episcopal Church, South.[7] By thus differentiating itself, the CME joined other black denominations in providing institutional infrastructure for many of the strongest churches of African Americans. C. Eric Lincoln and Lawrence H. Mamiya have called these churches "the cultural womb of the black community"[8] because they gave birth to economic and social institutions, provided opportunities for black people to practice public participation, and served as an institutional context for developing and expressing communal norms and customs.

Yet the very concept of the black church is a relatively recent development in the self-understanding of the churches of African Americans and in scholarship about them. Just as the change from "Negro" to "black" reflected a change in consciousness in the black community, so the idea of the black church reflects the impact on the church of the black consciousness movement of the 1960s and 1970s[9]—a movement to which many of the churches themselves had contributed as participants in the civil rights movement.

But change in black middle-class churches did not begin in the 1960s. As David Daniels, Lincoln and Mamiya, and others[10] have argued, black middle-class religion began to be identifiable as a distinct movement early in this century as part of the process of urbanization and class differentiation of African Americans. Beginning with the Great Migration, many urban middle-class congregations began to distance themselves from emotionalism and stressed a ministry characterized by education, reason, and refinement. The clergy became more professional, the lay leadership was drawn from—perhaps restricted to—the black middle class, and expressions of popular culture were increasingly excluded. By the late 1940s and 1950s, black middle-class churches with these characteristics were very substantial institutions. During these years, their members were beginning to move out of Chicago's first ghetto and into the Chatham and Greater Grand Crossing neighborhoods.

But before this relocation within the city had progressed very far, a second shift began. Many of these churches became involved in the civil rights movement, first in the South and then in Chicago. Little by little, some congregations affirmed an identity with a black popular religious culture and African American folk culture not tied closely either to values and lifestyles of the middle class or their denominations and congregations. The change was neither rapid nor universal. But during the last thirty years, not only the churches of the historic black denominations but the African American congregations of Baptists, Methodists, Lutherans, and Roman Catholics have increasingly identified themselves as part of the black church. They did not renounce their denominational affiliations, but the black church, not their denominations, defined their commonality as Christians who had survived slavery and Jim Crow and who still struggled against urban racism. All black churches had these historical and sociological experiences in common. The very concept of the black church expresses a solidarity that transcends class and denominational divisions.

Carter Temple CME Church was influenced by this redefinition and is contributing to it. Music and worship express the changing consciousness. While Handel's *Messiah* is still performed at Christmas and the choir sings anthems common to much of middle-class Methodism, music at Carter Temple also includes the beat, sound, and imagery of black popular culture. Drums are as prominently displayed and as constantly heard as the organ and piano. The newest assistant minister is a former blues singer whose Christianized rhythm-and-blues lyrics fill the church, evoking enthusiastic "Amens" and "Sing it, sister!" Preaching, particularly that of the senior pastor, is both learned and expressive. While not exactly a "Harvard hooper," Pastor Williamson might be called a "Garrett hooper"[11]—preaching a thoughtful, biblically informed, and inspirational sermon, which builds to a crescendo during the last ten or fifteen minutes and culminates in hooping. Congregational response is varied with some very expressive (standing, hands raised, audible praying, occasional shouting), and others very quiet and contemplative.

As part of a denomination that prides itself on its commitment to education, Carter Temple has a well-educated staff and lay leadership, and it devotes itself to the continuing education of all. Members receive book-length reading assignments for retreats and leadership training events, and teaching is central to church life. The books assigned and available for purchase after church are accessible to the lay reader and rooted in the biblical and black church traditions, but push the boundaries of those traditions. Walter A. McCray's *The Black Presence in the Bible* helps people find biblical warrant for the Afrocentric identity that is offered not only by elite black secular institutions, but from their own pulpit. The books of T. D. Jakes, such as *Can You Stand to Be Blessed?* and *Woman, Thou Art Loosed!*, recognize problems of domestic violence and questions of women's authority and place the issues in a biblical frame of reference. Many new currents in biblical studies, Christian education, and interpretations of the black family and the black community find their way into the study programs. In both worship and education Carter Temple is thus part of the process of redefining black middle-class religion that has been underway since the 1960s.

Carter Temple and the Crisis of the American Family

Simultaneous with the urban restructuring in Chicago and the redefinition of black middle-class religion, American family life has changed dramatically. These three changes span the three decades that Carter Temple has been in Chatham. Its ministry there must be understood in relation to these changes.

The publication in 1963 of *The Feminine Mystique*[12] by Betty Friedan began a critique of all gender relations in society, including families. While Friedan spoke primarily to and for white middle-class women, Angela Davis[13] spoke to and for activists of the New Left and the black consciousness movement, heralding a feminist strand within the radical social movements of the 1960s. Also in the mid-'60s, ethnographic studies like Carol Stack's *All Our Kin*[14] were conducted in African American neighborhoods, charting the complex, extensive networks of kinship and friendship essential to African Americans.

In the 1960s fundamental norms and assumptions about family life began to be questioned: that "nuclear families" of two married parents were best; that one (the father) should earn the income and the mother should be full-time at home; that the man should be the head; that the boundaries between the private family and public life should be as impermeable as possible.

The society, and especially women, became increasingly ambivalent about how individual freedom and communal nurturance were played out in social institutions. Women felt trapped in families and robbed of freedom, while the public sphere offered little nurturance, being so dominated by the spirit of the marketplace.[15]

Within this context of social ferment and nascent change in family paradigms, the "Moynihan Report," formally *The Negro Family: The Case for National Action,*[16] asserted not only that "the black family" (by which it meant the black nuclear family) was in deep crisis, but that this endangered all of American society. The Report was inevitably controversial, since it presumed the very assumptions about family life that were coming under scrutiny. But in linking changes in families to poverty, violence, and racism, the Report launched a national debate that continues into the present. The Children's Defense Fund has now documented that families of all racial and ethnic groups in America are changing in many of the ways the Moynihan Report attributed specifically to black families. Black and white families differ only in degree.[17]

It is, of course, the nuclear family, the family of two parents married to each other with children, that was the subject of concern, not primarily the extended family or more metaphorical notions of family such as the "church as a family" or friendship networks that people experience as "family to me." Though these have been important, and even though they are also under great stress today, they are seldom the subject of research or public discussion.

Compared with the first twenty years after World War II, fewer and fewer families are nuclear families. More people divorce. Single people are more likely to remain single, or to cohabit without making durable commitments. More unmarried people have children. Married or unmarried, teenagers, usually lacking parenting skills and income-earning capacities, are more likely to bear children. Domestic violence, mostly against women and children, or at least our awareness of it, is increasing.

These changes of the last thirty years may not be unprecedented. As Stephanie Coontz[18] and others have shown, family traits now critiqued as dysfunctional have been widespread at some previous point in American history. The nuclear family, independent of the kinship and friendship networks, was not firmly established as a norm until the 1950s. Yet the paradigms of the 1950s comprise the social and moral contexts inherited by middle-class black churches like Carter Temple. It is these they must reconstruct as they minister in the urban neighborhoods of the 1990s.

Among the resources for this reconstruction are scholarly perspectives on the black family that have emerged since the 1960s as competing interpretations. The earliest, identified with E. Franklin Frazier's *The Negro Family in the United States*[19] and with the Moynihan Report, is called the "cultural deficiency view" by Marian Wright Edelman[20] and the "cultural ethnocentric school" by Jualynne Dodson.[21] In this perspective, black families have debilitating characteristics, including instability, promiscuity, and matriarchy. The emasculation of black men during slavery and Jim Crow and under contemporary urban racism may be viewed as a cause or as an element of the matriarchal structure.

An alternative perspective, which Edelman calls the "cultural variance view," considers that differences in black and white culture and material circumstances require families of the two races to cope differently. People of African descent retained elements of African culture, developed a distinctive new culture in America, and evolved a family structure that is functional as a part of that culture. Andrew Billingsley, *Black Families in White America,* and Carol Stack, *All Our Kin,* supported this view in early rejoinders to the Moynihan Report and to its invocation of E. Franklin Frazier as a black authority for its point of view. A series of arguments for "retention" of African culture began with Melville Herskovits's *The Myth of the Negro Past,* published in 1941. One of the most recent, Peter Paris's *The Spirituality of the African American People,* published in 1995, emphasizes the ethical elements of African family life that have been incorporated into the moral culture of the African American family. These studies[22] are among many that suggest African cultural antecedents for extended families, including loosely constructed kinship and friendship networks, among black Americans. Yet the cultural variance perspective is not exclusively tied to the African retention arguments or to greater importance of extended, as opposed to nuclear, families. Some argue that extended family networks have helped black nuclear families to remain intact under pressure—or to reunite when separated.

A third perspective, or at least an area of research, emphasizes the significance of social class for the well-being of black families. Edelman[23] observes that for some scholars, social class determines whether (nuclear) families are functional and stable. In this view, black families differ from white families because poverty, racism, and marginalization affect them disproportionately. Others maintain that some of the differences of structure related to retention of African culture might remain, but white and black families would succeed equally in health, welfare, and participation in the society. William Julius Wilson and his colleague Mark Testa support this perspective by showing that black men with jobs tend to marry the mothers of their children.[24]

In sum, changes in the black family as a social institution, in the American family of which it is a part, and in scholarly perspectives on both, change the context for ministry at Carter Temple Church, as do structural changes in the city and historic changes in black middle-class religion.

Carter Temple in Times of Change

The pietism of the American black church flourishes at Carter Temple, and the close relationship between church and family is both a source of its vitality and a constant goal of its ministry. The innovation and change at Carter Temple do not detract from this fact, they develop it. Sunday morning worship is the central event of the church week, and it is expected to be the central event in the lives of families. Prayer meetings are held every weekday morning at 6:00, Saturday mornings at 8:00, Wednesday evenings, and on special occasions. Bible study is ubiquitous, at the church and in homes throughout the metropolitan area, and the Bible is the authority most frequently invoked as a guide to life's choices and a source of personal assurance.

Carters Temple's membership is comprised of about 50 percent married couples and 50 percent singles, of whom half have never married and half are either widowed or divorced. Church leaders estimate that about half of the children in the church are children of the single adult members, and that as many as 10 percent are children of singles who never married. However, the computerized church membership list records individuals by mailing address without indicating marital or kinship relations.

In its public rhetoric, Carter Temple generally assumes that the church is mainly composed of families. The "Church Family Album" features photos in family groups, and people being prayed for or honored are frequently identified by their kinship relations within the church. Such references disclose the importance attributed to nuclear families, and also to the extended families that have been important historically in the black community and the black church.[25] Explanations of how the church functions often refer to interweaving of cousins and siblings in the congregation. This overlay of nuclear families, extended families, and Carter Temple Church as a family is the locus of innovation in this church's ministry. Carter Temple affirms the nuclear family—two married parents rearing the children they bore—as an ideal, not as a norm. The Bible is invoked as an authority in family matters for instruction about how husbands and wives should treat each other, not—at least not primarily—about the importance of marriage itself. That is, Carter Temple affirms the nuclear family in limited, specific ways, never to restrict the status of individuals who are not part of nuclear families, and never to imply that nuclear families are capable of being autonomous or self-sufficient. The church seeks to be a communal context for everyone, regardless of whether they are part of a nuclear family, and regardless of how well such families are functioning. Single parents and married parents relate equally well to the church, as do their children. Two-parent homes are affirmed, but the extended, family-like network in the church is considered essential. The warrant for that network is to be found partly in the black church traditions. But at Carter Temple, these traditions are revised with the invocation of African traditions and articulated in an Afrocentric theology.

Carter Temple implicitly recognizes the value of nuclear families and enduring marriages. Husband-and-wife teams are regularly assigned leadership roles. They host and lead home Bible study groups. A husband and wife are co-leaders of the CYF, and another married couple lead the Junior Church. Pastoral leadership is often referred to as "the leadership of Reverend and Mrs." Support is given to helping marriages work, and to encouraging young people to choose marriage as the context for producing and rearing children. Books on successful marriage, mostly written by African American pastors experienced in counseling, are sold after worship. The pastor's sermons are sprinkled with advice about how to be a good husband or a good wife or how to work together as parents. He refers occasionally to dysfunctional families, violence, and abuse in ways that recognize that this church is not exempt from the negative side of family life and that encourage victims to seek protection and support in the church family.

Even when marriage is supported and promoted, care is taken not to presume that the listener is married or will choose to be—even if a parent. An eloquent Women's Day sermon by the "First Lady" (the pastor's wife) elaborated the positive side of being a single woman, in particular the freedom to serve God more fully and to grow in service and leadership within the church.[26] Instruction about parenting, particularly for men, stresses presence—"even if you don't live there. Be present to your kids." The literature table includes material on "life after divorce," not just on how to avoid it. The fact that the associate pastor is a divorced woman powerfully symbolizes the flexible attitude about families, and acceptance of individuals into service and full participation in the church.

What distinguishes Carter Temple, however, is not its flexibility and openness, but its vision of the kind of community it intends to be for its members and to model for others. This vision is linked to its evolving identification as an Afrocentric church. Even if the church could function without invoking African roots and articulating African culture as the source of norms for community, these cultural resources are prominent and resonate with the membership. Another distinctive feature of Carter Temple's approach to family life is its emphasis on "reclaiming" black men and boys. And while this does not depend on the resources of African culture, it is given a distinctive valence by references to the roles of elders—presumed to be men—in African villages. All in all, Carter Temple's vision of itself entails a moral flexibility and openness about the form of the family, but a heavy collective responsibility for the families in the church and the black community in general.

The long-standing black church traditions of worship, prayer, and Bible study provide the foundation for Carter Temple's life as a community. The verbal interaction among pulpit, pew, and choir loft reflects the call-and-response pattern characteristic of much African American worship. The centrality of the Bible as guide to life and assurance of salvation is always evident in worship and in the multiple Bible study groups and prayer meetings on the church calendar. Yet traditions at Carter Temple are developing and changing, particularly in their incorporation of African, not just African American, sources and symbols. The foundation for this development is the recent biblical scholarship concerning African people in the Bible and African sources of biblical literature. The African Heritage Bible is regularly studied and effectively marketed. Walter McCray's *The Black Presence in the Bible*[27] was the subject of a course taught by the author and required, in effect, for the church lay leadership, including the fifty-four-member Board of Stewards. Building on such writings, the pastor, other clergy, and lay leaders frequently refer to the Bible in an African context. Sermons and lectures assert that humanity originated in Africa; that it is the existence of the white race, not the black race, that needs to be explained; and that Adam and Eve, Noah, Abraham, and their descendants were black. Moses was certainly black, and so was Jesus—or, at least, he was not white. The fact that, until recently, most people thought of biblical characters, including Christ Himself, as white is the result of Eurocentric interpretation, the unfortunate consequence of the hegemony of Europe in Western culture. Accordingly, it is of great importance that Carter Temple establish the correct context for understanding the church. Christianity is not a "white man's religion"; it is a religion open to all and is the sole source of salvation for everyone. But people of African descent have a special status in the Christian church, because of the African roots that the church is only beginning to recognize.

Undergirded by the biblical warrant and propelled by the pastor's energy and vision, the church establishes an African dimension in its symbolic and cultural context. The African liberation colors of black, green, and red are prominent in choir robes, banners, and decorations. The prizes for the youth Bible quiz tournament are ribbons, and the colors are black (first place), green, and red. Kente cloth is worn by clergy, choirs, and laity. Artists' renderings of perhaps twenty kings and queens of countries of ancient Africa line the walls of the fellowship hall and theater—alongside photographs of bishops of the CME Church and heroes of the African American community. A picture of *The Lord's Supper* with a black Jesus and disciples hangs in the chapel, while the stained-glass image of a white *Jesus in the Garden* that used to be in the front of the sanctuary has been removed.

The annual African Festival Family Reunion Tea, which members say used to be "just another tea," has become a major event at Carter Temple, featuring exhibits of African crafts and culture, food, and clothing. The event reinforces what the pastor calls "our ties to the Motherland."

African imagery is particularly prominent in programs and events related to children and adolescents, and these tell us much about Carter Temple's concept of the family and its norms for relations among family members. The African proverb "It takes a whole village to raise a child" is rescued from being a cliche by the programs and patters of activity that give it tangible meaning. Occasions like the one reported at the beginning of this essay, in which adult members are called upon to take parental responsibility for all the children and youth of the church, are frequent, spontaneous, and essential to the image of parenting that the church seeks to project.

The Rites of Passage program, interpreted as an enactment of an ancient African village custom, is a significant event in the church year and the crucial event in the induction of a teenager into the responsibilities of adult participation in the church and the community. Preparation for the Rites includes study of African culture, the Bible, the black church, and the contemporary black community. Right living is stressed: not doing drugs, avoiding gangs and violence, men treating women with respect and not getting them pregnant, honoring elders, and recognizing that self-esteem is their birthright from God through their African heritage. Going to college is emphasized (and reinforced by the provision of ten thousand to twenty thousand dollars in scholarships), but not to the point of belittling those who do not see college in their future.

The Rites of Passage event includes an elaborate dinner, African and Caribbean music, dramatic productions depicting African and African American (including black church) traditions, and litanies and pledges of commitment to others, to church, and to the community of Africans and African Americans. All parents, not only the parents of the teens in the program, formally challenge the teens and pledge their support.

Boys and girls in about equal numbers participate in the Rites of Passage program and in its leadership.

The Save Our Sons program, however, reflects Carter Temple's priority commitment to minister to black boys and men. This is a project of Christian Methodist Men, the principal men's organization of the church. Each man is expected to mentor one or two boys, nine to twelve years of age, to build a strong relationship appropriate to their needs. Sometimes the mentor becomes, in effect, a surrogate father, sometimes just an additional older friend. If the boys live with, or have contact with, their fathers, the fathers are encouraged to participate. Mentors get to know each other and try to know the fathers and other family members of the boys. This practice of "intergenerational closure"[28] is believed by writers on educational reform to be a key support for educational success. Thus, it is possible that the SOS program provides the communal context for public school students that Christian academies and Lutheran and Catholic parochial schools provide for their students.[29]

Some of the boys in SOS are in church families, and others find the SOS program because they know some of the boys in the church or have some connection—friends, relatives, neighbors—to the men who are mentors in SOS. The church family is very extended in SOS, reaching into the neighborhoods around the church, bridging the boundaries of the black middle class to include the children of the working poor and unemployed. This extended church family also serves in a small way to offset the breakdown of extended family (kinship) networks that African Americans have experienced in the urban North and the loss of communal ties in disrupted city neighborhoods.[30]

The African imagery is less central in SOS than in the Rites of Passage program, but the boys are reminded of their African heritage, taught to be proud of it, and inculcated with a sense of responsibility that comes with being African. One of the leaders describes himself as a "mwaliamu" (teacher of the village). Recitation is in both Swahili and English. And while it is not a major image for the boys, many of the leaders see the African village as a model for SOS, with themselves as the elders, responsible for the welfare and rearing of the next generation of men.

The model or analogy of the African village is also important in Carter Temple's overall vision of itself as a community and in its central leadership structure. The village is an image that emphasizes the communal over the individual, the responsibility to the whole as a framework for such duties as those within the immediate family. The African village of-

fers rhetoric, frequently employed, to critique the larger society for what
it calls its "Eurocentric individualism" and differentiates Carter Temple
from it. "Eurocentric" is never explicitly connected with the cultures or
countries of Europe, but distinguishes white America from the black
community.

The employment of the African village model is also concrete. The
Board of Stewards, the highest lay authority within the church, is learning to think of the church "as a village" as a basis for understanding its
role. In the *CME Discipline*[31] the stewards are responsible for the lay role
in church governance and for caring for members. Stewards, like deacons in Baptist and Presbyterian churches, ensure that all members are
connected and that someone attends to their needs. Members are di-
vided among the stewards. Each steward is expected to maintain contact with those assigned to him or her, to know their needs for ministry,
to tell the appropriate person (usually the pastor), and to seek to engage
them ever more fully in the life of the church. This responsibility is challenging but feasible if the members live in the same neighborhood, regularly attend the same church service, and can keep in touch. But more
than half of Carter Temple's members now live outside the immediate
neighborhood, many of them in suburbs or distant neighborhoods
where they may be the only member of the church. What's more, with
three worship services, members may well not attend the same service
as their steward.

Training for the stewards now focuses on how to fulfill their responsibilities in this new context. Support networks, members meeting each
other's needs, is a different kind of challenge when the congregation is
large and geographically dispersed. Yet mutual aid is part of the black
church tradition and of the African village mythology. Carter Temple attempts to rise to the challenge in part by using new technology—a computer database of skills and talents members are willing to share with
each other, and lots of phone calls and automobile travel to make the
connections. Nevertheless, members testify that a lot still depends on
the pastor, who is renowned for his ability to connect people with others who can meet their needs.

Gender roles are also evolving in the life of Carter Temple. There is
significant attention to gender role differentiation in the church, reflecting both traditional understandings of male and female roles in church
and family, and the priority commitment "to reclaim the black male for
family, church, and community." In keeping with tradition, women and
men teach girls' and boys' Sunday School classes, respectively. The fe-

male and male assistant ministers counsel women and men, respectively. Women and men each have strong organizations and important roles that are defined by custom and tradition. The Women's Day, Women's Month, and Women's Retreat, and the Men's Day, Men's Month, and Men's Retreat are all very important events. They celebrate the contributions and achievements of women and men, respectively, and they define distinctive images and ideal roles for each.

Women are recognized for both service and leadership at Carter Temple. Pastor Williamson is frequently credited for encouraging and promoting women in ministry, including the fact that the only assistant pastor (to be distinguished from the several assistant ministers) is a woman. Both the Board of Stewards and the Board of Trustees are chaired by women (variously called chairmen, chairwomen, and chairpersons). Sermons and lectures frequently recall the traditional "servant" roles of women in the church, and seek to interpret these roles as models for discipleship for all rather than justification for subordination of women— without acknowledging the subordination often experienced by women and others in servant roles. Women's Day programs refer to changing roles of women, noting that "Christian women of the 1990s"[32] must not only nurture their families and serve the church, as always, but also must now take their role in the workplace and help earn the family income. The long-standing role of black women as wage earners is rarely mentioned, reflecting a nostalgic and unwarranted identification with the American middle class of the 1950s. The Women's Day program of 1995 referred to problems of domestic violence. With respect to abuse, a Women's Day sermon counselled, "This is not your fault. . . . . it's only your fault if you don't do something about it."[33]

The image of the Christian black woman is also projected in part as a point of reference in the discussion of black men, and this theme is complicated, experimental, and not always consistent. Women are appreciated for bearing more than their fair share of the family responsibilities, but called upon to be understanding of the plight of their men—not nagging them because they cannot get a job, or do not earn as much money as their wife or girlfriend or mother. Women are told that is what white society has done to our black men, and that the women's role is to support them and build them up. Sometimes speakers on the topic of the unemployment of black men grope for explanations that build up their self-esteem, but that line of thinking may be at the expense of black women. The claim has been put forward that employers feel threatened by the intellectual strength of black men, so they hire black women instead—implying that women have the jobs men ought rightfully to have.

Reclaiming black men to their "rightful place" is a very prominent theme at Carter Temple. The SOS program is not only a ministry to boys, seeking to save them from the pitfalls of drugs and violence. It is also a challenge to black men to step forward to their responsibility within the community. Just as the elders of the African village guided boys into manhood, so must the men of Carter Temple. Thus, in leading the SOS the members of Christian Methodist Men model one of the most important roles of the black man.

Other important roles of the black man are articulated and celebrated on Black Male Emphasis Sunday, the third Sunday of each month. Black men are both honored for their achievements and challenged to fulfill ideals of black manhood. Presented are men who exemplify many of these ideals—success in business, outstanding teacher or principal, faithful father and husband, leader in the church. Men who are successful in public roles are called upon to spend more time with their families, to be present with their children (usually in language that does not presuppose that they live with their children). Thus, the idea of reclaiming black men is not just applicable to street people, addicts, and gang members; it applies to the successful men of Carter Temple who are challenged to take responsibility within their families (both nuclear and extended) and their community (i.e., the black community). While the "rightful" place of the man as head of the family is occasionally mentioned and generally presupposed, it is not nearly as prominent in the church's rhetoric as are the responsibilities of being present, positive, respectful, and prayerful.

During the Black Male Emphasis Services, all the men and boys are instructed to join hands in a circle surrounding the sanctuary. The pastor prays that they achieve their rightful place as black men, fulfill responsibilities of discipleship, and enjoy the abundant life that God has promised. He often invokes African images and themes. He always assures the men of God's love and their own strength and calls them to responsibility. They are "Blessed to Be a Blessing."

Finally, there is the question of boundaries. Who is included in this extended family, this African village called Carter Temple? This church functions as a community primarily for its members and their friends who attend church regularly and participate in its many educational, social, and service activities. They receive phone calls from the stewards, go through the rites of passage or support their children in doing so, and lead the SOS. But the boundaries are porous. In some respects Carter Temple identifies itself with the black community as a whole, and in some respects with the local neighborhood as a community. The use of African symbols and culture identifies it with descendants from Africa, differentiates these descendants from Euro-Americans, and favors the Africans. The theme of reclaiming the black male is justified not primarily to meet a problem within Carter Temple, but to meet a critical need of the black community. When black men are lost, black families (both nuclear and extended) are weakened and the whole community is endangered.

The neighborhood surrounding Carter Temple is also part of what the church means by "the community." It is a neighborhood that exemplifies both the achievements of the black middle class and the erosion of those achievements with deindustrialization and urban restructuring. Carter Temple's identification with Chatham and Grand Crossing as neighborhoods under threat, and with the black community under threat, is seen clearly in the One Church/One School program, conducted with the nearby Ruggles Elementary School.

Pastor Williamson initiated the One Church/One School program as a project of PUSH while he was national president (1991–93). At Ruggles Elementary School, the program offers a two-week curriculum for seventh and eighth grade students led by Carter Temple ministers and lay people. Called "The Value of Life and the Value of Learning," this curriculum is designed to help students resist the temptations and pressures of drugs, gangs, and pregnancy, in which seventh and eighth grade students at Ruggles are regularly involved. The course warns the students of the dangers, costs, and suffering associated with drugs, gangs, and early pregnancy, and builds their self-esteem by presenting positive role models and teaching about the history of African peoples. Another component is called "deprogramming"—discrediting the negative images of African Americans by attributing them to alien and disreputable sources such as the entertainment industry, especially the video industry, and the mass media, generally associated with whites or Euro-Americans. The message is: We African Americans must see ourselves as we really are—and work to become all that we can be. We, the children of Ruggles School, can avoid the pitfalls that have befallen so much of the African American community.

The Carter Temple also sponsors events at the church for the children and parents of the children of the One Church/One School program, and these programs are much more explicit in their Christian content.

Through the One Church/One School program, boys are invited into the Save Our Sons program. For at least one year, the church offered a "Parenting Expo" for Ruggles parents, with workshops on teen pregnancy, gangs and crime, time and stress management, self-esteem, financial planning, and parent roles in the school. A Carter Temple steward who is a former school principal gave the keynote. She stressed very practical things children needed to do to succeed in school and in life: Increase their study time, decrease their television time, work hard at school. These activities depend upon values, structure, and discipline at home. She also stressed the community working together—church and school, parents, and other adults of the community—in rearing and educating children. This Expo was offered as a present-day manifestation of ways the African American community historically brought up its children.

Conclusion

Carter Temple's ministry to families is integral to its reconstruction of its identity as a church. So far as families are concerned, its primary emphasis is on ensuring that the church itself is a family-like community that welcomes, nurtures, and supports people regardless of their status as individuals and/or as members of biological, nuclear, or extended families. Within that framework it incorporates and attempts to support the other families to which people belong, and (except for rejecting homosexual relationships) it is self-consciously inclusive and nonjudgmental about the nature of those families.

Carter Temple finds normative sanction for durable and monogamous marriages in the biblical and black church traditions, and translates this into support for married people in the conduct of their lives together. It finds normative sanction for extended kinship families in the history of the African American community and the black church, and celebrates that history as part of its collective memory. (One does not, on the other hand, hear the Bible quoted about leaving one's father and mother and cleaving to one's wife or husband.) Finally, in both the history of the black churches and in certain aspects of African culture, Carter Temple finds normative sanction for the church as a family-like community that is needed to support and sustain families of all kinds.

The inclusion of African roots as a source of communal norms within the church depends in part on recent scholarship that locates the biblical drama partly within Africa. Thus, Carter Temple can uphold the authority of the Bible while incorporating new material attributed to the cultures of Africa. Carter Temple's theological contribution is to use these cultural resources in the rearticulation of norms for Christian community.

This new cultural and theological reconstruction has significant implications for Carter Temple's understanding of both the black family and the American family. It is often presupposed that people at Carter Temple would like to be in a two-parent, "intact," nuclear family, and they try to help those who are in such families to treat each other well. But the normative status of the nuclear family is relativized by the moral authority invested in the black extended family and, especially, in the church as a family-like community that is considered necessary for all kinds of families to thrive. This stance involves Carter Temple, at least implicitly, in the public debate about the black family, suggesting that the black family is indeed different by nature from the white family, and that this is not deviance, but rather a form of family life that is positive for African Americans and true to African heritage and culture. Intersecting with the church's interpretation of black families is its struggle to define a perspective on gender roles in which both men and women are accorded appropriate, though different, forms of respect and responsibility. This attempt is driven mainly by the perceived crisis of the black male, not by the resources of the black church or of African culture.

Carter Temple is staking its claim on a highly communal, collective interpretation of moral responsibility. Its flexible, multiple interpretation of family structures is offered as a corrective to the individualism that it associates with Euro-American culture and that it blames for the erosion of community (and therefore of morality) in American society. In its view, the black community, in the form of the black church reconstructed as an African village, has found what white America has lost.

But in attempting to be a truly whole community, Carter Temple is not only up against an individualistic morality—or amorality—that it associates with the white community. It is up against a process of urban restructuring that makes it harder and harder for people to know each other well enough to be a supportive community. The question remains whether the theological development within the church will provide a sufficiently powerful spiritual center to sustain the sense of community against the forces of fragmentation to which it will continue to be subject. If so, then families of diverse kinds—intact, nuclear, single-parent, foster, intergenerational, and widely extended—may be sustained as well.

NOTES

1. These and the subsequent quotes are careful paraphrases based on notes taken during the revival service.

2. About the overlap of church and household during slavery, see Cheryl Townsend Gilkes, "The Storm and the Light: Church, Family, Work, and Social Crisis in the African American Experience," in *Work, Family, and Religion in Contemporary Society*, eds. Nancy Tatom Ammerman and Wade Clark Roof (New York: Routledge & Kegan Paul, 1995). She also discusses the family rhetoric and imagery of church life as evidence of the church's family-like structure and function. See also Don S. Browning, "Family Ethics and the Ethics of Ministerial Leadership" in *Clergy Ethics in a Changing Society*, James P. Wind, et al. (Louisville, Ky.: Westminster/John Knox Press, 1991), 198–214, for a discussion of three overlapping families—the congregation as family, the families that make up the congregation, and the minister's own family. These three meanings of family overlap at Carter Temple.

3. I am assuming an understanding of practical theology drawn from Don S. Browning's *A Fundamental Practical Theology* (Minneapolis: Fortress Press, 1993) and his unpublished lecture, "Practical Theology and Congregation Studies" (December 1995), which includes a brief discussion of Carter Temple. In Browning's terms, I believe Carter Temple is engaged in a "practice-theory-practice" model of theological inquiry. It is "reconstructing inherited practices" of ministry to families, in order to respond to the needs of families in an environment it perceives to be in crisis, and in so doing it operates within a normative framework that is embedded in a larger narrative of which the church is a part. In this case, at least, the construction of the practice of ministry entails some theologically substantive rearticulations of the larger narrative—in particular, the syncretism of African culture and biblical Christianity.

4. William Braden, "Chatham: An African-American Success Story," in *Ethnic Chicago*, 4th ed., eds. Melvin G. Holli and Peter d'A. Jones (Grand Rapids: Wm. B. Eerdmans Publishing Co., 1995).

5. Arnold Hirsch, *Making the Second Ghetto: Race and Housing in Chicago, 1940–1960* (New York: Cambridge University Press, 1983).

6. David Bensman and Robert Lynch, *Rusted Dreams: Hard Times in a Steel Community* (New York: McGraw-Hill Book Co., 1987).

7. For a detailed history of the CME Church, see Othal Hawthorne Lakey, *The History of the CME Church* (Memphis: CME Publishing House, 1985). For a survey of the history of the seven major black denominations, see C. Eric Lincoln and Lawrence H. Mamiya, *The Black Church in the African American Experience* (Durham, N.C.: Duke University Press, 1990).

8. Lincoln and Mamiya, *The Black Church and the African American Experience*.

9. This process is outlined in Lincoln and Mamiya, *The Black Church and the American American Experience,* chaps. 6 and 7.

10. David Daniels, "Chatham and Greater Grand Crossing: The Dominance of Religion and Race," in *Religious Organizations and Structural Change in Metropolitan Chicago: The Research Report of the Religion in Urban America Program,* ed. Lowell W. Livezey (Chicago: Office of Social Science Research, University of Illinois at Chicago, 1996). Daniels refers to the writing of Clarence Joseph Rivers, James Cone, Gayraud Wilmore, E. Franklin Frazier, and others.

11. Pastor Williamson is a graduate of Garrett-Evangelical Theological Seminary, a seminary of the United Methodist Church.

12. Betty Friedan, *The Feminine Mystique* (New York: W. W. Norton & Co. 1963).

13. Angela Davis's early impact was as a speaker and organizer. However, see also Angela Y. Davis, *Women, Race, and Class* (New York: Random House, 1981).

14. Carol B. Stack, *All Our Kin: Strategies for Survival in a Black Community* (New York: Harper & Row, 1974).

15. These themes provide the structure for *Rethinking the Family: Some Feminist Questions,* eds. Barrie Thorne with Marilyn Yalom. (New York: Longman, Inc., 1982), and are discussed in the introductory essay by Barrie Thorne.

16. Daniel Patrick Moynihan, *The Negro Family: The Case for National Action* (Washington, D.C.: U.S. Department of Labor, Office of Policy Planning and Research, 1965).

17. Marian Wright Edelman, *Families in Peril* (Cambridge, Mass: Harvard University Press, 1987).

18. Stephanie Coontz, *The Way We Never Were: American Families and the Nostalgia Trip* (New York: Basic Books, 1992).

19. E. Franklin Frazier, *The Negro Family in the United States* (Chicago: University of Chicago Press, 1939; rev. ed., 1969).

20. Edelman, *Families in Peril,* 8.

21. Jualynne Dodson, "Conceptualizations of Black Families," in *Black Families,* ed. Harriette Pipes McAdoo (Beverly Hills, Calif.: Sage Publications, 1981), 24ff.

22. Melville J. Herskovits, *The Myth of the Negro Past,* (Boston: Beacon Press, 1969), and Peter J. Paris, *The Spirituality of African Peoples* (Minneapolis: Fortress Press, 1995).

23. Edelman, *Families in Peril,* 9.

24. William Julius Wilson, ed., *The Ghetto Underclass* (Newbury Park, Calif.: Sage Publications, 1993), 6, and Mark Testa, et. al., "Employment and Marriage among Inner-City Fathers," in *The Ghetto Underclass,* ed. Wilson, 96–108.

25. Wallace Charles Smith, *The Church and the Life of the Black Family* (Valley Forge, Pa.: Judson Press, 1985), 22, claims that "the black family's chief strength is its extended nature" and urges churches both to draw on this strength and to nurture it, rather than to assume the nuclear family as a

sufficient model. A profile of the black extended family, based on ethnographic research, is provided in Elmer P. Martin and Joanne Mitchell Martin, *The Black Extended Family* (Chicago: University of Chicago Press, 1978), and additional perspective is provided in Stack, *All Our Kin.*

26. Doris Y. Williamson, *Women's Day Sermon,* Carter Temple CME Church, March 26, 1995.

27. Walter A. McCray, *The Black Presence in the Bible* (Chicago: Black Light Press, 1990).

28. James S. Coleman, "Social Capital in the Creation of Human Capital," *American Journal of Sociology* 94 (1988).

29. In addition to Coleman, "Social Capital in the Creation of Human Capital," see Anthony S. Bryk, Valerie E. Lee, and Peter B. Holland, *Catholic Schools and the Common Good* (Cambridge, Mass.: Harvard University Press, 1993), especially chaps. 8 and 11.

30. See Martin and Martin, *The Black Extended Family,* and Stack, *All Our Kin.*

31. *The Book of Discipline of the Christian Methodist Episcopal Church* (Memphis: The CME Publishing House, 1990).

32. "Christian Women of the '90s" was the theme of the 1993 Women's Day at Carter Temple. These comments are based on observations of Women's Day events in 1993 and 1995, supplemented by interviews.

33. Mrs. Henry Williamson, *Women's Day Sermon,* Carter Temple CME Church, March 26, 1995.

2

Saint Vincent de Paul Parish

MICHAEL MCGINNIS
MAUREEN KELLY SIMONE

Ministry to families in Saint Vincent de Paul Parish (hereafter most often referred to as St. Vincent Parish) in the Germantown section of Philadelphia is woven into many, if not all, aspects of the parish's life. It is no exaggeration to say that ministry to families is inextricable from the many specific things that this parish does to carry out its mission. At the same time, not many events bear a specific "for families" designation. Thus, the following case study describes a parish in which ministry to families is an ever present subtext, if not always the main text, in every aspect of parish life.

Our method of gathering data on St. Vincent Parish has combined both formal and informal participant observation strategies with individual and small group interviews. "Informal" participant observation refers to the fact that the coauthors of this case study had been frequent participants in St. Vincent's liturgies and other activities for many years prior to undertaking this research in a formal manner. In addition, Maureen Kelly held a position with a coalition of parishes in which St. Vincent Parish took part. The "formal" participant observation refers to the coauthors' involvement in any way with St. Vincent Parish from January 1994 to June 1994, when the interviews were conducted.

Admittedly the coauthors have considerable familiarity with this particular Roman Catholic parish, and, not surprisingly, considerable appreciation for the success of the parish's ministries. In order to establish some critical distance between their parish experience and their representation of it in this format, the coauthors have introduced pastoral-theological perspectives drawn from the writing of Dr. Evelyn E. Whitehead, Rev. Philip Murnion—particularly in his capacity as director of The Parish Project, an undertaking of the U.S. Conference of

Catholic Bishops—and selected documents from the Episcopal
conference itself. Selection of those particular sources implies some level
of interpretation of the parish's ministry to families. The coauthors believe that the parish's ministries reflect a pastoral-theological perspective that calls for ministry willing to engage people's real life experiences,
even when those experiences do not appear to fit within the framework
of church law. The coauthors also note that the language of intimacy,
present in ministerial guidelines of the church, cannot be easily melded
with the structures of intimacy, particularly family intimacy, when
translated for a larger group such as a parish. The staff at St. Vincent realize these basic pastoral principles and accompanying difficulties. This
realization underlies the pastoral leader's reflection on parish ministry
as family to family. The accent is on the experience first: experience acknowledged, celebrated, and critiqued within the community of the
church.

Preamble

The church stands—broad, beautifully detailed, soaringly majestic—
in an urban neighborhood that is aging and in some ways declining. Inside, Eucharistic liturgy is being joyfully celebrated under the interior
flying buttresses of St. Vincent Parish church. The congregation, economically and ethnically diverse, is solidified in a church ritual expressing their common search for the presence of God, in the events of
their lives and in one another. They have come together amid the chat-
ter, clatter, and bustle of the neighborhood, friends uniting in worship.
Their pastor has just completed his preaching on the Sunday scripture
lesson. Following a pregnant pause, the pastor rises from his presider's
chair to announce that the liturgy cannot continue—the sacred Eucharistic worship cannot proceed—as yet, for the most important
guests–gifts–members had not returned. With that, the doors to the
body of the church were flung open, and the smiling young children entered the church. Father Greg, standing at the altar, announced to all
present, "We can now proceed, as our most important members are now
among us."

At the entrance to this same church one encounters a sign, insignifi-
cant in size, perched at eye level near the main entrance. It proclaims
the primary mission of the parish members to all who enter: "Enter to
learn. Leave to serve." This statement epitomizes the mission of the people of St. Vincent Parish.

Liturgy—Hospitality—Service

In preparing its parish mission statement, the congregation reflected on areas of parish life felt to be most significant—liturgy, hospitality, and commitment to service. As to the latter, service is seen as addressing social justice issues, particularly among the residents of the neighborhood that surrounds St. Vincent Parish. Because of these commitments, this worshiping community is a vital, vibrant link between the members of the congregation, whose spiritual lives are enhanced by the service work that they do, and the population of the neighborhood, whose physical and emotional needs are met in part through the work of the congregation.

Staff

The parish is staffed by members of the Vincentian community of priests and brothers. At the time of our interviews, the pastoral leadership consisted of a priest pastor, as well as a priest acting as an associate pastor. In addition, several members of religious congregations fulfilled various ministries. Among these, a religious brother coordinated the pastoral care ministry from a central location known as the "Inn Dwelling." Care of the sick, the hospitalized, and others with physical needs is coordinated by a woman religious who works on a full-time basis. She is assisted by a professional woman from the parish who works part-time. Another woman religious serves in a very varied job that includes coordinating the soup kitchen, publishing the parish newsletter, preparing for the children's liturgy of the Word, and facilitating the religious development of the adults of the community. In addition, a layman works part-time as an important link between the families and individuals of the parish and the neighborhood in the role of Parish Services Coordinator. He develops programs of interest for the parish or responds to the voiced needs of recipients of parish social ministries. This man also attempts to place interested individuals and/or entire families in social ministries. Finally, the church employs the services of a full-time liturgy consultant, who coordinates all of the ministries of worship by directing four individual choirs, preparing the worship space for liturgy and other special rites, and assisting the community in preparing seasonal themes for parish worship.

History and Locale
of St. Vincent Parish

St. Vincent Parish was established in 1851, at its current location of Price and Lena Streets, in Philadelphia, Pennsylvania. While the predominant ethnic identity of the area known as "Germantown" was Euro-Germanic, this parish was created to meet the needs of the Italian-speaking population. The church architectural plans included flying buttresses, Italian frescoes on the ceiling, an abundance of Italian marble, and as much gold filigree as the community could afford. This church structure was a source of great pride to its membership. Other facilities on the property included a rectory, convent, and school. These buildings, while not as ornate as the church, also reflected the taste and design of qualified artisans.

For many decades, the neighborhood remained quite stable. Younger members of extended families tended to mature, marry within the community, and return to build or buy another home in the Germantown area. This cycle contributed to the stability of the neighborhood and the parish. Slowly, shortly after World War II, change came to Germantown. No longer were immigrant families being supported by and assisted by a community that spoke a common non-English language. Children who married looked to developing neighborhoods in the northeast section of the city, where more modern homes were being built. The infrastructure of the Italian-based community began to change. At that same time, African American families began to experience a prosperity that allowed them to purchase homes in the Germantown area. Some of these members of the African American community already worshiped in the Roman Catholic tradition. Because of social, economic, and racial barriers then existing, the membership of St. Vincent Parish resisted the efforts of the black community to worship in a common space. Instead, a chapel space was prepared to serve the needs of the black community. Located some distance from the main building of the parish, the chapel became known as the St. Catherine Parish Annex. While nothing of this segregation was recorded publicly, it remains a fact that by the mid-1950s, St. Catherine's was a thriving black Roman Catholic community. It was served by the same Vincentian priest community that served the Italian membership at the main center of worship on Price and Lena Streets.

By the mid-1970s and continuing into the present decade, the general makeup of Germantown had become largely African American. Today, the area's population breaks down ethnically as follows: black, 66 percent; white, 32 percent; Hispanic and Asian, 2 percent.[1] This profound change in ethnicity also affected the socioeconomic characteristics of the neighborhood. Today, the properties on the west side of St. Vincent Parish's boundaries are largely industrialized and commercial. On the residential east side, two distinctly different areas are merged together. In one area, many urban professionals have taken advantage of the locale's proximity to the downtown area and purchased homes there. In this area, median income is high.[2] Here, too, the median housing values are high, close to ninety thousand dollars, while unemployment figures are low. However, in the area of Germantown just abutting the church property, the poverty level averages close to 13 percent.[3] In addition, unemployment statistics show the jobless figures at a staggering 23 percent.[4]

However much Germantown has changed ethnically and economically, its physical aspect has changed relatively little. While walking through the streets of Germantown, one encounters stately homes on tree-lined streets and well-maintained, prewar apartment complexes. These streets house both a young professional population and a somewhat wealthy elderly population. Other homes, particularly the large Victorian homes, have been subdivided for group homes for young adults, patients who need skilled nursing, and adults with emotional and/or mental problems who have been mainstreamed into the community. Finally, government-owned tract housing accommodates marginalized families.

Near the geographic center of the parish is a large commercial strip. The neighborhood families' needs can be met to some extent here. There are two banks, two supermarkets, many small family-owned businesses, two large parks, and a few day-care facilities. There are several private schools, reminders of previous eras that continue to exist in Germantown's changing environment. In addition to the public schools, there are two academic magnet schools nearby, which bring youth from various neighborhoods together in order to study in a diverse situation. One medium-sized urban Catholic university is also located nearby. Faculty members from that institution contribute to the parish's adult and religious education programs.

Just as Germantown has changed in its physical makeup, so too has the population of St. Vincent Parish. With fewer Roman Catholics among the growing African American population of the neighborhood, one would imagine that it would be very difficult for St. Vincent Parish to act as a fiscally responsible parish without visible funding sources. Many inner-city parishes have been merged or suppressed in many dioceses in the United States. Yet St. Vincent Parish continues to be a vibrant center of Catholic Christianity in the northwest section of Philadelphia. It has survived and even thrived for many reasons, some of which are explored or suggested below. However, the predominant factor conducive to the survival of this parish has been its ability to minister effectively to a variety of families, peoples, and cultures.

Today, the makeup of the worshiping community at St. Vincent Parish can be characterized by using the term *intentional faith community*. This term denotes the fact that the membership does not necessarily come only from the surrounding neighborhoods. In fact, many parishioners come to Germantown from suburban communities, with a few traveling great distances to bring their families to worship here. These people, some of whom have been interviewed in this study, have formed this intentional community at St. Vincent Parish because they appreciate the attempt by the parish staff to make the Eucharistic liturgy central to the inner working of family life, while at the same time centering that same family life into the mission statement of the parish.

Recent Pastoral History:
The U.S. Scene

Evelyn Whitehead notes that although the hierarchical Roman Catholic church would prefer to view itself in a familial context as "the family of God," she notes that, "in the language of intimate family life, we are called upon to love one another, to care for each other's needs . . . to view ourselves as members of the same family. . . . This language seems to stand in direct contradiction to their [the people's] experience of church as an institution."[5] For many obvious reasons, in many Catholic parishes today, one can see typical styles of ministry. In Model Number One, Father knows what is best for the parish community. He alone as pastor makes the decisions. In Model Number Two, parishioners are the children of God who are to understand the efforts of the loving, pastoral father. Prior to the relative freedom of educational opportunities offered by the post-Vatican II church structure, these particular models worked well in many Roman Catholic parishes. Model Three developed in the late 1970s and well into the 1980s, when education, discussion groups, the challenges of ministry in diverse situations, and declines in the number of ordained priests combined to open the doors of ministry to the entire church community. Ministry to and by community members became very important to some individual church congregations, if not always to the hierarchical structures.

In the early 1980s, many Roman Catholic scholars, theologians, and writers began to challenge hierarchical positions concerning women, examining in particular the rights of women in family life and in situations during and after divorce and/or separation. In general, that questioning examined the vitality of the church from the standpoint of its ability to integrate pastoral and family ministries relevant to the changed and changing situation of women. On the other hand, some official church documents from this era contain notes of caution against the tide of social change, reflecting—and creating to some degree—fear among those who ministered in the parishes. Among the concerns of the hierarchy at this time were those connected to women and the new freedom deriving from the cultural revaluation of the contributions of women, both to the parish community and to the secular world.

During this time, and from a pastoral perspective, Father Philip Murnion was director of the United States Catholic Bishop's "Parish Project." One of the project's purposes was to mentor to the bishops and the entire U.S. church through a weaving and integration of current theology into the pastoral practices at the parish level. Seeking such integration often required walking a tightrope between conflicting and sometimes contradictory theological and pastoral perspectives. Exploration papers associated with the project noted that the vitality of the church would and could only coincide with its firm commitment to, "[the] ability of ministry to be open to the broadest variety of human concerns, the most profound questions of individual and social life."[6] Murnion saw the implementation of a new parish social order and policy committed to social ministry as deeply important to the role of the modifications of Vatican II. While acknowledging that there were normative theological foundations for the institutional response of the church leadership, he noted that there are many opportunities for pluralistic expressions and actions in an individual parish program. He believed these opportunities would lead to a renewed vitality in Roman Catholic parishes. The Parish Project's working document suggested that this "ability of ministry to be open to the broadest variety of human concerns, the most profound questions of individual and social life"[7] would assist in the integration of families into the broader structure of the church. In addition, it suggested that the church retain its concerns for morality and the justification of its beliefs, yet—through the use of a variety of ministries at the parish level—attempt to acknowledge the diversity of the peoples served in an individual community. Even in the hierarchical structure, changes were being effected. Serious references, not just lip service, to family structures as true and respected roots in the educational processes began to appear in church documents nationally and internationally.

Recent Pastoral History in
St. Vincent Parish: Focus on Households

In meeting with the staff members who were described in the first section of this essay, the coauthors were struck by the broad nature of their utilization of the term "family." *Family*, in general, referred to a "household." In fact, the staff had used this generic term for a number of years in an attempt not to exclude anyone from joining the parish family. They wished to express the thought that those willing to practice their faith communally and worship with others committed to the parish mission could become members. Clearly, the staff members were motivated by a desire to include all persons, regardless of gender, race, age, ethnicity, marital status, or sexual orientation. As the leaders of a parish struggling to survive in a rapidly changing neighborhood, the staff felt the need to include all people in their vision of parish family. As evidence of this desire, during our interview with the pastor, he noted that families and individuals filling out the paperwork necessary to become parishioners were asked why they wanted to join the membership at St. Vincent Parish. His point was that a person's worldly status meant little in terms of belonging. Rather, one's expressed desire to serve others plus a willingness to be hospitable to all—along with a desire to worship communally—were needed to really "become" a part of the St. Vincent family. Clearly evident here was the parish's encouragement of a broad community among its individual and family members. Evelyn Whitehead refers to this stage of a community's development as one "that challenges the sometimes impersonal and outdated structures that many experience as [a] parish."[8] In these developments in St. Vincent, one can see evidence of the movement out of impersonalities that for Evelyn Whitehead characterized some Catholic parishes.

Since the people of St. Vincent no longer wished to remain anonymous and distant from each other—a cold, impersonal parish—many changes had to take place in the parish's structure and daily operations. During interviews, the pastor acknowledged several developments that assisted the parish in becoming a more person- and family-oriented community.

In order to renew itself and to be more alive to the parishioners and more representative of the ethnic makeup of the neighborhood, the parish recognized a need to develop closer relationships among its own parishioners. It was also during this period, in the mid-1980s, that the staff began to see a new mission statement forming for the parish, one expressed in the light of social justice issues and community woes such as fractured family life and diminished services caused by cutbacks in social spending in designated federal funding. The parish began to understand the tremendous need for mutual support systems between the parish and the surrounding neighborhood. Two vignettes express the pervading need for mutual program support.

A young woman, currently a staff member, had just graduated from college. She was a talented musician but had little chance of finding work in her field. She was one of the few African American members of the parish. This woman had talent to share. She also had a secret: She was an unwed mother. She gathered up her courage to ask the pastor to hire her. She expressed a wish to make overtures to the African American population of the neighborhood. She offered to use her musical talents to provide choirs at church worship services. In return, she asked that the parish provide both financial and emotional support for herself and her son.

In the second vignette, a young man and his companion sought membership in a parish community. They did not feel welcomed in any of the neighborhood churches they had previously visited, not because they were an unmarried couple, but because they were an openly gay couple. These two men also had talents that they wished to share with the community. In return, they were seeking understanding, a sense of familial concern that was lacking in their lives, and a place to be able to seek out mutual fellowship.

In both of these vignettes, which read as portraits of very real lives, one can look clinically at these descriptions of family life in the community near St. Vincent. In both stories the characters are integral parts of fractured families. They were hurt deeply by life. All of the individuals were despairing of finding a community that would accept them in the conditions to which they were bound. In both vignettes, we see human beings who seek to find their place in a social system, the Roman Catholic church—a system that they hoped would value their gifts and talents, and welcome them as individuals with needs to be met and gifts to share with a community.

For this parish, the movement toward greater inclusiveness had its start in 1969 when a Vincentian brother began his ministry. For the next several years, he, with the support of the parish staff members, began to put into place a better system for the parish to respond to the social woes of the families of the community. He planned and executed the renovation of the former parish convent into the parish center that serves all of the families of St. Vincent, new or old, rich or poor. Through this activity and others like it, the parish began to personalize its mission. It identified the needs of its own members and those of the residents of the surrounding community. The parish center allowed for a far-reaching social service to the people of Germantown. With a sense of oneness of purpose, the parishioners began to work in the center along with the staff members. After a short time, this building was no longer large enough to house all of the programs that the parish envisioned, so a second building, the former school, was utilized. With the help of parish members and with some community and foundation funding, the buildings were transformed. They now housed a soup kitchen, a food storage area, referral center, and an intake center where trained parishioners supplied information, particularly to the homeless and to emotionally disturbed and mentally incapacitated members of the larger surrounding community. In addition, rooms were set aside as a furniture bank and as a thrift clothing operation. The parishioners did not hire people to run these centers. Instead, they themselves became assistants under the direction of various staff members. What had previously been impersonal neighborhood disputes and difficulties now had names and faces attached. What becomes personal can no longer be ignored or passed by unseen. Rather, in addressing the oppression of some members and families of their community, the parish had internalized the experiences, which became the mission of the community of St. Vincent Parish.

Evelyn Whitehead identifies this form of growth as the beginning of the development of true community in the spirit of family life. She notes that in generating feelings of oneness and in living a shared personal existence with the neighborhood, parish members gained a sense of oneness of purpose with each other, which was to lead families to identify the vision and values of their very intimate parish.[9] Ms. Whitehead also notes that in acting as it did, early in its new state, the parish "as a large organization" began "to facilitate communication and interaction on a continuum used to describe the development of family forms and group interaction."[10]

Because the church community came together in the early 1980s and developed a mission, people and families like those in the two vignettes were able to become active members of a vibrant community. In fact, the parish developed its mission statement to reflect its desire to serve its families and its neighborhood, through the development of good liturgy, by offering excellent hospitality to all who entered the property, and through the skilled social services they provided. The initial step in parish family development helped to bridge the gaps among many of the parish membership and their neighbors in Germantown. This step also allowed for some intense relationships to form, as people reached out toward one another. Many parishioners and neighbors began to meet in small sharing groups, as they set about identifying further communal needs that could be addressed. In meeting the needs of the parish and neighborhood community, these people feel they were responding to their Christian duty.

Recent History: United States
Episcopal Conference Statements

More recent church teachings—both at the international level of the church and at the level of the writings and exhortations issued by the United States Catholic Conference of Bishops—have been very encouraging compared to the compilation of documents concerning family life developed by this same group over the past thirty years. The United States' bishops have given considerable leeway in their description of the nature of being family. These documents have also produced some new modifications in strategy for parish planning with families, as a particular theme and circumstance. Also encouraging are signs that texts issued by many of the Roman Catholic publishing companies are more representative of the Catholic families involved in parish life today. In addition, in a variety of the larger diocesan structures, there are Family Life offices with staffs that more closely resemble the peoples, cultures, and family situations present in the parish communities that they serve. In providing these services, the Family Life offices are following the directives of individual bishops and the conference of bishops in general.

One document in particular has had a great deal of impact: "Follow the Way of Love: A Pastoral Message of the United States Catholic Bishops to Families."[11] This document recognizes from its roots that the definition of family life is a transitional one at best. The document seeks to heal strained relations between the institutional church and the families that make up individual parishes. It addresses issues that are relevant to the various forms family life can take in the 1990s. This document also recognizes and supports the rights of a Roman Catholic to be, at once, both part of the temporal world, yet a true child of the kingdom of Heaven. Pastors, Family Life Centers, and Christian families—even people who choose to remain single—have found encouragement, opportunity, and resources for assistance in carrying out the responsibility of being the "way of love, even as Christ loved you."[12]

In the initial section of the document, "The Way of Love" clearly recognizes the individual nature of today's families, and it treats the diversity of such individualism as a gift, rather than as a problem. In this profound document, the American bishops speak of celebrations and struggles, the good news of the world, and that which is prejudicial. More importantly, it points out one very clear fact: regardless of the family structure one is called to form, and in whatever circumstances an individual may have undertaken the path of life, all people are called to share in the saving graces of God's love. That is, those who are heterosexual as well as those in homosexual unions, and those in solid marriages as well as those for whom divorce has become a reality will share in God's plan for families. This view is perhaps the most encouraging of all: that all families have a vision in which to grow and that parishes are to respect that vision and encourage its development.

"Follow the Way of Love" asks that families carry out the gospel message by sharing belief in God, experiences of familial love, and intimacy—both in family life and in friendships; evangelizing others who are in need of nurturing; pursuing an active education; assisting others to a renewed prayer life; and serving the community. In addition, this document binds all parishioners in the common causes of reconciling broken relationships, celebrating wonderful moments in the lives of others, acting in a just manner in the community, welcoming those who have no family, and affirming the value of all lives. This document gives value and structure to the gospel message of Jesus and vilifies the lives of those who struggle in their daily life. The Bishop's paper also calls for an acknowledgment by individual parishes of all families in their community, be it those who suffer through divorce, death, blended families and relationships, and so forth. All share in the grace that is God's gift to God's community.

Recent History:
St. Vincent Parish

The staff and parishioners are constantly bringing pressure upon the leadership in the neighborhood to help others face the many social problems that face the families in their community. In fact, seeing the pain and despair of the neighborhood drives the social justice programs at the parish center. Just as the Catholic bishops have asked of them, the people of St. Vincent Parish give witness to God's goodness by their acceptance of people, and by sharing their giftedness and talents. Many share their professional talents in the legal and medical fields and others assist in fulfilling the promises of mutuality and love.

There were many end products generated through the initial steps taken to serve the needs of others. These steps reflect the need of the parishioners to reach out to families in order to continue to grow communally. One of the greatest end products was growth in membership generated as word of the work being done at the parish level began to filter into Germantown. This payoff was generous indeed. Many individuals and young couples began to travel to the church from many surrounding suburban communities, especially seeking concern for their family. As the parish grew, it became much more diverse, even more diverse than the community that sustained it. As with any new situation, the enormous changes began to affect the people-to-people interactions. One intense area of concern for the staff and parish leadership was how to plan for, service, and commune with others among the diverse ethnicity of people that now made up the worshiping congregation of St. Vincent Parish. As the leadership reviewed their mission statement during the boon years of the mid-1980s, they began to look at particular segments of the community rather than at the community at large. This scrutiny led them to reflect on the population segments that were not previously receiving direct parish attention: needy families, the rather large African American community that surrounded the church buildings, families who were raising small children, and the elderly population.

Other Roman Catholic documents reflect on the partnership between the parish and the family. One of the newest and most celebrated is called "Families at the Center: A Handbook for Parish Ministry with a Family Perspective." Written in 1990 by the Bishop's Committee on Marriage and the Family, this handbook offers carefully worded suggestions for those who staff parishes. Although this booklet strives to give a Christian perspective on the development of family, it also recognizes diversity. It asks that each parish look inward—perhaps at its mission statement—then outward, to be certain that those of their community who are diverse racially, culturally, through sexual preference, and ethnicity are truly being served by the parish community. The program asks if there is a "preferred family structure in the parish? Does the parish reward only certain types of structures?"[13] Implicit here is the wish of the Bishop Committee to establish and celebrate a richness of diversity within a given parish. This attitude is certainly prevalent at St. Vincent Parish. The parishioners recognize the fact that they as a group of people are not representative of the diversity of those who live in the boundaries of the parish. The membership of St. Vincent de Paul has spent the past several years trying to establish better contacts within the neighborhood. They ask that their many parish pastoral and planning councils, while keeping in mind the traditional teaching of the institutional church, allow an individual to face any type of humiliating situation with regard to their complicated family situation or lifestyle. If families are considered at the center of any parish, are planning commissions and church services convenient for the types of families in the congregation? Are listening sessions held so that the parish may understand the needs of its individuals and its families? In the Bishop's document, "Families at the Center," the church hierarchy called for parish leadership that are open to questioning and personal reflection, in order to maximize family involvement. The Bishops wish to find ways for individuals to come to know God in a more intimate manner. In light of this document, when visiting the campus of St. Vincent Parish, one is struck by the fact that the vision of "Families at the Center" is carried out in its fullest measure. As an example, there is a twelve o'clock service daily, both for the working people of the neighborhood and for those families who are availing themselves of the parish's social services. One day, when I chanced into the church for the noontime service, I recognized one of the homeless men of the area who had also come into the worship space. Immediately, the priest presider led the man to a front pew, greeted him by name, and thanked the man for his prayers during the liturgy. Other parishioners welcomed the man as well. Following the liturgy, a staff member met the gentleman and brought him to the social services area. No, there would be no back pew for this gentle person, but only the best accommodation the parish had to offer, a front-row seat. This is a true gesture of the warmth offered by the people of St. Vincent Parish.

In order to reflect on many parish and neighborhood issues, the parish held several Sunday sessions to redevelop its leadership among its parish council. The council was to be responsible for addressing the above issues and develop ideas and the means to assist the many homogeneous groups that populated the congregation. They would assist these groups to grow in maturity of faith, theology, and leadership abilities. They were to be given the opportunity to worship together, mindful of the many cultural flavors of the people. In addition, the council was charged with assisting the growth of families in positive ways. In using this method as an avenue for change, the staff of St. Vincent Parish, according to Evelyn Whitehead, interacted as an "intermediate group." Mediating the various discrepancies and diverse problems that faced the parish community brings a new level of intimacy to the relationships present in the parish community.[14] As an intermediate grouping, the council and staff urged the church community to think of itself not as "households," but as "familial structures." During this time the generic term, "household," became to both the staff and the parish in general an inadequate description of the parish membership.

Several factors seem to have redirected the community's attention and purpose toward family structures and problems. For instance, many of the younger couples, most of them professional, were raising children or contemplating beginning their family. While there had previously been a small group of families with young children present at the Sunday liturgical rites, there were so few Roman Catholic children in the immediate Germantown area that the parish school had been forced to close during the 1970s.

This fact changed during the renewal of the parish. In addition to the influx of children from the immediate neighborhood, many families from the suburban areas were bringing children to the Sunday worship services. This situation—along with the relevance of the needs of the elderly community and the poor of the area—demanded a new response on the part of the parish community, a whole new method of planning for the parish. The parish leadership was assisting the community in redeveloping itself, thus creating new life through its reaction to the variety of new situations that were occurring among its membership.

Several "town meetings" were held, usually following a selected Sunday Mass. Monthly forums were also conducted by the leadership. They were held at times that the committees felt were convenient to all community members. Coffee hours were also added. All of these sessions were designed so that the staff and leadership could hear and understand the needs of its people. It was also expected that these meetings would generate responses from the membership to answer the many issues to which the community was attempting to respond. During these sessions, the community acknowledged that it had and was continuing to undergo dramatic cultural, traditional, and familial transition. These changes were impacting every aspect of parish life. Through these sessions it was determined that creative means of rethinking religious experiences were necessary.

Out of this rebirthing process, the parish community made a firm commitment to reorganize four specific areas of communal life: to offer hospitality, by any means necessary, to all who requested assistance; to create a liturgical worship environment that would free each member to pursue the Spirit of God through his or her own cultural, ethical, and personal images; to commit to value, accept, and plan educational and social activities for families with younger children; and finally, to raise the respect for and awareness of certain practices in the community, that are designated to assist the needs of the elderly. In addition, the parish renewed its commitment to its mission to evangelize and care for the needs of the marginal peoples of St. Vincent Parish.

There are many small communities within St. Vincent Parish. They come together for prayer, at the hour they agree to meet. One of the associate pastors, a woman religious, provides the material for their Bible study. These groups are, like the examples above, designed to meet the expressed needs of the community membership. And, here, as always, there is baby-sitting service available to all who attend. This in itself is an invaluable aid to parents, especially single mothers and fathers, who wish to avail themselves of the gifts and programs of the parish. St. Vincent de Paul is a parish that has responded to the call of the Bishops to really look toward the needs of others. They have thought out many of the details that help rather than hinder families in coming together for worship and social services.

Unresolved Agenda

While in the process of assessing the parish's offerings, people are gathered in a process of reflection. As a result, the parish has made some painful discoveries. Racism existed among its membership at both the practiced and at the perceived levels; cultural and ethnic differences separated some members of the community from others. These differences, while they were not a staggering burden for a growing parish, were certainly cause for concern. The parishioners acknowledged that differences among peoples did occur and needed immediate redress from a community that purported to offer hospitality to all who participated. Other family life issues, among them the care given to the gay membership and single members of the community, prevented the people of St.

Vincent Parish from becoming the seamless garment that they envisioned for their membership.

One issue that raises its ugly head in the neighborhood surrounding St. Vincent Parish is racism, or a separation. The parishioners worry about the segregating of the worshiping community from its surrounding neighborhood. The staff and the parishioners have worked very hard to alter this situation, but the development of trust takes a great deal of time to come to fruition. This parish has not given up hope. They continue to reach out to the neighborhood through personal invitation, evangelization, common worship services, and friendly gestures, in the hope of breaking the remaining racial and ethnic barriers. To some degree their persistence has reaped its reward, but much is still to be done in this area of ministry.

There also remains the issue of the frustration of the single people in the community, some of whom are homosexual. Although many feel welcomed, as we read in the earlier vignette, the parish is still wrestling with responses to the needs of those who are single. Discussions recently have revealed several possible social service leads that might assist the people of the neighborhood. St. Vincent Parish may in fact respond to those with the AIDS virus. Perhaps they will find new methods of gathering the lonely and address the problems faced by those who live alone. The parish council is working to address these issues at future parish forums.

Among all of these issues, the one of immediate concern seemed to be responding to the need for religious education for youngsters. After several meetings in the late 1980s, the parish procured the capable services of a Sister of St. Joseph. The St. Vincent Parish community challenged her to evangelize among the children of the immediate neighborhood. She was to identify each child and determine their needs, which proved to be quite a challenge. The hierarchical structures of the Roman Catholic church in Philadelphia had failed to do its best to encourage membership among minority communities. Many of these families were suspicious of any attempts on the part of the Sister to meet with and develop educational programs for their children. To make this project more difficult, the parish council asked that any new program be woven into current programming available for the middle-class children already being served by the parish.

Undaunted, this Sister visited with the families in the neighborhood to ascertain their spiritual, emotional, and physical needs. In order to meet the spiritual needs of all of the children of the parish, a religious education program was developed, one that simply flowed out of the liturgical rites of the Sunday worship, the Mass. The young members of the parish would exit the body of the church, following the opening greetings and prayers. Carefully trained group leaders oversaw small group reading and discussion of the lesson. The scripture of the day, albeit a watered-down version, was discussed by the children, and at times reenacted by them. At other times, artwork and crafts were produced. All of the discussion and the project were designed to respect all of the children who were present from the community. In addition, the discussions were rooted in the values and mindful of the mission statement of St. Vincent Parish. Thus, what was professed by the worshiping community concerning family was being put into practice. As a case in point here, a friend's son was a five-year-old child when his family, who lived comfortably in a neighboring suburban community, began to attend St. Vincent for Sunday worship. The child's mother, herself a professional theologian, had been the primary source of religious education for her son. She had used her skills to help her son appreciate the Mass and make an adult ritual more palatable to a young child. Thus, the young man became familiar with the Roman Catholic rites. However, after the family joined St. Vincent Parish, the child began to point out the many differences between his former church community and the parish life he experienced at St. Vincent's. To him, new children, experiences, and families from a variety of ethnic ancestries proved quite interesting. He began to call the Mass the "Eucharist," because he now understood that the ritual was intended as a sharing among friends, neighbors, and family. He expressed an interest in sharing, too. The family signed up to serve meals at the parish soup kitchen. The young man prided himself in sharing! He also opined that the Eucharistic liturgy, along with the "Children's liturgy of the Word," was a much shorter rite than the "long Mass" presided over at his former parish. In fact, however, the liturgy of sharing at St. Vincent's was almost twice as long as the formal Mass the family had previously attended. This vignette is proof positive of the nature of the parish's commitment to family life. It shows how a parish should be able to join together, in a ritual of sharing, while providing for all the needs of the parish, even the needs of its youngest people.

Just recently, one of the researchers had the opportunity, after almost a year, to revisit St. Vincent Parish. The occasion was the liturgy of the Easter Vigil, perhaps one of the holiest celebrations in the Roman Catholic calendar. What was witnessed at that liturgy gave me hope for all Christian parishes.

Several new members were being baptized into the Roman Catholic tradition. With a great deal of song and celebration, the four adults to be received gathered for the Mass. The celebrant of the liturgy was the pastor of St. Vincent Parish. At his side was not the usual assistant pastor of the parish, a cleric, but a lay presider of prayer, a term coined by fringe members of the church. The lay presider of prayer was a woman. She, like the main celebrant, was dressed in the colors of the season. She too wore a mantle of cloth, a sign of respect for her role in the liturgy. One sensed that every individual at the liturgy understood that a moment such as this was new and refreshing. This was meaningful for the Roman Catholic community as a whole. It was not as if the parish were breaking any liturgical rule in a legalistic way. But in bending the current structures, they were breaking new ground for women in the Roman Catholic Church.

As the evening continued, the four who were to be officially received into the church community walked individually to the baptismal pond. Then, each person was dressed in a white garment. One by one, each stepped into the pond. Three times, they were blessed by the priest, the lay presider, while the community sang a song of welcoming for each of the new members. Following the immersion, as each person came out of the water, the pastor was there, holding a huge, white, fluffy blanket. Using the motional range of his entire body, he engulfed the individual into the blanket by folding them into his arms, smothering each new parishioner with the love of the entire community.

Yes, all parishes can truly be graced with the complete presence of God, if they persevere throughout the difficulties, the official red tape. By doing so, each parish will stand enriched, as we believe that St. Vincent de Paul Parish is enriched, with a true love for the individual membership, with respect for the rights of all diversification of family life, with a caring for the entire community, and with a true love for the strangers in their midst, for any of these among them might be the one called the Savior.

NOTES

1. "Total Population by Race," *1990 Census* (Philadelphia: Philadelphia Planning Commission, 1990), 16–17.
2. Ibid.
3. "Total Population by Race," 5–6.
4. Ibid.

5. Evelyn Whitehead, *The Parish in Community and Ministry* (New York: Paulist Press, 1978), 36.

6. Philip Murion, "Parish Projects: The Unmet Challenge of Vatican II," *Origins* 8, no. 2 (1981): 30.

7. Ibid., 30.

8. Whitehead, *The Parish in Community and Ministry,* 47.

9. Ibid., 37.

10. Ibid., 39.

11. Ad Hoc Committee of U.S. Bishops, "Follow the Way of Love: Message of the U.S. Catholic Bishops to Families, 1994," *Catholic International* 5 (February 1994): 86.

12. Ibid., 5.

13. Bishops Ad Hoc Committee on the Family, *Families at the Center: A Handbook for Parish Ministry with a Family Perspective* (New York: United States Catholic Conference, 1990), 3.

14. Whitehead, *The Parish in Community and Ministry,* 37–38.

3

The Braid of Generations

A Model of Family Ministry

BRITA L. GILL-AUSTERN

Prelude

The sounds of Congregation Beth El open one to hear the rhythms and reoccurring themes of this synagogue's life. These sounds carry something of its unique character. To hear the *niggunim* (chants) sung by the congregation during a Shabbat service is to feel the spirituality and sense of community that knits this synagogue together. The *niggunim* become, as the rabbi says, one path to help people get from where they are to where they want to be, the critical analytical side shuts down and opens one to experience the holiness of the present moment.[1] To hear the cries of restless children in the service is to know that they are welcome in the center of this congregation's life. To overhear private whispered prayer in the midst of community is to know that relationship to God is taken very seriously and the communal and individual expressions of piety are interwoven intimately here. To listen to the *shofar* on Rosh Hashanah is to be reminded that this house of worship is a part of a history spanning generations and continents. To hear the arguing with the rabbi and the bantering over Torah in the bat/bar mitzvah class or on Shabbat morning is to know the intellectual vitality that undergirds this congregation. To feel your feet and hands moving involuntarily to the music of the klezmer (Yiddish revival jazz) band as the congregation dances with the Torah on Simchat Torah is to know the joy that is at the heart of Judaism and that permeates this congregation, drawing its generations close to one another.

Beth El is a special place. The rhythms, cadences, and themes that define its being pull one in and link one with past and future generations. I have been drawn into the life of this congregation as observer and participant. My Jewish husband and Jewish children belong to Beth El, and therefore it is integrally interwoven into our family life. As a Christian, it is not my primary religious home, but participating in its life has deepened and enriched my faith and enlarged my vision about the possibilities of family ministries within congregations.

Reoccuring themes in the life of Beth El contribute to the special character of this congregation's ministry to families: a ministry as vital, dynamic, and joyous as I have seen anywhere. Beth El holds a vision of family that is inclusive of diverse forms and views family within a generational perspective that vastly expands the meaning of "family." The family is seen as central to the passing on of Jewish identity, and helping parents raise children with a strong Jewish identity therefore is key to the synagogue's ministry to families. The primary vehicle for ministry to families is through educational programming. Here the braid of generations is woven together and people are helped to find authentic religious experience through the normal developmental changes in the family life cycle.

Participation in and observation of this community of faith, interviews with staff and several members, documents written by members of the congregation, as well as the rabbi's sermons and writings are the resources for the writing of this essay.

Background and History/Foundations

Beth El is young, established in 1962 when twenty-three families met to explore establishing a new Jewish community in a suburb of Boston. Its building program began with thirteen families pledging forty-four thousand dollars over three years, and a very unpretentious prefab structure was constructed. It has been recently remodeled to accommodate its ever-growing religious school and congregational ministries.

In January 1971, one year after the dedication of a new temple and two years after a search for a full-time rabbi, 66 members out of 120 came to see if agreement could be reached to affiliate with one of the organized religious movements. On that day five voted for affiliating with the Orthodox, eleven with the Reconstructionists, nineteen with the Conservative movement, and twenty-three with the Reform movement, with the rest voting against any of these. Beth El's identity became and remains officially Reform, affiliating with the UAHC (Union of American Hebrew Congregations), but the congregation decided to observe these practices:

1. The second day of Rosh Hashanah was to be observed.
2. Skull caps and prayer shawls were to be voluntary.
3. Shabbat morning services were to be held in addition to those on Erev Shabbat.
4. A kosher kitchen would be maintained.[2]

These decisions created a synagogue with a unique character that draws many into its fold because it blends the traditional and the modern into a creative synthesis. Heavy use of Hebrew in the service, the chanting of *niggunim,* emphasis on study, and the more traditional celebration of holidays give the resonances of a more traditional *shul* (synagogue). The radical embrace of equality between men and women in all aspects of its life and its many intermarried couples contribute to its Reform character.

Insiders affectionately call Beth El "Neo-Hasidic Reform" or "Reconservorthodox," because it does not easily fit conventional labels. To say it is a Reform synagogue simply fails to describe it. The rabbi, Lawrence Kushner, likes to think of it as "post-denominational in the sense that the Reform movement was originally meant to be—that we'll try anything that works and avoid any kind of orthodoxy."[3] This congregation draws members from all the movements within Judaism and develops a strong religious identity in its members. People take their Jewishness very seriously and celebrate it joyfully. This unique identity, weaving the traditional and the modern, profoundly shapes its family ministries.

Beth El currently embraces around 450 households, with over 100 joining in the last three years. Sixty percent have school-age children. The rabbi has been there for twenty-five years and has shaped strongly the ethos and character of this congregation. The staff also includes a director of education, a cantor and a Jewish Life educator.

Reoccurring Egalitarian Theme

Critical to Beth El's approach to family ministries is a pervasive egalitarian ethic. There is no "separate but equal" category here. Women wear the *yarmulke* (skull cap) and *tallis* (prayer shawl), read Torah in the service, and are involved in all leadership roles. There is a faithful observing of the ritual of naming, *Simchat Bat,* for Jewish girls as a counterpoint to the *Brit Mila,* (circumcision of boys). Bat mitzvah is as important as bar mitzvah.[4]

Perhaps one of the most revealing things about this synagogue and descriptive of its character is its *siddur* (prayer book), *Vetaher Libenu* (Purify Our Hearts). In 1975 the Ritual Committee responded to the congregation's increasing dissatisfaction with the lack of Hebrew in the "newly revised" Union Prayer Book and the archaic translations of the liturgy found in other prayer books. The Ritual Committee organized thirty individuals into a working group to create and compose a *siddur* to meet Beth El's specific needs. In May 1975 *Vetaher Libenu* was published and became a central part of the life of Beth El. With its publication Beth El became more nationally known. Many individuals and communities requested copies. In 1979 members decided that it was time to write a new prayer book, as the first one thousand copies were exhausted. The Ritual Committee ripped up the first draft of the *Vetaher Libenu II,* unanimously deciding that exclusive use of male and medieval imagery for God invited idolatry. In October 1980 Beth El published the first nonsexist Jewish prayer book, now in its sixth printing. This prayer book with its inclusive language for God and humanity and its eloquent poetry is foundational to its life. Other prayer books for the high holidays are now being written by members of the congregation.

Family and Family Ministry:
Meanings and Definitions

Synagogues traditionally count membership by families, not by individuals. This orientation reverses that of most Christian congregations. About ten years ago Beth El began to define a family as those who shared a household. Thus, families at Beth El have many different configurations. Though its understanding of family for membership purposes is those sharing a household, its theological understandings of family are deeper and broader. Family is not simply a nuclear family, a household, or any of our private understandings of family. Family can only be understood within the context of generations.

Beth El's family education program begins with the kindergarten program called *Shalshelet HaDorot* (the great braid of generations). Family includes connection to generations past and future. Both are essential to carry forward the Jewish tradition faithfully. Thus, though its definition of family as household is very contemporary in its inclusiveness, the rabbi states that the purpose of the family is to raise Jewish children. Without Jewish children the braid of generations and of Judaism breaks. Its theology of family underscores the parents' responsibility to raise their children

within the Jewish tradition and to give them a strong, healthy Jewish identity. Family ministry focuses not simply on strong religious education, but
on connecting the generations. As Rabbi Kushner put it in one interview,
"Family life is the raison d'être of everything we do; it is absolutely fundamental to my conception of what a congregation is to be."

Beth El bears witness to the rabbi's conviction that we meet God in
the faces of our parents and in the faces of our children, because our parents' faces tell us that we have been born, and the faces of our children
tell us we will die. We meet God in the cycle of generations (Kushner
1988, 1). Stefan Zweig, the Austrian Jewish author, wrote: "One who
looks at his father is like one who sees God, because he can look beyond
his father to creation. And one who looks at his children sees God, because he can look beyond his children through the generations to see
the Messiah."[5] This theology leads to a family ministry that celebrates
developmental transitions of those in the community as places of encounter with the holy.

While Beth El works to increase commitment to Judaism and its practices, such as the observance of Shabbat, it recognizes pressures and
stresses on family life. Beth El accommodates the realities of today's families, while maintaining a commitment to making a place for Judaism in
the rhythms of modern life. If a family can't have a Shabbat dinner together, its members are advised to try to light the candles and have the
blessings over bread and wine before people leave home on Friday
evening. This openness to changing realities is also evident in the embrace of varying family configurations, including intermarried couples
and gay and lesbian couples.

Intermarried Couples
and Their Families

One of the many family forms that Beth El embraces and welcomes
is that of intermarried couples. The congregation has many intermarried
couples—15 to 20 percent of the congregation—and it reaches out to
them intentionally. The outreach attempts to involve non-Jewish members of the congregation in learning about Judaism and becoming a part
of the life of Beth El. There are four or five conversions each year of intermarried congregants, often around the bar/bat mitzvah of a son or
daughter. Proselytizing among the intermarried couples is absent, but
Beth El reaches out consciously to give them the tools to feel a part of
the community.[6]

The rabbi maintains the official position of Judaism against participating in intermarriage ceremonies. Research demonstrates that children of intermarried couples are much less committed to Judaism over
the long haul. The rabbi tells people this. Yet, if someone is already intermarried, even if there is a certain amount of cognitive dissonance,
there is no conflict. His attitude reflects a Talmudic passage that says, "If
you ask me before, I'll tell you no; if you ask me afterwards, it is O.K."
Intermarriage is discouraged, but there is great tolerance of it where it
has taken place. A desire to reach out to these families as much as possible is demonstrated in the encouragement of their full participation.
The synagogue and Reform Judaism fully support intermarried couples
who wish to raise their children Jewish.

Gays and Lesbians Are Also Families

One Yom Kippur (the day of atonement in the Jewish high holy days)
service I attended, the rabbi spoke on gay and lesbian relationships. That
he would choose this topic for Yom Kippur says volumes. I asked him
how he came to his stance of openness and inclusiveness. He shared that
it was in meeting with members of the congregation who were gay or
had gay kids. He said, "In every meeting, they wept." This affected him
powerfully. He had friends who were, as he put it, "further along than I
was at that time and it became very clear to me that the real issue was
what kind of community do you want gay and lesbian Jews to have?" He
would like to think that the congregation doesn't pay much attention to
sexual orientation or gender. For him, the best thing to say to someone
who "comes out," is "So what?"

The congregation does not do anything explicitly for gay or lesbian
couples; they are accepted and counted as families. There is less concern
about homosexual behavior and more concern about whole people and
their becoming committed Jews.

In response to the argument of many that homosexuality destroys
family life, Rabbi Kushner said in his sermon for Yom Kippur:

> What ruins family life even more is dehumanizing and exiling one
> of its children, attempting to compel them to lead celibate lives,
> and denying them equal social and religious status. Inability to par-
> ent one's own children for whatever reason is no reason to deny
> any loving couple the joys of sexual love and children, either
> through artificial insemination or adoption. There are plenty of or-
> phans in need of a loving home. We encourage the creation of lov-

ing, nurturing Jewish homes where children can grow into loving and mature adult Jews.[7]

Rabbi Kushner stated that the goal of the synagogue is to fashion a Jewish community that welcomes and respects everyone regardless of sexual preference. He declared that, "There is no moral or religious reason why two men or two women cannot establish mutual, monogamous, nurturing, loving relationships and families. Homosexual couples are perfectly able to raise healthy children."[8] Gay and lesbian members and their relationships are a part of the fabric of Beth El. They belong as threads in the braid of generations. They are included as families and accepted as families in all aspects of ritual and synagogue life.

Torah—the Tree of Life
for Family Ministry

Much of family ministry at Beth El centers around the holiness of the Torah. In the Talmud it says that there are three ways we serve God: by study, prayer, and acts of loving kindness. Study of Torah is regarded as one of the ways we serve God, and it is an essential part of the spirit that animates this congregation.

There is perhaps no better symbol for the centrality of Torah to this synagogue's life and to its family ministry than the very festive and joyous celebration of *Simchat Torah*. This Jewish holiday celebrates the completion of the year's cycle of Torah readings and the commencing again of the reading of Genesis. Children love this holiday for its spontaneity, frenzied dancing, spirited music, and singing, all which convey abandon and intoxicating joy around the Torah. At Beth El the tradition is that everyone forms a circle, lining the walls of the sanctuary, and the entire Torah scroll is slowly unrolled from hand to hand, with babies to the elderly gently holding the parchment of the sacred scroll. When the unrolling is complete, the story of creation in Genesis touches the story of Moses' death in Deuteronomy. Groups are assigned sections of the Torah from which they create presentations in music, rhymes, riddles, or mini dialogues. Then the scroll is rewound ready to be read from the beginning. The music of a klezmer band invites all into dancing with the raised Torah as it is passed from person to person in ecstatic jubilation. The Torah becomes the partner with whom everyone wants to dance.

The Torah is the tree of life in this synagogue; its nutrients feed the minds, bodies, and souls of its families. The Torah focuses families on what is important and helps them sort out the essential from the trivial in their lives. Torah is the heart that pulsates in all the rhythms and movements of the congregation and gives families a sense of their unique place and identity.

The Jewish approach to scripture is also critical to Beth El's family ministry. Christians tend to look to the Bible for stories that lift up ethical ideals to model. In Judaism there is less search for biblical ego ideals and more recognition that often the family stories of the Bible are horrific. Families are destroyed and demolished in the Hebrew scriptures. As the rabbi put it:

> It is not just like they have problems, they are terrible; there is murder, rape, lying, cheating, thieving; families are not just injured, but destroyed week after week. One Jewish teacher said, there is no one in the Hebrew Bible that you want your kid to grow up to be like. Therapists have told me that around December they do record business, especially with alcoholics, because the disparity between the idealized family and the reality of their own family is excruciating and intolerable. Jews have less of this. The scriptural lessons diffuse the idealism.

Psychologically astute people know that the gap between expectation and reality causes suffering. Overidealization of the family creates images of the perfect family that are impossible to emulate. The rabbi says clearly, "We are not Ozzie and Harriets here, we name what is, as well as what we would like to be." Scripture lessons defuse the idealization of the family and help people recognize themselves in the discord, deceit, sibling rivalry, and messiness of family life, and opens them to share from the depths of their experience. In conversation with the rabbi, he pointed out the Hebrew Bible is notorious for not hitting you over the head with a lesson. You can be instructed by seeing the consequences of actions. For instance, when Rebecca pits one son against the other in service of her bizarre dream, what happens? She never sees her beloved son again; Jacob never sees his parents again.

Family-Centered Also Means
Home-Centered

Traditionally, Judaism has been passed on through the generations, not primarily by participation in the synagogue, but by faithful familial observance of Shabbat and other Jewish holidays and rituals. Judaism is not learned first through cognitive acquisition of concepts or principles, but through the repetition and participation in ritual observance in family life.

Education Director Sheila Goldberg noted a critical turning point in the congregation's thinking about religious education when they realized that the present generation of children may know more about Judaism than their parents. Many in the congregation were raised in nonreligiously observant homes and had minimum exposure to what they should be passing on to their children. To strengthen the braid of generations, the parents must be educated with the children, for ultimately the parents in Judaism must teach the children. Abraham Heschel stated it well:

> Significantly, the biblical injunction does not say that we are to appoint a teacher to train our children. The biblical injunction is that the parent be the teacher. . . . Thou shalt teach them diligently, not vicariously.

The synagogue does not try to take over the role of the parents, but to support, undergird, and give them resources to do their job raising Jewish children. The synagogue's job is to empower and teach parents the tools to model a Jewish way of life for their children. There is a commitment to including parents and grandparents wherever possible. Parents are expected to be students, too! This high expectation has its rewards. One parent expressed it this way: "My daughter knows I'm studying while she is studying and it has a way of putting us on equal footing as we learn together."

Family Ministry Requires Family Education

The metaphor one might choose to speak of Beth El as a congregation is not family but *shul* (school). Yet it is a *shul* organized for families to help create more Jewish families. Study is taken seriously and playfully at Beth El. It is seen as a part of what Jews are commanded to do and what it means to be a Jew. Beth El's family ministry grows out of the conviction that faithful ministry to families must deepen their Jewish identity and enable them to see how the tradition can speak to the most significant issues and concerns of their life together.

Family education must link the generations to enable the parents and children to reconnect through the tradition. The Family Learning Program booklet states:

> The difference between family learning and religious school is that the religious school ceases to be a surrogate for parents teaching

children. Instead, the Family Learning Program becomes both an arena where parents and children learn together and an enabling mechanism for parents to become their child's primary teachers. Religious school becomes a place where children begin to form their own Jewish peer community through informal Jewish learning experiences.

Family education enables families and friends to do Jewish things together. A grant from the Combined Jewish Philanthropies has supported Beth El's commitment to strengthen the family through an educational approach that emphasizes family learning rather than the individual child. To do this, Beth El links family education to developmental stages and transitions more than to specific ages.

Family Education Linked to Developmental Milestones

There is one great life issue, leaving one's parents and returning time and again, according to Rabbi Larry Kushner:

> We spend our lives trying to get away from our parents and keeping our children close, but since everyone is both a child and a parent of the next generation, you don't have to be a rocket scientist to figure out that we have a problem here. Lots of kids who want to get away. Lots of parents who want to keep their kids close. Lots of kids wanting to go home, but not being able to stand it when they get there. Lots of parents eager for their kids to go back to school, but not being able to stand it when they're gone.[9]

Our relationship with God is characterized by the same dance of leaving and returning to our source and destiny. Beth El helps people enact leaving and coming back every week. On a Saturday morning, coincidentally when there is a bar mitzvah and a baby naming, at the Kiddush table where the blessing is said over wine and bread, the rabbi doesn't know whether he should say first we have the baby, bar mitzvah, and then bridal couple; or bar mitzvah, couple, and then baby; or bridal couple, bar mitzvah, and then baby. The theme of leaving and returning dances through all these developmental life cycle observances.

Borrowing from family systems theorist Edwin Friedman, the rabbi speaks of nodal events as the times when family structure is open to new information and healthy growth, especially during the period six months before and six months after these pivotal times. Friedman has observed that "rites of passage" were the first human efforts to deal with modern psychotherapy's major concerns: change and separation.[10] These developmental shifts and the rituals marking them are religious because they touch people at their core. They touch what is most real.

Family systems change and rearrange themselves at developmental transition points. The homeostasis that resists change may crack, bend, or somehow be shaken. New possibility for healing appears and new opportunities for imagining ways of being in relationship arise. Because the ground of family life may shift significantly then, anxiety and exaltation accompany such turning points. The congregation and the rabbi help in significant ways in offering a structure and ritual to guide families through these transitions.

Beth El is extraordinarily intentional in ritualizing and making the most of the nodal events. They become not mere obligatory rituals, but life occasions filled with a sense of *kedushah* (holiness) for family and congregation. The rabbi says:

> One reason synagogues refuse to roll over and die is that Jews keep coming back to reenact the generational transmission, the most irreligious Jews meet God at baby namings, weddings, bar mitzvahs, because the generations are there. The generations point to something that is beyond use.[11]

Judaism has two calendars of sacred time—the public and the personal. The public calendar is the festival and holiday calendar; the private calendar revolves around the life cycle.[12] While Beth El misses no chance in the public calendar to bring families into full participation, our focus in this chapter is on the private calendar of Jewish sacred time: the nodal events in the life cycle. Here the congregation has a unique opportunity to help parents and family members with transitions and changing roles.

The families of Beth El are mostly dual-career couples with children. Most are professional and many are in high-powered positions. These families need a synagogue that provides centeredness and cohesiveness, and helps integrate the many threads of their lives. Beth El strives not only to avoid further fragmenting stressed and strained families, but to bring them together in ways that create more than the illusion of family togetherness. Family ministry seeks ways to help parents and children reconnect; the primary approach is through family education focused on life cycle events.

Bat/Bar Mitzvah

The life cycle may not begin with the bat/bar mitzvah, but it has become the most celebrated of the life cycle rituals in Reform synagogues and thus a natural beginning point for family education. Bar/bat mitzvah literally translates as "son or daughter of the commandment." It signifies that now one is old enough to be responsible for the *mitzvot* (commandments). With the bar/bat mitzvah one becomes able to fully participate in the ritual life of the synagogue. One becomes bar/bat mitzvah at or after one's thirteenth year. Thirteen was considered in the Mishnah and the Talmud as the time of spiritual, moral, and religious maturity. Some rabbinic sources explain that at thirteen a youth becomes able to make mature choices. It is only then that the youth possesses both the *yetser hatov* (the good inclination) and the *yetser hara* (the evil inclination), the twin forces of good and evil that Jewish theology sees struggling against one another in the human psyche.[13]

Bar/bat mitzvah is commonly understood as a coming-of-age ritual where one becomes a man or a woman. The real hope underlying the bar/bat mitzvah is that one will become a *mensch,* a full and decent Jewish human being. This is only possible if one knows the importance of being faithful to the commandments and keeping the *mitzvot.* It is not an initiation into privilege, but into responsibility. At thirteen, one inherits both the rights and responsibilities of keeping the *mitzvot.* It is critical to remember also that bar/bat mitzvah is about developing a special and sacred relationship to the Torah, to know experientially and intuitively the unique power of the scroll to evoke history, continuity, and tradition. Reading the Torah scroll a bar/bat mitzvah is not simply participating in an act that marks a coming of age. He or she is brought into contact with the mystery and awe of God's presence in this sacred text. Bar/bat mitzvah is a rite of initiation and a recognition of God's presence in the holiness of the encounter with the sacred scroll.[14]

It is not just the celebration on the day of the bat/bar mitzvah that makes Bat/bar mitzvah a transformative event, but the time spent together in advance preparation and study. Bar/bat mitzvah is a process as much as an event. Bar/bat mitzvah facilitates a sense of competence and mastery by requiring the learning of the Torah blessings in Hebrew, reading or chanting the week's Torah portion, and preparing a *D'var Torah,* a short sermonlike talk, for the event. Every bar/bat mitzvah child at Beth El must, in addition to attending Hebrew School twice weekly, attend a Torah study class with their parents and the rabbi for three months. This class is referred to as the "X-rated" one: children must be accompanied by one or both parents. The rabbi preaches that what we are teaching kids is what parents should be learning.

To sit in a room with children seated around the table with the rabbi and the parents grouped in a circle outside of the table, all learning together, is quite an experience. One parent described it:

> We sit behind our children for many Sunday mornings, sometimes proud of their wisdom, sometimes mortified by their frankness. We watch as the Rabbi deftly takes the ancient text and makes it come alive for them. Parents and teenagers learn from each other. The Torah class retreat is a special moment in time, a chance to witness what we thought impossible, our children grappling with Martin Buber, a chance to share Shabbat with other families as one extended family. Torah class adds a special dimension to an already special time in the lives of young adults and their families.[15]

Every child and parent who attends the Torah class for bar/bat mitzvah must attend a weekend retreat prior to the bar/bat mitzvah. The rabbi says, "They may not remember much of what they learned, but they will remember they came with you." The weekend begins Friday afternoon with kids and rabbi discussing Buber's "Way of Man." The parents sit on the outside of the circle, sometimes engaging in the discussion with the kids. The evening starts with a Shabbat meal and service, planned by the different families with much singing. The kids do a fun activity together while parents gather to share memories of their own bar/bat mitzvahs and something about their own Jewish journeys. A special bonding between parents happens during this time. Saturday morning begins with a Shabbat service, study around the Torah text, and then free time games and fun, followed in the late afternoon by some individual time for parents and children to work on questions about adolescence and Torah separately, and then parents meet individually with their own child to discuss their responses. Twilight brings the sweetness of the Sabbath to a close with a *Havdalah* service that marks the parting of the Sabbath from the rest of the week. On Saturday night parents talk about issues confronting kids of this age, sharing parenting expertise and struggles. The rabbi speaks about the importance of the bar/bat mitzvah's participation in the high school program after the bar/bat mitzvah. The retreat strengthens Jewish identity and parents and the bar/bat mitzvah class members forge closer friendships. Thus, all participants customarily invite other class members' families to their bar/bat mitzvah.

Bar/bat mitzvahs at Beth El are an integral part of the regular Shabbat morning service. This life cycle event is not set apart from the regular liturgical life of the congregation, but is made part of it.

The whole family tribe gathers for bar/bat mitzvahs. Members of families traditionally come from great distances to be present. It is a time of great emotion, as Rabbi Salkin describes it, a "river of tears."[16] Having experienced my eldest son's bar mitzvah this last year I can testify to the many streams that make up this river of tears. Tears come from tribal memory, reconnecting everyone present to the past and traditions of a people. The braid of generations is symbolized ritually in the moving act of the rabbi placing the Torah scroll in front of the ark, in the hands of the grandparents, then the grandparents passing it to the parents and then the parents to the child. One cannot help but be moved by this simple act that reminds us how tradition is handed down from one generation to another. This concretizes for the bar/bat mitzvah the truth that he or she is now part of a people whose roots are deeply woven into the past and reach to the future. This meets a fundamental need of an adolescent for a profound sense of belonging that links him or her with something much larger than the self.

There are also tears that flow from a sense of mortality and eternity. Professor Jacob Neusner describes it this way, "At a bar or a bat mitzvah, a parent thinks not so much of the future as of the past, especially if a grandparent or a parent is deceased; the entire family one has known has assembled, and that is as much the past as the future."[17] The frailty of aging grandparents, the absence of grandparents already dead and the unmistakable aging of the parents, all underscore not only the fragility and fleetingness of life, but that we are a part of a braid of generations, whose beginning and end transcends us as individuals. Meaning transcending the moment is touched, pulling one into the great stream of generations that bear witness to the life-giving and sustaining power of a God who redeems and delivers a people.

The tears also flow because the parents are moved. Most parents are entering into middle age, and they need rites of passage as much as their children. At bar/bat mitzvahs one sees the braid of generations and feels the poignancy of time's passing; the years are passing and cannot be recovered. And parents see that they are not so young anymore. Their children are becoming individuals with identities of their own, and grandparents are cherished in the awareness that time with them is very limited. Indeed, in the bar/bat mitzvah one sees the face of God in the generations and streams of tears touch all that is most real. One of my friends said following my son's bar mitzvah, "Every child should have one of these." She is right; through the preparation and through the liturgy celebrating this day, the power and holiness of this event transform both adolescents and parents. The event is not simply an individual developmental transition, as important as that is, but the dawning of profound knowledge that one belongs to a people and something larger than the self. Adolescents stand with a new pride and self-confidence in this knowledge.

More bar/bat mitzvahs at Beth El complete the high school religious school program—75 percent—than at any other synagogue in New England. Why do an extraordinarily high number of its bar/bat mitzvahs return to the religious school here, when nationwide more than half of youth end their Jewish education soon after their bar/bat mitzvah? This may have less to do with the programming, which is very good, than with the fact that the rabbi puts considerable pressure on the parents at the bar/bat mitzvah retreat. He believes that high school kids like most of all to be with their peers; if parents stick together and require their teenagers to attend the program then all their friends will be there. It will not be an issue with the kids about whether they should attend. The commitment of the parents to present a unified front has helped the high school program be such a success. This approach has been highly effective at Beth El, partly because the rabbi holds a good amount of authority in the synagogue. His injunctions are taken very seriously. This is part of the synagogue's commitment to life-long Jewish learning. It arose also in the awareness that dropping out after the bar/bat mitzvah is disastrous to the growing identity of Jewish youth.

Hanukat Banim

When the congregation found they had such success with the bat/bar mitzvah program and family education, it asked, "Who else might we get involved in studying and learning?" Rabbi Kushner and Education Director Sheila Goldberg decided to emphasize parental involvement more when families first came to the synagogue to help them see learning as a life-long process that takes place in a community. Sunday morning, when parents bring children to Sunday school (kindergarten through second grade), was the one time window, the one crack at people's schedules, for pulling them in. A child's entry into kindergarten was another major event to lift up. It provided an opportunity to help parents understand the importance of family education and to give them resources to become a more fully Jewish family. Thus began the Family Learning Program, which starts for families whose children are in kindergarten and continues through junior high. Eighty to 90 percent of children now start in kindergarten as opposed to less than 50 percent ten years ago. Parents meet often with their children, but more often separately, to learn how to become their children's teachers and to learn to create meaningful Jewish experiences in their homes. Three-fourths of parents from kindergarten through junior high participate.

The education program begins with a focus on three themes: The Cycle of Shabbat and Our Relationship to God; Sacred Texts and Other Stories of Our People; and Jewish Historical Experience. The program also involves study of the Hebrew Bible, study of Jewish prayer and symbols, the celebration of Jewish holidays, and the meaning of *mitzvot* for children. Throughout the year there are family-centered activities such as building a *Sukkah* (harvest booths to celebrate Sukkot), making menorahs for Hannukah, shared Shabbat dinners, *Havdalah* ceremonies, and creating family stories.

Hanukat Banim (consecration) marks the beginning of a child's religious education. The occasion calls out for ritualization in a *shul* and tradition that takes study and developing a Jewish identity with great seriousness. As kindergarten children take their first steps in what hopefully will be a life-long journey learning about Judaism and its traditions, they come to a Sabbath morning service in December and are blessed. Families are encouraged to invite lots of family members, especially the grandparents, to emphasize the continuity of righteousness through the generations. The rabbi blesses the children individually in front of the open ark. He gets down on one knee to be at eye level and places his hands on each child's head and says a blessing. He asks each child to point to his or her parents and grandparents in the congregation. He whispers, "Do you know why your Mommy and Daddy and Grandma and Grandpa are so proud? Because of where you are standing and what you will learn. I hope you like this place very much and have a good time when you come here."[18] Rabbi Kushner describes:

> What is happening here is root-level synagogue life. The ceremony is so spiritually primary that no matter how disorganized (two dozen six-year-olds can get very disorganized), no matter how apparently irrelevant the liturgy, or boring the speeches, there is no way to diminish its immense personal and religious power. All anyone will remember is this "sacred" moment in front of the scrolls which means, "Now the little one is a student of Torah." The par-

ents look to their parents. The words are never spoken, "See, Mom, see, Dad, I brought them here."[19]

At the conclusion of the blessing, the director of education gives each child a small *tallis* (prayer shawl) that he or she may wear in services. The pictures of all the kindergarten classes throughout the year are displayed together in the hall of the synagogue. They are a visible and symbolic reminder of the braid of generations and the commitment to the study of Torah for forming a Jewish identity.

Siyyum

During the high school years, fifty to sixty students gather on Monday nights to eat pizza, study, and talk with one another and the religious school faculty. The religious school's best teachers and the rabbi are present every Monday night. The primary focus of the program is the study of texts (Torah and other sacred texts, the Jewish historical experience, and contemporary Jewish philosophers) and seeing how these texts relate to their lives and connect them to past and future generations. The program also involves the high schoolers in undertaking projects aimed at "improving the world" and helping them understand their social responsibilities as Jews. The projects include such activities as working in a soup kitchen, visiting the elderly, and protecting the environment. Beth El emphasizes *Tikkun Olam* (the repair of the world) in all areas of its life as a congregation. Children and adults, therefore, are encouraged to find many channels for participation. A celebration of the completion of study, *Siyyum,* marks the student's graduation from religious school. In preparation during their senior year, they study great twentieth-century Jewish thinkers and theologians like Buber, Steinsaltz, and Heschel and develop their own personal philosophies of religion. Each student reads an excerpt from his or her paper at the *Siyyum,* which is a part of the Friday evening Shabbat service. An example of one excerpt read at a *Siyyum* service:

> Another time that I came to feel God occurred at Beth El's memorial service for Yitzhaq Rabin. He was so far away in relation to the world itself, yet we all felt attached to the great man. As those in the room joined arms and swayed to the notes of Rabin's peace song, I felt spiritually glued to everyone there. We were united. God was present. The room was filled with God's presence as he flowed throughout all of the congregants swaying, singing, and crying.
>
> While praying on that tragic day, I lost the limits of my own

person. I did not stop to think of my own separate tile on the mosaic, but rather I focused on the big picture. A passage from *Or Ha-Emet* (2b.) says that people in prayer should not notice themselves as individuals. When thinking of God it is necessary to give in to the fact that we are small tiles; there is something far more important than we are as separate people. We are a part of a much more powerful being.[20]

At the *Siyyum* the graduates also receive *shofars* (rams' horns) as gifts and are invited to play them at future high holiday services. The *shofars* symbolize celebration and a new beginning, but also their ongoing relationship to Judaism and its sacred public calendar.

Beth El Adult
Jewish Literacy Program

Undergirding all ministry to families at Beth El is the assumption that as adults grow in an understanding of the depth and richness of their tradition they will have an invaluable resource to share with their entire family. To be a responsible family member requires commitment to a life-long process of learning what it means to live as a Jew. Three years ago, under the leadership of Cantor Lorel Zar Kessler, Beth El instituted the Adult Jewish Literacy Program as a foundation for life-long Jewish learning. This program includes classes, dinner seminars, individual projects, and Hebrew readiness. Classes include Jewish Religious Thought; *Mitzvot:* What Does It Mean to Be Commanded?; Liturgy and Prayer; Jewish Historical Experience; *Tannakh;* The Life Cycle; and Rabbinic Literature.

The Adult Literacy Program is an essential component of community building because it addresses "Jewishly" issues that all families confront. Often the bar/bat mitzvah or *Hannukat Banim* celebrations and their preparations serve to launch parents into this extended commitment of study spawning an ever-growing group of Jews and congregation members interested in serious study of Judaism. This commitment to learning is seen in the many well-known scholars-in-residence that come to Beth El and are greeted by large audiences.

In the course of the year, in addition to the Adult Literacy Program, programs are offered that address family life directly. In one year, topics included The Psychology of Jewish Mourning; Ten Commandments of Parenting Adolescents; Aging: What's Normal? What's Not?; Distant

Care Givers; How to Die, How to Live?; Crossing the Bridge Together—Constructive Ways to Communicate with Your Pre-Teens; Grandparents, Parents, and Children: Sorting Out Mixed Traditions; Living in a Stepfamily: What Works? What Doesn't?; Dilemmas of Multigenerational Loyalty; Struggles as Parents and Children—Passages in Genesis; Making the Bible Come Alive; *Midrash:* How We Can Shape Our Family Lives; Abraham, Father and Husband—How Successful Was He?; and The Seduction of Judah: Responsibilities and Potential for Change in Our Families.

Honoring the Aged— *Hevra Kibud Zekaynim*

Beth El is a young congregation with few elderly. The older people have largely moved to warmer climates, and the vast majority of grandparents live in faraway cities. Yet Beth El attends to education about caring for aging parents. This develops a community of concern and support among members struggling with these issues. Many in the congregation are part of the sandwich generation simultaneously caring for elderly parents and young children. The education program assists them in meeting this dual challenge. Outreach to the elderly in the larger community and in nursing homes undergirds the congregation's commitment to honor the aged.

Mourning and Grieving— *Hevra Kadisha*

Judaism has many customs and rituals that both honor the dead and comfort the bereaved. They are a critical part of care to families. Death is recognized as final, devastating, and traumatic. Rituals are provided to accompany and care for the grieving after a loss. Every member is notified by phone when a member of the synagogue dies so that the community can extend its care to the family. *Hevra Kadisham,* the group responsible for attending to the needs of the bereaved, makes arrangements for the week following a death including: seeing that the body is prepared and brought to the sanctuary, seeing that the body is never left alone, sitting *shiva* (keeping company with the mourners in their home for three to seven days), conducting evening services at the home of the bereaved, and seeing that enough food is provided. Several members spoke of the importance of the attentiveness and presence of both the rabbi and *Hevra*. In the liturgy the Kaddish (mourner's prayer) is recited every week. On the *Yahrzeit,* the anniversary of a death in the family, the rabbi asks persons in the congregation to say the name of the person whose *Yahrzeit* is being observed when his eyes meet theirs, before the reading of the Kaddish.

The community acknowledges one important loss, miscarriage, that many pass over. Several members expressed a sense of being helped in this loss, not simply personally, but publicly, by having it acknowledged in the liturgy in prayer before the Kaddish.

The Role of Leadership in Family Ministry

The levels of leadership at Beth El are multiple and diverse. The rabbi's self-understanding as primarily a teacher has set the tone for the congregation and has supported its strong emphasis on study. Rabbi Larry Kushner enthralls young and old as a teacher of Torah, making the tradition come alive to his audiences. Equally important is his leadership, which focuses on building a spiritually and ethically mature community. He has encouraged families to form *havurot,* family groups, where they meet regularly and celebrate holidays together. He has encouraged family participation in all synagogue events.

Director of Education Sheila Goldberg, an extraordinarily competent professional with immense personal warmth and concern, deserves much credit for the family educational program now in existence. She provides outstanding leadership to the religious school and highly valued guidance to parents, and she works closely in a team relationship with the rabbi, the cantor, and the Jewish Life educator.

Cantor Lorel Zar Kessler brings a soulful presence and exquisite gift of voice that knits people into community with one another and into closer relationship to God through singing and chanting together. Her presence in liturgy, in the religious school, and in the lives of members of the congregation deepens the spiritual connection for all.

Jewish Life Educator David Sherman embodies the love of Torah and Jewish study for young and old. His role is integral to weaving the braid of generations through observance and study.

The lay leadership in the congregation is also very strong. The initiative of members is responsible for many programs, events, and activities at Beth El. With unusual talent and expertise in the congregation, gifts for leadership abound. The rabbi has encouraged and strengthened that leadership, without diminishing his own authority.

Missing Notes

In a congregation as alive and vital as this one, one still needs to ask, whose needs are not being met? Who feels somewhat marginal or peripheral to the main ethos of the congregation? With such a heavy emphasis on children and the importance of children to the continuity of Judaism, childless couples, whether by infertility or choice, might experience Beth El as painful at times. Although opportunities for involvement are many, it may be harder for them to feel fully part of the community. Some have expressed concern that the synagogue is too focused on young children.

Older members also might feel marginal at times because of the emphasis on families and children. They may sense that they no longer are in the mainstream of congregational life. Beth El's few elderly attendees may reflect that the congregation lacks intentionality and focus on the needs of older members.

No groups in this congregation are oriented to the elderly, the single, the recently divorced, or widowed. This absence could reflect a conscious strategy of including them and linking them to the life of the congregation as a whole. It might also point to a lack of conscious outreach and ministry to these people.

Though Beth El does not hold on to notions of the ideal family, severe dysfunction and what it means in family life are given little attention. The extremities of what plague and break families seem to be absent in its programming. Workaholism, alcoholism, adultery, incest, or sexual abuse are seldom discussed.

Postlude

Family ministry in this congregation, as we have seen, is intimately related to family-centered education. It cares for the family less by taking care than by teaching resources from the tradition that enable members to make sense of the issues and problems they face in their lives. The focus of family ministries is not primarily therapeutic or pastoral; it is first and foremost educational. This, no doubt, grows out of the strong emphasis on study and learning in the Jewish tradition, an ever-deepening concern to strengthen Jewish identity in an increasingly assimilated and secularized Jewish population, and a long history valuing the continuity of righteousness through the generations. It also grows out of the rabbi's identity and commitment, which is above all to be a teacher. Beth El does not focus its ministry to families on being particularly solicitous of individual need or particular families. Rather, it emphasizes creating a community where the bonds are strong enough among people that care emerges within the context of deep relationships. Members unite in common search of the values, practices, and insights of their tradition that can support and nurture healthy families.

This congregation offers important insights to becoming a vital and dynamic congregation that ministers effectively to families: a family-centered, not child-focused approach to education that deepens Jewish identity by making accessible the resources of the tradition; an emphasis on the continuity of righteousness through the braid of generations; a focus on developmental transitions in the life cycle as key moments when religious experience can be touched and deepened; a congregation that is not overly dependent upon the clergy for initiative; a leader who is clear and consistent about his own identity and sense of mission, and who supports and encourages initiatives from members; a high level of programming that reflects the theology and mission of the congregation; participatory and spiritually uplifting worship; and a constant willingness to change to adapt to their members' needs and the changing times. Beth El remains most true to its unique identity as it continually seeks to be faithful to the Jewish tradition while simultaneously remaining open to new ways of embodying that faithfulness. One member articulated this well:

> What we have to fear is not change, but complacency. When we stop experimenting, when we become too satisfied with what we do, we will lose what we are. And the only way to avoid that is to learn to examine what we do in light of who we want to be.

Beth El creates an inviting melody, one that many who have been drawn into its life would say is irresistible. The power of the joyful and celebrative embrace of the tradition, the life cycle of families and family life, awaken a sense of the holy that opens people to want more. This community of faith lures people into the beauty and meaning of being part of something larger than themselves, the great braid of generations—*Shalshelet HaDorot*.

NOTES

1. Anita Diamant, "Why I Daven Where I Daven," *Reform Judaism* (fall 1995): 16.
2. Nancy Gossels, ed., *1988/5748 The First Twenty-Five Years: Congregation Beth El of Sudbury River Valley,* (Sudbury, Mass., 1987), 25.
3. Diamant, "Why I Daven," 17.
4. The first bat mitzvah in Jewish history occurred in 1922, conducted by Reconstructionist rabbi Mordecai Kaplan for his daughter. Bat mitzvah has since become integral to the tradition of Reconstructionist and Reform synagogues, but with less status or meaning than bar mitzvahs.
5. Jeffrey Salkin, *Putting God on the Guest List* (Woodstock, Vt.: Jewish Lights Publishing, 1993), 20.
6. Few of the intermarried couples in the congregation have a spouse who is an active committed Christian. Most have drifted away from their religious homes and affiliations and thus are often open to making Beth El their primary religious home.
7. Lawrence Kushner, "Yom Kippur Morning 5750: For the Sin of Homophobia," unpublished sermon.
8. Ibid.
9. Lawrence Kushner. *Invisible Lines of Connection* (Woodstock, Vt.: Jewish Lights Publishing, 1996), 52.
10. Edwin Friedman, *Generation to Generation: Family Process in Church and Synagogue* (New York: Guilford Press, 1985), 7.
11. Lawrence Kushner, "Imagining the Synagogue: These Are the Generations of Abraham and Terah" (Sudbury, Mass., 1988).
12. Salkin, *Putting God,* 21.
13. Ibid., 4.
14. Ibid.
15. Gossels, ed., *1988/ 5748 The First Twenty-five Years,* 30.
16. Salkin *Putting God,* 17.
17. Ibid.
18. Kushner, "Imagining the Synagogue," 3.
19. Ibid.
20. Dana Emily Shulman, "On the Occasion of *Siyyum* 5756," unpublished article, 1996.

4

A Pentecostal Megachurch on the Edge

Calvary Church, Naperville, Illinois[1]

PAUL D. NUMRICH

Introduction

Calvary Church finds itself "on the edge" in several respects. First, the church is located in a so-called Edge City, an exurban enclave ostensibly offering everything that young, upscale families need in life. Yet the stresses of the Edge City experience bring many to Calvary's doors seeking emotional and spiritual healing. Second, like the Assemblies of God movement generally, Calvary Church stands at the border between the peculiarities of its Pentecostal heritage and a growing identification with middle-class American culture. In the metaphor of one observer, the larger movement faces a crossroads;[2] in our imagery, it walks the line of accommodation, adjusting and adapting traditional emphases to contemporary realities (hopefully) without compromising its essential identity. Finally, as a megachurch, Calvary Church rides the cutting edge of what some hail as the quintessential American congregational form of the future.[3] Yet, Calvary's insistence on retaining a modicum of Pentecostal practices places it along the margins of the "seeker-oriented" megachurch movement.

This essay examines the challenges of family ministry in a Pentecostal megachurch on the edge in so many ways.

Address:
Naperville, Edge City, USA

According to Joel Garreau,[4] metropolitan America has moved past the suburbanization stage into the era of the Edge City, those attractive, outlying ("exurban") areas containing all of life's essentials—job, home, marketplace, cultural offerings. Naperville lies on the western edge of an

Edge City hugging the Illinois Research and Development Corridor in DuPage County west of Chicago.

A defining characteristic of an Edge City is that three decades ago it looked nothing like today. The city of Naperville was suburban home to less than twenty-three thousand people in 1970. By 1994, Naperville's population exceeded one hundred thousand, and it had become the tenth-fastest growing municipality in the nation. Today, some three hundred people move into the city monthly. The Indian Prairie School District 204 is the fastest-growing school district in Illinois, with 1996–97 enrollment expected to top fifteen thousand.

Employment opportunities in the county are astounding: two national research and development labs, fourteen industrial and business parks with over one hundred acres each, and twenty-six major employers with one thousand or more employees each (including AT&T's ten thousand-plus in Naperville and neighboring Lisle). Between 1965 and 1989, DuPage County accounted for over 37 percent of all new jobs in northeastern Illinois (which includes Chicago); in 1992, retail sales in the county stood at $10 billion. The so-called East-West office market exceeds any other single suburban market in the area both in total office building inventory and in total office space under construction. Occupational transiency is endemic to the area: nearly half of DuPage County's population changed residence in the period 1985–90. Not surprisingly, as a consequence of tremendous exurban growth and development, area farm land declined 93 percent between 1950 and 1992.

Over 90 percent of Naperville residents are white, though blacks and Asians comprise a significant new presence. Median family income for Naperville is about sixty-seven thousand dollars, while less than 2 percent of its residents fall below the poverty level. Naperville's blacks rank sixth in per capita income among blacks in all Chicago-area municipalities. The average home value in Naperville approaches two hundred thousand. Commenting on a recent marketing analysis by Virginia-based Claritas Inc., the *Chicago Tribune Magazine* stated that "wealth is a major characteristic of DuPage County." Claritas identified Naperville as an "Elite Suburb" with predominant "lifestyle clusters" wherein residents "[b]uy trivia games, own a piano, read parenting magazines," and "[p]lay racquetball, own a video camera, listen to jazz radio."[5]

By most indicators, this Edge City offers a high quality of life for its residents. "Naperville has a good reputation," remarked one local real estate agent. "It's got a family atmosphere and a nice downtown. People just want to live here."[6] The city's Internet home page, Naper View, was accessed in its first summer by over twenty-two thousand people from as far away as California, Costa Rica, and Malaysia. Educational opportunities stand out as a major attraction. "DuPage rolls on as one of America's premier counties for public education," reported the *Chicago Tribune* in 1995.[7] DuPage spends more money per student (over $5,800) than any other county in Illinois. In 1995, the Illinois Association of School Boards granted a two-year exemption from improvement requirements and quality review visits to all public schools in Naperville, perhaps the only such exemption in the state. Several local colleges provide a cultural milieu potentially rivalling that of Chicago. For the civic-minded citizen, the local Naperville newspaper lists over two dozen clubs and interest groups; for the spiritually inclined, Naperville is home to fifty congregations.

Life is good here, but not unmitigatingly so. In 1989, *Atlantic Monthly* ran a story entitled "From Naperville: Stressed Out in Suburbia," chronicling the ambivalent lifestyle of local people. "In Naperville the word 'stress' came up constantly in conversations," the story noted. "They complain that between working long hours, traveling on business, and trying to stay in shape they have no free time."[8] Between that 1989 story and today, a more insidious stress factor has arisen for Napervillians: corporate downsizing. On the first business day of 1996, AT&T announced an anticipated nationwide layoff of forty thousand employees. The *Chicago Tribune* commented that "some AT&T workers greeted the news as yet another thunderclap in a place often shaken by such storms."[9]

In its 1995 report on the status of children in Illinois, the nonprofit group Voices for Illinois Children identified DuPage County as perhaps "the best place in the state to be a kid." "Yet for all its affluence and top-notch statistics, DuPage County also is home to a rapidly growing population of at-risk families and children who must rely on social services such as food stamps."[10] The Illinois Coalition to End Homelessness estimates that DuPage County is home to about 8,200 homeless people; "some say 150 people spend their nights sleeping in their cars or on the streets" of Naperville,[11] the same city where a car wash and detailing center features a Starbuck's coffee shop. Rapid change and new diversity have brought contention to town as well: homeowners protesting construction of an apartment complex they feel will tarnish Naperville's image, the Diversified Parents Association confronting the local school board over minority hiring practices, and neighbors opposing an Islamic center over renovation plans and parking problems (and, according to sources at the center, showing anti-Muslim bias).

Of course, the very growth that creates prosperous and attractive Edge cities like DuPage County carries its own inherent limitations. A recent study admitted that "the county currently is facing the combined problems of simultaneously addressing overall jobs/housing imbalances, dealing with major traffic congestion problems, and meeting the housing needs of its newly created workforce." The study identified Naperville as one of several areas in the county where the jobs/housing situation is "extremely out of balance."[12]

The history of Calvary Church is intertwined with the Edge City growth of Naperville. Sandwiched between the openings of Bell Labs in 1966 and Amoco's research and development facility in 1969, Calvary Temple Church began its corporate life in 1967, purchasing a small frame church building near the center of town. (Today this houses Calvary's ministry to the poor, mostly from the neighboring city of Aurora.) Eleven years later, the congregation relocated to an area of new growth in Naperville, eventually constructing a worship and educational facility of over eighty thousand combined square feet on forty acres of land. (Calvary Christian School and Daycare/Preschool remain here today.) In 1993, Calvary Church occupied its current massive structure on 116 acres of former farmland along the fast-growing southwest side of Naperville. The $20 million site stands between a major shopping mall and a prestigious subdivision designed around an Arnold Palmer signature golf course. In 1994, the congregation voted to drop the potentially misleading term "Temple" from the church's name.

A Pentecostal Megachurch

Calvary Church is big by any standard, physically dominating the landscape around it and attracting great numbers of people each week. For several years, Calvary's Sunday worship attendance has exceeded the two thousand mark that quantitatively defines a "megachurch."[13] On a single Sunday morning in the dead of winter during our field study, 2,978 attended worship and 1,063 attended Sunday school, a grand total of 4,041 souls.[14]

But size is only one aspect of the recent megachurch phenomenon. By other measures, Calvary Church presents a more ambiguous case. In some ways, Calvary resembles the archetypal Willow Creek model of the megachurch, but Calvary has chosen to retain certain distinctively "traditional" Christian emphases that "seeker-targeted" or "seeker-oriented" megachurches consider obstacles to reaching the unchurched, skeptical,

and disaffected—though spiritually hungry—"seekers" of contemporary society.[15]

Calvary Church stakes its claim at the front door, where a free-
standing, forty-foot-high white cross and architectural lines reminiscent
of a traditional steepled church mark the facility as definitely a house of
worship, rather than possibly a corporate headquarters, junior college
campus, community center, or shopping mall.[16] In Calvary's spacious
"auditorium"—here retaining seeker-oriented terminology, rather than
"sanctuary"—the silhouette of a cross appears on the overhead video
screens welcoming people to the church, while an impressionistic cross
configuration hangs at the center-rear of the large stage. Seeker-oriented
megachurches consider even such understated Christian iconography to
be potentially off-putting to the unchurched visitor. Other than the
crosses, however, Calvary's interior, like other megachurches, has a
comfortable Edge City ambience to it, feeling far more like a mall or convention hotel than a traditional church.

Again, as at other megachurches, Calvary Church's full-service programming offers mega-options to a consumer-oriented potential clien-
tele. Virtually every need can be met and every talent accommodated, as
a perusal through Calvary's ten-page ministries brochure reveals. Moreover, everything about the place says, "This is a well-run operation.
These people know what they're doing." And that's "a start" for getting
the unchurched in the door.[17] Once inside, an extensive fellowship
group ministry metes out the "big church" experience in manageably
small doses for the membership.

The linchpin of the seeker-oriented megachurch approach is the distinction between the weekend services, which eliminate the "cringe factor" for unbelievers, and the midweek believer services in which the
faithful gather more traditionally as a worshiping church.[18] At Calvary
Church, this distinction is minimally maintained at best. Founding Pastor Robert Schmidgall's Sunday morning sermon, with its numerous
points, subpoints, and biblical references, marks the highlight of the service for most of Calvary's Bible-toting and Bible-friendly congregation.
Seekers often criticize such "long walks through the sticky pages of the
Bible, where you hit six or seven topics at one time. . . ."[19] Calvary's music is upbeat and professionally executed, but never the "slick" presentations toward which some megachurches tend. Moreover, Calvary
steers clear of "smooth jazz" muzak and religiously neutral lyrics, pre-
ferring to mingle traditional favorites like "Blessed Assurance" and
"Trust and Obey" with unambiguous "CCM" (contemporary Christian

music). All attendees receive an offering envelope upon entering the auditorium, and the offering time is prefaced by the admonition that this
act symbolizes Christian commitment. Such an approach is anathema to
the seeker-oriented megachurch, where the uncommitted are directed
to "take a pass, sit back, and enjoy the music" as the plates make the
rounds. At Calvary Church, Sunday morning services conclude with a
good old-fashioned altar call for the unsaved to come forward and give
their lives to the Lord. At Willow Creek Church, in contrast, the Sunday audience heads for the exits instead of down front.[20] In short, Calvary Church worships on the weekends, not just midweek as do
seeker-oriented megachurches.[21]

"What's wrong with that lady, Mom?" asked a child sitting near me
when someone in the congregation spoke in tongues during a Sunday
morning service. This incident, plus the immediate interpretation of the
tongues-message by another person in the audience, the handraising by
many of the worshipers, and the modest emotionalism of the worship
experience all reveal Calvary Church's underlying Pentecostal identity.
When I asked the assistant pastor whether such behavior might frighten
off the unfamiliar visitor, he admitted that Calvary's Pentecostalism is
"seeker-hostile" rather than "seeker-sensitive." But, he continued, instead of discouraging such behavior in the Sunday morning services (as
does another Assemblies of God megachurch he knows), Calvary's
pastors matter-of-factly explain the behavior to the audience when it
happens. He noted that even non-Pentecostal Christians have initial
misgivings about attending a Pentecostal service; the key is whether a
person's pain is great enough to risk anything, even walking into a Pentecostal church, to find healing.

Calvary Church is affiliated with the Assemblies of God, the largest
Pentecostal body in the world and, according to some sources, the
fastest-growing Christian body in the United States. The Pentecostal
branch of contemporary Christianity has roots in the nineteenth century, particularly in the Holiness and Healing movements within American Christianity, but counts its birth from the manifestation of certain
distinctive spiritual experiences, commonly called "charismatic gifts"
or "gifts of the Holy Spirit," that occurred at the Azusa Street Mission
in Los Angeles in 1906. From the beginning, modern Pentecostals
have understood their movement as a restoration of conditions present
during New Testament times, an understanding that distinguishes
Pentecostalism from Christian fundamentalism (the latter restricting
charismatic signs to the apostolic Church). Over time, Pentecostalism

has found common theological ground with the wider evangelical movement within contemporary Christianity, and both movements have found growing acceptance within middle-class American culture.[22]

The Assemblies of God represents what may be called classical Pentecostalism, which typically eschews dramatic manifestations of charismatic gifts such as public healings and exorcisms. Moreover, it should be noted that the Assemblies of God predates the so-called Third Wave charismatic renewal movement following World War II, which eventually swept across denominational lines (and into mainline Protestant and Roman Catholic churches) and formed new groups such as Vineyard Ministries and Maranatha Fellowships. The Assemblies of God offers a relatively staid and moderate form of charismatic Pentecostalism that stresses the present availability of spiritual gifts through the "baptism of the Holy Spirit" (a postconversion experience into the fullness of the Christian life, initially signified by glossolalia or "speaking in tongues"), the immediacy of God's divine guidance in everyday life, and the urgency of bringing others to a belief in Jesus Christ. Observers suggest that institutionalization of the movement over time, identification with generic evangelicalism, recent growth, and cultural mainstreaming of its constituency (i.e., moving from the disinherited "other side of the tracks" to the solidly middle class) have all threatened the Pentecostal distinctiveness of the Assemblies of God. The challenges and risks of adapting Pentecostal peculiarities to contemporary middle-class American needs are perhaps most evident in the ministries to Edge City people provided by Assemblies of God megachurches like Calvary Church.[23]

Family Ministry at Calvary Church

When I asked the assistant pastor why people come to his church, the first attraction he listed was Calvary's quality programming for all age levels within the family. The norm at this church—by virtue of being the biblical norm, in their understanding—is an intact, harmonious relationship between husband and wife, around which a nuclear family can form. Calvary Church seeks either to facilitate or to restore this norm in people's lives, whether they be disaffected youth, new parents, unmarried singles, or families suffering the general stresses of Edge City life. Calvary applies its Pentecostal understanding of the Christian faith to all such needs.

Family Night and
Senior High Youth Ministry

Significantly, Wednesday evening is Family Night at Calvary Church. A typically megachurch twist is given here to the traditional church programming notion that the whole family should worship together midweek, as age-specific services divide up the family unit into parents (who gather in the auditorium) and various groupings of children (who worship elsewhere throughout the facility). Calvary's senior high worship service is particularly noteworthy in its approach to the life issues of today's Edge City youth.[24]

The scene could be any teen mixer in the area, as three hundred or more youths mingle to the deafening blare (and indecipherable lyrics) of rock music coming from huge speakers on the sound stage. As many as seventeen local high schools may be represented in the crowd tonight, though most of the young people attend one of the three Naperville schools. There are a few more girls than boys—what's new at teen mixers?—and though most are white, a significant showing of minorities is evident. Blue jeans, shorts, and T-shirts abound. Not a few of the guys sport long hair. Floating unobtrusively through the crowd, members of the volunteer leadership team greet regulars and newcomers alike.

One of the guys in blue jeans, T-shirt, and long hair grabs the microphone to invite everyone to find a place in front of the stage. Lead guitarist and vocalist—and senior high pastor—he takes the six-member band through fifteen minutes of "rockin'" good music, now with patently obvious Christian lyrics: "Ain't No Rock (Gonna Praise in My Place)," "Great and Mighty Is He," "The Name of the Lord Is My Strong Tower." Most in the crowd clap and move in place to the music; many, though by no means all, raise their hands in typical Pentecostal style as they sing.

After a short prayer of blessing for the offering, large buckets (the kind for popcorn at the movies) are passed through the crowd, though they collect very little cash. The youth pastor asks how many had "a great thing" happen to them in last Sunday's worship service. About half of the group raise their hands. "For those who didn't," the pastor continues, "I hope you'll get to the point where you can be pumped up for the Lord!" He then explains the meaning of worship for those who don't understand what it's all about, several times asking for quiet and attention from the young people. Human beings were created to worship God, he summarizes. "I talk to God and tell Him that I love Him and that He is awesome to me. Put yourself before God in worship now."

After more singing, the pastor offers prayers for those present who don't know the Lord, for the graduates going away soon to college, and that the young people here tonight might change the world through their Christian commitment. Some of the teens whisper praises softly, a few speak in tongues (which elicits questioning glances from those nearby). Two girls sing "Jesus Will Still Be There," the gist being that Jesus will help you when the going gets rough.

Tonight's sermon is given by a guest speaker. It is very long, longer in fact than the typical Sunday morning sermon at Calvary Church. Though the audience is mostly well-behaved, the speaker often fails to hold their attention. A few of the youth seem put out by being here at all. The speaker invokes numerous biblical texts to build his case for the main themes of the message: Stick to God's path of righteousness, no matter what your peers are doing, so that you will not come under God's judgment; maintain fellowship with other Christians; share God's saving message with the lost. The sermon moves seamlessly into a closing time of commitment to the Lord, as both non-Christians wishing to give their lives to Jesus for the first time and Christians wishing to rededicate their lives to Jesus come forward for prayer with the youth leaders. The rest of the audience is rather summarily dismissed.

According to Calvary's youth pastor, over 95 percent of these teens attend Family Night at least monthly, and two-thirds to three-fourths come to the church with other family members. To my observation that the band gave a professional-quality performance rivaling any in town, the pastor pointed out that if entertainment were the only goal, the Wednesday night program could easily draw five hundred young people. By retaining the present format, with sermon, prayer, and challenge to Christian commitment, the program remains faithful to its mission despite the consequent loss in numbers. Though most of the regulars are unaware of Calvary Church's Assemblies of God identity, and most probably would not even recognize the term "Pentecostal," the youth ministry neither hides nor apologizes for glossolalia and other gifts of the Holy Spirit. First-time visiting youth typically express curiosity about such things, often asking "Why are they speaking in Spanish?" in reaction to the glossolalia. The key to overcoming negative impressions lies in whether the visitor comes with a friend from Calvary. A positive, preexisting relationship mitigates the initial tendency to see tongues as a freakish sideshow.

The youth pastor considers it unhealthy for the family when spouses attend separate churches according to their upbringing. In some cases, as younger kids get involved in Calvary's program, the whole family begins to attend, and even unchurched parents may show up. The majority of teens come from nominally Christian families, which represents an uphill battle against real commitment to Christ. Several have rebellious siblings, or an alcoholic or abusive parent who provides an improper model of what it means to be a Christian.

Many of the teens live with their single mothers. These seem to act out the most, the pastor observed, probably because their homes lack the "good cop, bad cop" of two parents. Without a father to provide a positive adult male role model, some of the girls drift toward promiscuity out of their longing for male relationships, while some of the boys become "ladies' men" since they never learned to relate normally to other males. Youth ministry leaders, some of whom experienced similar situations growing up, seek to provide positive adult relationships with these teens, often serving as surrogate father figures. A newly instituted small group approach to Calvary's senior high ministry hopes to develop "a sense of family, accountability, and purpose" among the youth.

Less than 10 percent of the youth attend Christian high schools, where incidents of serious immorality seem fairly uncommon. For those who attend public schools, Calvary's message is that they model a righteous character in an environment where tolerance appears to be the only moral standard. Simply to walk the straight and narrow today is a worthy accomplishment, contends the pastor, who himself attended Naperville Central High School only a few years ago. A key strategy has been to cultivate a sense of unity among Christian students from all churches, particularly through organized Bible studies at the schools. Waubonsie Valley High School, for instance, will begin this school year with forty to sixty youth in Bible study under the direction of a teacher who belongs to Calvary Church.

Clarifying the function of the heavy moralism of the youth services, the pastor explained that Calvary Church teaches first and foremost about Jesus Christ and faith in him, from which will spring a moral life. These youth might not be interested in minor moral issues, and neither does the program dwell on them, focusing rather on the major problems of substance use and sexual activity. Citing Romans 12:1–2 and 2 Corinthians 5:17, and drawing from Calvary's Healing and Holiness roots, the pastor stressed that deep down these youth need emotional healing and transformed lives. "I won't be shy about offering them that. Many are thirsty for it." Commenting on those who seemingly attend youth services under duress, the pastor noted, "You never know whether Joe Hardhead who attends each week because his divorced mom dragged him here might be grabbed by something in a message."

Other Programs for Families

In addition to Wednesday Family Night activities, Calvary Church offers many programs targeted at special interests within the family, including groups for men only, women only, and seniors (age 55 and older). Life Changing Ministries coordinates support groups for people facing serious issues such as sexual abuse, substance use, dysfunctional family relationships, and grief over loss of loved ones. Those in need of serious counseling can engage the services of two full-time staff Christian counselors. (As one counselor told me, Naperville is a "scary area" for many people, and the church provides a comfortable context in which to deal with their anxieties.) The extensive Sunday school provides numerous age-graded classes during three separate time slots every Sunday morning. Sunday school also includes ACTS, the Adult Christian Training School, "Calvary's Sunday morning teaching arm for adults," with regularly scheduled topics on family life.

Calvary's largest demographic unit is the twenty-five to forty age group, that is, a mix of younger "baby boomers" and older "baby busters."[25] Two recent ACTS courses addressed their concerns about newly married life and parenting small children.

The month-long class for newly marrieds, which drew around a dozen couples in their twenties and thirties, featured sessions on the topics of love, communication, and Satan as the enemy of marriage. The concluding session considered ways to respond to the inevitable conflicts in married life so that they might become the means for establishing the intimate, loving relationship God wishes for everyone. The session was led by Calvary's staff pastor for outreach, who drew his lesson plan and worksheet from a source put out by David C. Cook, an evangelical publishing house. Advice comprised a blend of conservative Christianity and commonsense tips about human relationships. For instance, the pastor expounded a list of five Bible passages concerning conflict resolution, followed by the five steps of "Problem Solving 101": define the problem, brainstorm solutions together, evaluate alternatives, find points of agreement, and agree on common ground and act on it.

I overheard a conversation between two class members prior to this session, a man and a woman (not married to each other) who shared very personal anecdotes about the difficulties in their respective marriages, commiserating that they hadn't realized what they were getting into. Throughout the session, people did not hesitate to offer examples of serious conflict in their relationships, some perhaps warranting professional counseling.

The ACTS course entitled "Growing Kids God's Way," an eighteen-week series based on the evangelical videos and workbook of the same name, drew around eight couples with children ranging from infant to elementary school age. A lay couple who had taken the course twice led the concluding session I attended. It was clear that most of these parents struggle with the normal demands of good parenting; one couple appears to struggle mightily with several personality disorders, both in themselves and in their children.

The woman leading the session opened with a long, well-articulated prayer that included a petition for a "relationship with Christ and a relationship with our children." The freewheeling discussion summarized the most helpful learnings from the course, generally revolving around the importance of parental authority.

"Child-centered parenting" does not work, the group agreed. The primary relationship is between husband and wife—Adam and Eve are the basic family unit, children being extensions of that relationship.[26] Stable parents who set appropriate boundaries bring stability and security to their children's lives. One couple shared illustrations of instilling self-control in their eleven-month-old daughter by saying "No" to her in a consistent manner. Another couple appreciated the way the course helped them to identify principles and articulate reasons for what they tell their eleven-year-old daughter to do or not to do. Several people spoke approvingly of the advice that a child's only options in responding to parental discipline should be "Yes" or "May I appeal?" The appeal process is a privilege, not a right, its purpose being to give the child an opportunity to inform the parent of extenuating circumstances that might mitigate the discipline. Some class members reported instituting another suggestion from the course into their families' lives, that of children addressing elders, even relatives like aunts and uncles, as "Mr." or "Mrs." instead of by first name. This shows respect and bestows a mantle of authority, rather than treating adults as peers.

When one class member advocated spanking as a disciplinary method, the woman leading the class challenged the notion that physical punishment should become routine in parenting. Parents should employ discipline in ways that make correct behavior attractive to children.

Address your children eye-to-eye and tell them clearly what you expect of them. Since they don't really want to obey, they pretend not to hear. Once they've heard, they can obey and be blessed; if they don't obey, parents must hold them accountable for the consequences of their choices, an approach that does not violate their individual freedom.

As in the ACTS class on new marriages, members of this class shared personal difficulties openly with each other. "Every day I ask the Lord to show me what to do," one woman admitted, noting that she knows she will never reach perfection as a parent. Many nodded sympathetically as another woman described her foster son's many emotional problems. "God is healing him," she testified. One man confessed that, even though he's been through the eighteen-week course twice, he sees no change in his children yet.

The session ended with everyone holding hands in a circle as several people gave prayers about being godly parents and shedding small rays of light in a dark world. While one person prayed, others whispered praises like "Hallelujah," "Thank you, Father," and "Jesus, Jesus, oh Jesus." One woman spoke in tongues briefly, several times. After class, the woman coleader of the group walked over to the couple suffering from the personality disorders and prayed quietly with them. In small ways such as these, Calvary lends a Pentecostal air to an otherwise generically evangelical ministry to young parents.

One of Calvary Church's major programs for families is its day-school operation. As its Statement of Purpose indicates, "Calvary Christian School exists to aid Christian parents in their God-given task of educating their children." Now in its sixteenth year of operation, Calvary School has an enrollment of over 180 students in kindergarten through eighth grade, with 140 in a separate preschool/daycare program (30 of whom overlap with the grade school). Plans to consolidate these programs at the new site of the church have been put on hold as congregational leaders pray about the future of the school.

According to the current principal, Calvary Church views the Christian school option as a matter of parental preference rather than conviction. Just over half of Calvary School's students come from Calvary families, the rest mostly from other conservative churches. The primary motivation for enrolling children in the school appears to be the parents' desire to integrate the academic and spiritual aspects of their children's lives.[27] On the other hand, a few parents enroll their children simply for the convenience of having both a grade school and a daycare program at a single site. The vast majority of Calvary School's families are nuclear.

The school awards a handful of scholarships to needy families, all of which are single-parent.

For at least ten years, Calvary School has embodied a typically evangelical Christian perspective, summarized by the principal advocating a "personal relationship with Jesus." Only on rare occasions will themes from Pentecostalism or the Assemblies of God be mentioned in the biweekly chapel services. The dayschool appears to be one program where Calvary Church's accommodation to broader evangelicalism has obscured its distinctively Pentecostal identity.

Singles Ministry

"Lifelight Singles Ministry is a Christ-centered ministry for single and single-again persons . . . designed to address the unique needs of singles through biblically based teaching, fellowship, education, and Christian community." As Calvary Church's singles pastor explained, the term "singles ministry" is somewhat misleading in implying a homogeneous group. In reality, there is no such thing as a "typical" single adult. Singles fall naturally into three different categories: 1) the never-marrieds, generally in their twenties to early thirties; 2) the divorced, mostly in the thirties to fifties age range; and 3) the widowed, usually older ages. None of these groups feels completely akin to the others. For instance, the widowed are typically faithful to one spouse their entire lives, whereas the divorced typically remarry; at the same time, the divorced carry emotional scars and stigmas that differ from the situation of the widowed. (The pastor noted that the stigma of failure in divorce is found not only in society but in the church as well; even the Bible favors the widowed over the divorced.) The fact that both the widowed and the divorced no longer have spouses constitutes only a superficial likeness between the two groups.

Nevertheless, the pastor offered some generalizations about Calvary Church's singles ministry and the individuals served by it. Calvary offers a wholesome atmosphere of friendly, caring people that satisfies a single adult's need for companionship (which, of course, finds ultimate fulfillment within the marriage relationship). Some singles feel out of place in their own churches where programming caters exclusively to married couples and families.[28] At one singles Sunday school class I struck up a conversation with a thirty-something factory worker. Having recently broken up with his fiancée, he needed to distance himself from the church they both had attended. He participates in Calvary's singles activities to offset his feelings of isolation both at work and at home.

The leaders of Calvary's singles ministry are not naive. They know that some singles attend "on the make," as it were, searching for a mate. A few may even be desperate to find a person who will validate their individual self worth. Occasionally two such needy, incomplete people marry each other and quickly discover that it takes whole persons to make a marriage work. When the singles pastor recognizes such cases, he refers them to Calvary's counseling professionals; unfortunately, such people usually do not admit their need and thus do not follow through on the referral.[29] The pastor hopes someday to offer a "marriage encounter"-type program for never-married singles that will both provide the proper preparation for marriage that is lacking in society's current dating practices and present a "major reality check" regarding marriage as it is portrayed in the popular media.

According to the singles pastor, many attend Calvary's singles activities in search of an experience with the Lord that they can share with other people. He senses that singles today have work, friends, and exercise routines, but still carry a spiritual emptiness, a void that needs filling.[30] Calvary's singles ministry provides a safe and familiar context for spiritual experiences, using upbeat music similar to what they hear on the radio (though with biblical lyrics), and relevant messages they can appreciate and apply to their lives. Singles from the Bible that provide useful illustrations include the apostle Paul, Ruth and Naomi, and Jesus himself.

Vocational stresses are among the most frequent prayer requests of Calvary's singles. Usually these concern job dissatisfaction and workplace conflict, though some relate to layoffs. The pastor remarked that singles are tempted to throw themselves into their jobs and seek the entire meaning of their lives there. He tries to encourage them to devote their undivided attention to service for the Lord.

Calvary Church runs an annual twelve-week divorce recovery workshop that draws many local people who turn to the church for understanding and explanation of their grief. (The pastor pointed out that society has no established customs for consoling the divorced comparable to those for the widowed.) The church advertises this workshop in the same forums that local bars use for advertisement since so many recently divorced people quickly return to such premarital haunts. The advertisements clearly identify the workshop as church-related—in other words, no "bait and switch" here. The majority of the participants are non-Calvary people. The program is run very tightly, with trained facilitators who steer people out of the "badmouthing-my-ex" syndrome. Christian jargon is kept to a minimum for most of the series. Emphasis is placed instead on common sense, good counseling techniques, and general Christian principles of forgiveness and freedom from bitterness and anger. Only the concluding session zeroes in on specific biblical (though not peculiarly Pentecostal) teachings, the rationale being that by then participants will have seen the practical benefits of such teachings and developed an openness for more.

The issues of divorce and sexuality mark poignant areas where Calvary Church's Pentecostal/Holiness/Healing principles confront typical Edge City adult lifestyles. As to divorce, Calvary takes its stand on 1 Corinthians 7 and Matthew 5, which identify a non-Christian spouse or fornication as the only legitimate reasons for divorce. On this basis, a person who divorced for incompatibility or some other nonbiblical cause cannot legitimately remarry. As the assistant pastor noted, matter-of-factly, Calvary loses members over this stance. He went on, however, to say that Calvary is not just about doing what is scripturally lawful, but also what is good for the person. Many divorced people today remarry without having worked through the problems that led to the divorce in the first place. Such cases simply become "same problem, different address."

Remarriages are handled by the entire pastoral staff on a case-by-case basis. Calvary will remarry an individual whose ex-spouse is still living if the situation fulfills scriptural criteria; even so, the staff will try everything possible to restore the original marriage. In cases where the ex-spouse has remarried, Calvary chooses not to seek the breakup of that marriage in order to restore the previous one.

On the matter of sexual activity, Calvary makes no compromise over abstinence outside of marriage. Not long ago, a single woman at Calvary became pregnant. The counseling staff advised her to go to Pastor Schmidgall. She repented of her sin in his presence, and he forgave her. But then she asked to confess her sin before the congregation, which the church does not require. At a Wednesday Family Night service she stood before the assembly and asked forgiveness. The congregation wept with her, Pastor Schmidgall publicly affirmed his support for her, people came forward and prayed over her. The church supported her throughout the pregnancy, after which she decided to give the child up to adoption to a Christian family. (Other women in similar circumstances have kept their babies, even dedicating them in services at

Calvary Church. No stigma attaches to such women if they repent of their sin, though the church makes every attempt to establish a loving, Christian, nuclear family around these children.)

That woman continues to attend Calvary at this writing, sitting in the second row during worship services. Recently she stood before the congregation again, this time to thank them and to announce that she is going on a mission trip to Europe, her way paid by a church member. As the assistant pastor put it to me, commenting on this case: "When there's repentance, there's restoration, and we're the agents of restoration. God instituted the Body [of Christ] and we experience a sense of community and a tangible expression of God's grace through it. We don't bind people up in guilt and the law, though neither do we condone the sin they commit. If they've sinned and repented, we ask what we can do now to help them through the situation so that they can lead a Christian life again. The bottom line is that Christ will heal you." Here we see the Holiness and Healing roots of Calvary's Pentecostalism being applied to the wounds of Edge City people.

Conclusion

Calvary Church, like the larger Assemblies of God movement, has drifted away from some of its early Pentecostal peculiarities. For instance, former "sins" of a severe Holiness code—like card playing, movie going, bowling alleys, women's slacks—now constitute merely "fringe issues" of personal preference, as one Calvary pastor who remembers the old days put it to me. Moreover, the Assemblies' slow drift into evangelical theological territory, and evangelicalism's steadily growing acceptance in middle-class American culture, have likewise compromised the movement's Pentecostal distinctiveness to a certain extent.

Calvary Church would appear to qualify as one of those large Assemblies congregations identified by Blumhofer as willing to walk the risky line between conservation of its Pentecostal heritage and evangelization of people unfamiliar with, yet perceived as desperately in need of, that heritage.[31] In many ways Calvary Church "remains a defiantly 'peculiar people'" by contemporary social standards.[32] Calvary's uncompromising stances on major moral issues, as well as its retention of at least a modicum of Pentecostal practices, suffice to cut against the grain of both typical Edge City baby boomer tastes and, by extension, important aspects of the seeker-oriented megachurch approach.[33] I recall the forty-something woman at a singles activity who told me that she likes attending Calvary Church but won't join because of disagreement over one theological point. No doubt other local baby boomers don't even attend because of such disagreements over Calvary's distinctive emphases. As for the many who do attend Calvary Church, however, Poloma's words seem apropos: "They encounter a God who personally leads and directs, who speaks through dreams, visions, and inner senses, who confirms their religious beliefs, who performs miracles and healings, and who in other ways manifests his presence to them."[34] For Edge City families in need, this could be both a holy and a healing God.

Postscript

In January 1998, Calvary's Church's founding pastor, Robert Schmidgall, age 55, died of a heart attack while attending a prayer breakfast at a local restaurant. Speaking for the family, his brother noted that Pastor Schmidgall's "heartbeat was for the world to hear about Christ." At the celebration service for his life, he was remembered as "a humble, big-hearted family man."

NOTES

1. Field research conducted in 1995–96 under the auspices of the Religion in Urban America Program, University of Illinois at Chicago.
2. Margaret M. Poloma, *The Assemblies of God at the Crossroads: Charisma and Institutional Dilemmas* (Knoxville, Tenn: University of Tennessee Press, 1989). The Assemblies of God prefers the designation "movement" rather than "denomination."
3. For example, Charles Trueheart, "Welcome to the Next Church," *Atlantic Monthly* (August 1996): 37–58.
4. Joel Garreau, *Edge City: Life on the New Frontier* (New York: Doubleday, 1991).
5. Patrick T. Reardon, "The new geography," *Chicago Tribune Magazine,* 5 November 1995, sec. 10, pp. 15–28.
6. Courtenay Edelhart, "Naperville sprawls contentedly," *Chicago Tribune,* 30 November 1995, sec. 2, pp. 1+.
7. Casey Banas, "DuPage schools get usual 'A' for top-notch student scores," *Chicago Tribune,* 2 November 1995, sec. 1, pp. 1+.
8. Reprinted as Nicholas Lemann, "The New Suburbia: A Different Entity," *Current* (February 1990): 15–20.
9. Stephen Franklin, "40,000 at AT&T now await word," *Chicago Tribune,* 3 January 1996, sec. 1, pp. 1+.

10. Quotations from Jeffrey Bils, "Study counts children's blessings," *Chicago Tribune,* 3 January 1996, sec. 2, pp. 1+.

11. Karri E. Christiansen, "They're hard to count, but Naperville's homeless exist," *Beacon-News* (Aurora, IL), 8 June 1996, sec. A, p. 3.

12. "DuPage County Jobs/Housing Study," DuPage County Regional Planning Commission (February 1991): 26–27.

13. John N. Vaughan, *Megachurches and America's Cities: How Churches Grow* (Grand Rapids: Baker Book House, 1993). Vaughan himself is inconsistent as to whether worship attendance alone grants "megachurch" status (compare pp. 19, 53, 78).

14. Of course there would be some overlap between attendees at worship and Sunday school.

15. For the Willow Creek model, developed at Willow Creek Community Church in northwest suburban Chicago, see Lynne and Bill Hybels, *Rediscovering Church* (Grand Rapids: Zondervan Publishing House, 1995). Calvary Church does not belong to the Willow Creek Association, an international network of over one thousand seeker-oriented churches. Neither is Calvary Church affiliated with the several hundred Calvary Chapels nationwide, modelled after Pastor Chuck Smith's Calvary Chapel of Costa Mesa, California; see Randall Balmer and Jesse T. Todd, Jr., "Calvary Chapel Costa Mesa, California," in *American Congregations,* vol. 1, eds. James P. Wind and James W. Lewis (Chicago: University of Chicago Press, 1994), 663–98.

16. On megachurch architecture, see Paul Goldberger, "The gospel of church architecture, revised," *New York Times,* 20 April 1995, sec. B, pp. 1+.

17. Quotes taken from a description of the Willow Creek approach, in Robert McClory, "Superchurch," *Reader: Chicago's Free Weekly,* 7 August 1992, sec. 1, pp. 1+.

18. Hybels and Hybels, *Rediscovering Church,* 172–77.

19. The quote comes from a comment made to Pastor Bill Hybels of Willow Creek Church (Ibid., 30).

20. The Willow Creek approach creates a "safe place" for unbelievers to consider the Christian message during the seeker service, relegating commitment to the midweek services (Ibid., 41, 133, 161, 206). An altar call is designed to "pressure" the unbeliever into an immediate decision. In a recent Sunday service at Willow Creek, Bill Hybels concluded his message with a powerful but rhetorical appeal for commitment to God. At Calvary, the auditorium stage is bordered by steps for use in "coming forward" at the altar call. Willow Creek's stage has no such provision.

21. "We don't *worship* here on weekends," Bill Hybels told his Sunday morning audience on the day I visited Willow Creek; of course, he hoped they would return to do so midweek.

22. For a concise overview of Pentecostalism's larger context, see Mark A. Noll, *A History of Christianity in the United States and Canada* (Grand Rapids: Wm. B. Eerdmans Publishing Co., 1992). On the Assemblies of God, see Edith

L. Blumhofer, *Restoring the Faith: The Assemblies of God, Pentecostalism, and American Culture* (Urbana, Ill.: University of Illinois Press, 1993), and Poloma, *The Assemblies of God at the Crossroads.*

23. As others have noted, the megachurch phenomenon is indigenous to ex-urbia. In addition to the many nondenominational cases, the Southern Baptist Convention and the Assemblies of God lead the way in numbers of megachurches nationwide (Vaughan, *Megachurches and America's Cities*).

24. Following are composite highlights of two youth services observed in summer 1996.

25. The "baby boomer" generation was born between 1946 and 1964, the "baby busters" after that.

26. Homosexual unions are simply assumed to be "sinful" and thus not belabored at Calvary Church.

27. The excellent public school system in Naperville at least partly accounts for the existence of only four parochial schools (two Catholic, one Missouri Synod Lutheran, and Calvary Christian School). Contrast this to the neighboring city of Aurora, which has at least three times as many parochial grade schools as Naperville with virtually the same number of residents.

28. Calvary offers such specialized programs as a single parents support group, a child-care service, and an annual winterization service for single women's cars. Calvary encourages members of other churches to maintain those ties even while attending Calvary's singles activities.

29. One lay leader observed that the singles attending Calvary today are generally much healthier than a decade ago when the singles ministry seemed to attract "life's losers."

30. Along this line, an article in the local Naperville newspaper featuring a large and selective (secular) singles club listed "Bible study" as one of many interest groups in the organization.

31. See Blumhofer, *Restoring the Faith,* 273–74.

32. Poloma, *The Assemblies of God at the Crossroads,* 160.

33. As one of Calvary's pastors told me, agreeing with Blumhofer's assessment, Assemblies of God Pentecostalism runs counter to typical baby-boomer tastes (*Restoring the Faith,* 272). Of the several baby-boomer characteristics identified by Blumhofer, "the yearning for affirmative rather than prophetic preaching" seems most crucial in my mind. This fits well with Wade Clark Roof's characterization of baby-boomer preferences for less authoritarian and absolutist churches; see Wade Clark Roof, *A Generation of Seekers: The Spiritual Journeys of the Baby Boom Generation* (San Francisco: HarperCollins, 1993), 204–12. (By the way, Roof's profile of "Linda Kramer" provides an apt description of the typical Calvary Church baby-boomer member.)

34. Poloma, *The Assemblies of God at the Crossroads,* 91.

5

"No Doubtful Disputation"

A Ministry of Restoration and Reconciliation at City of Refuge Community Church

SANDRA BLAIR

> Him that is weak in the faith receive ye, but not to doubtful disputations.
> —Romans 14:1, KJV

The conviction that persons who are weak in faith should be welcomed but not subjected to controversial disputation undergirds an inclusive theology and biblical hermeneutics. This view of inclusiveness, acceptance, and healing is embodied in the ministry and belief system of the City of Refuge Community Church in San Francisco, California. This congregational case study examines two major social institutions that shape lives and values. It highlights a liberating praxis that has characterized the black church's prophetic role as an agent for social justice and change.

The rapidly growing, vibrant new congregation was organized in 1991 by Pastor Yvette Flunder, a dynamic African American woman in her late thirties, and six other persons. Beginning with about eighteen persons meeting for prayer and Bible study in Pastor Flunder's home, the membership is now almost four hundred, with an annual operating budget of $100,000 to $125,000. The largely lower-middle-class congregation, composed primarily of residents of San Francisco and East Bay cities, is predominantly African American but also includes Anglos and Latinos. The membership is at least 75 percent gay/lesbian/bisexual and pre/postoperation transgender (referred to in this article as g/l/b/t).

Pastor Flunder was previously associate pastor at Love Center—the Oakland, California church founded and pastored by Rev. Walter Hawkins—which she left to launch an autonomous, more proactive ministry addressing substance abuse and the human immunodeficiency virus/acquired immune deficiency syndrome (HIV/AIDS) epidemic. In mid-1994 City of Refuge opted to be in care of the United Church of Christ (U.C.C.), and in April 1995 was installed as a full member of the denomination. This balances the need for institutional support and the desire to preserve a degree of independence as well as to retain its Afrocentric, Pentecostal worship. The U.C.C.'s congregational polity guarantees City of Refuge's operational autonomy, and the liberal statement of faith allows doctrinal and theological freedom. Additionally, Congregationalism is progressive and has historically been committed to social action and justice. Following this tradition, the U.C.C. General Synod has since 1975 adopted resolutions supporting the human rights of all persons in church and society, regardless of sexuality. A 1991 resolution affirmed gay, lesbian, and bisexual persons and their ministries.[1] Notwithstanding dissension over the issue, a 1993 resolution reiterated the unity of the church in spite of diversity and reaffirmed the 1991 legislation.[2]

Originally located in the largely gay Castro district, City of Refuge has been housed in a diverse selection of San Francisco neighborhoods. It moved in August 1984 to the exclusive Pacific Heights, and in December 1995 began sharing the First Congregational Church building on the borders of the elegant Union Square shopping and hotel district and the economically depressed Tenderloin district. At the end of 1997, City of Refuge relocated to 1025 Howard in the South of Market district that has a high concentration of transients and the homeless, persons living with HIV/AIDS, recent immigrants, substance abusers, and prostitutes.

City of Refuge was so named because the theme of restoration and reconciliation is central to a ministry that offers the assurance of God's eternal love for and acceptance of persons who often find themselves excluded in the mainstream church. Its doors are open to those with a history of incarceration, substance abuse, and irresponsible sexual activity, as well as to persons living with HIV/AIDS and AIDS-related complex (ARC). Its affirmation that a personal relationship established with God through Christ cannot be lost because of one's actions and lifestyle is important for persons who have experienced considerable rejection and condemnation in their religious and social contacts.

The members have experienced multidimensional oppression based on race/ethnicity, gender, sexual orientation, and class. Theologically and ethically, the congregation challenges sexism, racism, and homophobia in church and society. Pastor Flunder confronts the oppressive aspects of the traditional male-dominated black church, and she both critiques patriarchal structures and epitomizes the opposite of patriarchy. Though she feels it is culturally inappropriate for the black church to eliminate all male images of the divine, she re-presents God as the creator of a nurturing, inclusive community.

City of Refuge is concerned with reconciling human sexuality and spirituality, but does not engage in the more political advocacy of sexuality of explicitly gay and lesbian churches such as the Universal Fellowship of Metropolitan Community Churches and the Unity Fellowship Movement. In fact, public reference to sexual orientation is rarely made. However, City of Refuge insists that g/l/b/t's should be extended full acceptance and fellowship in the body of Christ and not merely tolerated as second-class and subordinate members. A history of homophobia in the African American community—compounded by an intentional campaign by the heterocentric, conservative religious right to pit the black church against gay, lesbian, and bisexual people—makes acceptance a position that few black churches are willing to adopt. City of Refuge is nonetheless committed to establishing dialogue between the African American community and g/l/b/t's, and to addressing the deep-seated denial prevalent in the black church. Coalitions have been built with some black churches in the San Francisco-Bay Area (in particular, Allen Temple Baptist Church in Oakland and, in San Francisco, Glide Memorial United Methodist Church and St. James Baptist Church) and across the country.

Pastor Flunder's upbringing in the Church of God in Christ (COGIC) has helped to shape the City of Refuge's theology. Characteristics of COGIC's Holiness revival roots find expression in City of Refuge's doctrine: the firm belief in the inspiration and authority of Scripture, emphasis upon sanctification, concern with inner conversion and personal piety, centrality of pneumatology, understanding of sin and substitutionary atonement, stress on doctrinal truth, explicit Trinitarian teachings, and the Pentecostal practice of speaking in tongues. However, her personal spiritual and theological evolution has in many ways separated her from her Pentecostal heritage. Her ministry contrasts markedly with the Pentecostal movement's historical disassociation from social engagement and belief in the primacy of spiritual conversion over socioeconomic and political conditions and issues. The conservative COGIC theological and hermeneutical perspective is rejected in favor of liberation theology and liberal hermeneutics. The eclectic nature of the congregation is epitomized in its self-identification as an actively inclusive "Metho-bapticostal" body.

Pastor Flunder has integrated black and womanist theologies with her evangelical tradition. Elements that inform City of Refuge's theology are the concern with social justice; the challenge to transform oppressive socioeconomic, political, and religious structures; the understanding of the contextual nature and cultural underpinnings of theology; the emphasis on God's immanence; the understanding of the work of the Holy Spirit as being foundational to personal and social liberation and transformation; and the importance of ethics and praxis. However, issue is taken with black and womanist theologians for not being as informed and as open as they need to be about aspects of human sexuality.

Pastor Flunder believes the refusal to engage in doubtful disputation (that is, not quarreling over or passing judgment on disputable matters) was fundamental to Paul's ministry. Her reading of Paul has led her to conclude that nothing is sin in and of itself but is sinful only in how it impacts the call of Christ. Christians are thus free from guilt but also accountable because of their love for Christ.

Stressing salvation by grace and not by works, City of Refuge reiterates the Holy Spirit's power to bring about personal inner transformation, and to reveal to believers the life of Christian responsibility they should live. The official policy is neither to condemn homosexuality as a sin nor to be permissive, but to assist individuals to discover God's will for them within God's conciliatory plan of redemption through Christ. Convinced that salvation is available to all, City of Refuge believes the rejection of persons because of their sexual identity is inconsistent with its understanding of Jesus's ministry.

The church's statement of purpose establishes its worship life and social ministry as the means by which it embodies the empowering presence of the incarnate Christ in the world and by which it brings relevance to a changing community. This twofold mission evolved from an understanding of the nature and function of the church as a locus of healing, restoration, and reconciliation. According to the church's statement of purpose, the function of worship is to ". . . respond to God with adoration and praise, preach the Word of God, nurture the believer to maturity in Christ and thereby receive the impetus to evangelize and serve God in the world . . . "; and the function of social ministry is ". . . to integrate forgiveness for transgression with psycho-social and physical healing by meeting the profound social issues . . . with a liberating Gospel of restoration which affirms ethnic, political, social and individual diversity."

The charismatic worship services contribute to the sense of the congregation's openness. In the Pentecostal liturgical tradition, the order of worship is simple and without prescribed rubrics. The emphasis is upon spontaneous, ecstatic prayer and praise that celebrates the Holy Spirit's gift and work in effecting personal and social change.

Pastor Flunder has several years experience as a social worker and was the executive director of the Ark House, Love Center's communal shelter for AIDS patients. Many members are employed in the areas of HIV/AIDS advocacy, public health, substance abuse counseling, and social services. A strong sense of social justice and activism is evident in City of Refuge's ministry. It engages in community-based political action, particularly on behalf of disenfranchised sectors of the African American community. For example, it has lobbied for passage of laws affecting housing and fiscal assistance, been active in the struggle for the civil rights of g/l/b/t's, addressed HIV/AIDS issues, and intervened for youth caught in the foster care system.

A primary concern is the HIV/AIDS epidemic. A large part of the church's resources is invested in addressing the overwhelming needs of both those living with HIV/AIDS and persons whose partners or parents are dying from the disease. The church has established the Ark of Refuge, a nonprofit advocacy and direct service agency that serves the counties of San Francisco and Alameda. Operating on a $1 million budget from public and foundation grants and donations, the agency maintains four houses in San Francisco and Oakland that provide residence, direct services, and educational training for persons with HIV/AIDS and in recovery.

City of Refuge also conducts outreach to substance abusers as well as to survivors of incest and sexual molestation, and several Twelve-Step recovery groups meet at the church weekly.

The official leadership of City of Refuge—including the Senior Pastor, Auxiliary Pastor, Elders, Ministers, Deacons, and directors of departments—consists of thirty persons, the majority of whom are gay and lesbian. Approximately 20 percent of the congregation is heterosexual. The small number of heterosexual men (3 to 5 percent of the membership) is attributed largely to the reluctance of straight men to be identified with gays. Although the ideology and ministry of the church are strongly influenced by the needs of g/l/b/t's and persons living with HIV/AIDS, the power dynamics do not exclude or discriminate against heterosexuals, and the church is eager to broaden its outreach to heterosexuals.

City of Refuge's emphasis on issues affecting the g/l/b/t community is understandable given its social location in the San Francisco/Bay Area, where there is a large population of g/l/b/t's and greater social tolerance.

Although the State of California does not legally recognize same-sex marriages, a 1991 San Francisco ordinance permits gay and lesbian couples to register as domestic partners. A February 1996 ordinance authorizing a civil ceremony to solemnize domestic partnerships for persons over the age of eighteen preceded a mass ceremony on March 25, 1996, when 175 couples publicly affirmed their commitment to each other.

The Bay Area also has a concentration of persons living with HIV/AIDS. Nationwide, AIDS is the main cause of death for African American men between the ages of twenty-five and forty-four, and the second-leading cause of death for African American women in that age group.[3] The California Department of Health Services has reported that between 1981 and September 1994, 76,840 cases of AIDS were recorded in California.[4] San Francisco, with nearly a quarter of the state total, has the highest incidence of the disease. The number of AIDS cases in San Francisco is 18,092, with 11,901 deaths (for a fatality rate of 65.8 percent) and 2,405 cases per 100,000 population. Corresponding figures for neighboring Alameda County—where 40 percent of the congregation resides—are 3,750 cases, 2,253 deaths, and 280 cases per 100,000 residents. There are up to 8,000 new HIV infections in California each year, and one in every 180 to 250 residents is HIV-positive. Of those infected with HIV, 70 percent are gay; 13 percent are women or heterosexuals who inject drugs; 8 percent are gay, lesbian, and bisexual persons who inject drugs; and 4 percent are women infected through heterosexual contact.

Many members of City of Refuge are alienated from their families of origin by childhood histories of sexual and physical abuse or of neglect; or because their sexuality or substance abuse conflicts with their families' moral values. The largest problem for some congregants is a sense of disappointment and loss in personal and family relationships. The church serves as a needed "family" structure that supports members in the processes of recovery, reestablishing trust, building self-esteem, overcoming guilt and anger, working through feelings of isolation and abandonment, and developing healthy relationships. Pastor Flunder often finds herself viewed as a surrogate mother, and has the challenge of not being drawn into codependency. City of Refuge also functions as an extended family for persons who have not joined the church but who utilize the services and are included in the fellowship. The family ministry is shaped by the congregation understanding itself as a safe place where people can work out relational issues while knowing they are forgiven.

Consistent with a trend evident in the United States since the 1960s, the concept of family has been redefined to include alternative family structures as well as the traditional heterosexual nuclear family unit. In response to the members' life situations, the prevailing definition of *family* in City of Refuge is two or more persons sharing the same life chances (that is, opportunities, threats, and resources or lack of resources) who may or may not be sexually intimate but who have made the decision to be accountable to each other; to care for each other; and to be responsible for each other's physical, mental, emotional, and spiritual health and well-being. The members' family culture is primarily same-sex couples with and without children, as well as single g/l/b/t's and heterosexual parent families. City of Refuge must balance the tension that, with the predominance of same-sex families, those desiring support for the heterosexual family structure may not find their needs addressed as adequately.

Interviews were conducted with a cross-section of the congregation: lesbian and gay couples with children, individual lesbians and gays with and without children, bisexual males and females, and heterosexuals. The results indicate that the family ministry and the forms of family culture are appropriate for the congregation, and that the family culture shares the values of the congregational culture.

Family life is nurtured through various components of the church's ministry. The intergenerational worship services are family-oriented and address issues pertaining to family relations. The weekly new members' class and Bible study, and discipleship training class address topics such as relationships and parenting. A six-week series on relationships is conducted that includes such topics as conflict resolution, monogamy, child-raising, and personal spirituality. Recreational activities, such as picnics and camping trips, and cell group meetings held regularly in members' homes help strengthen the collective and individual family bonds. Counseling on family issues is offered, and plans are underway to initiate a parenting training series.

Teaching, preaching, and counseling are central to the congregational family ministry because they inspire spiritual and emotional development as well as social action. The importance of ritual as a vehicle for self healing and for undergirding and empowering the church community is acknowledged, but ritual is not the primary embodiment of the family ministry's ethos. Instilling what a member termed "Bible survival skills" is viewed as paramount to recovery and wholeness. Also, for many members the ritual in their prior church experience was essentially meaningless because neither during nor outside of the ritual did they feel fully a part of the community.

People in long-term familial relationships compose approximately 50 percent of the congregation, and about one-third of the adult members are parents. The congregation accepts and validates the committed relationships of both heterosexual and g/l/b/t couples. Although Pastor Flunder affirms and has performed same-sex unions, she is not ready to take the radical step of conducting them as a public ritual at City of Refuge. This action would characterize City of Refuge as a gay/lesbian/bisexual church, not just a church that is open to g/l/b/t's, and would seriously jeopardize the relationship with the black church that is culturally important to the congregation. Unions and covenantal relationships are legitimized liturgically in other ways. During the weekly worship service and at an annual service, members are invited to the altar for prayer with their partners and children. The church does not practice infant baptism but conducts a ceremony of blessing for children up to the ages of twelve or thirteen. Couples are frequently recognized by name, and the clergy and elders are encouraged to take their partners to the church's leadership retreats.

The majority of the congregation are in their twenties and thirties. The oldest member is a woman in her seventies, and there are about fifteen persons in their fifties. Because there is not a critical mass of elderly members, the need for services to them has not been pressing, and this aspect of the congregation's family ministry has yet to develop fully. Though the greater need at present is that of younger members who are struggling with issues of parenting and sexuality, the goal of the leadership is to increase evangelism to seniors.

City of Refuge has recently had a large influx of children and youth as a result of parents being reunited with their children, particularly after completing drug recovery and regaining custody of their children. At the time of this writing, there are about fifty young people, fifteen of whom are teenagers. Some of them are children of g/l/b/t parents, but most identify sexually as heterosexual. Sometimes teenagers have concerns or conflicts related to their parents' sexuality, mainly because society presumes gay/lesbian/bisexual family patterns are abnormal. To counteract this pressure, the church offers counseling, instruction, and support-group activities that provide positive reinforcement on human sexuality. The church leadership reinforces the need for children and youth to be raised in and involved in the church, and is committed to expanding programs for them. The still-evolving youth and children's ministry includes such activities as a children's choir, weekly children's Sunday school and children's church, a monthly youth and young adult meeting, and youth participation in worship.

City of Refuge has responded to the rapid increase in youth orphaned by HIV/AIDS, a nationwide phenomenon with tremendous implications for family ministry. A relative lack of attention to this population contributes to the lack of empirical data on their numbers. From approximately 18,500 in 1991, the number of "AIDS orphans" (80 percent of whom are African American and Hispanic) is estimated after 1995 to surpass 17 percent of children and 12 percent of adolescents whose mothers die of all causes and is projected to reach 72,000–125,000 by the year 2000.[5] As a member of the Black Adoption Agency's Board of Directors, Pastor Flunder advocates on this issue—as do other members involved in the social service system. At Ark of Refuge's houses in Oakland, counseling is provided to dying parents and to prospective adoptive parents. Some congregants serve informally as foster parents, and efforts are made to ensure that affected children participate in church activities.

The family theology of City of Refuge assumes that the responsibilities of heterosexual relationships are also applicable to g/l/b/t relationships. Although not all members are ready to accept that promiscuity is unhealthy and some interpret freedom in Christ as giving them liberty to be licentious, a primary expectation is that relationships be monogamous and that the choice of one's partner be governed by God's will. Respect for oneself and for the integrity of others is reinforced. The scriptural injunction for believers to present their bodies as a living sacrifice, holy and acceptable to God (Rom. 12:1), is understood as requiring a healthy and responsible sexual life.

Pastor Flunder's hermeneutics has molded the congregation's understanding of how scripture functions in social relations. She believes traditional interpretation has alienated society's marginalized and powerless, and insists that g/l/b/t's struggle—as have African Americans and women—to free themselves from oppressive hermeneutics. Her overriding desire is that g/l/b/t's will not have to hide their sexual identity because scripture passages are used to condemn them.

In the Christian community, the Bible is commonly the arbiter for determining traditional family values—as though the nuclear family is the

Judeo-Christian biblical norm. In fact, prevailing notions of family and the value system associated with it are grounded in Victorian sexual mores and the context of postindustrial modernity. Recognizing this, the congregation seeks out a more liberating hermeneutic.

One source is New Testament scholar Cain Hope Felder, who argues that the variations in biblical family patterns implicitly broaden the notion of who constitutes the members of God's household. In the Old Testament, the continuation of the blood line through successive covenants was achieved through diverse patterns of family and household life. Although blood relations and ethnic purity were a primary concern in patriarchal society, traditional family arrangements based on blood kinship become less significant in the New Testament—especially in the earlier writings that reflect the apocalyptic eschatology of a period when the Parousia was thought to be imminent. Writings after C.E. 70, when the Early Church was becoming institutionalized, reflect a growing concern for household codes to ensure mutually responsible domestic relations that represented a paradigm for relationships in the family of faith. A central theme is the new spiritual kinship and obligations that the blood of Christ creates for the Christian community. "*Blood relatives and language were no longer decisive criteria for the new Household that God and the ministry of Jesus make possible. . . .* God is the pre-eminent parent and householder in the Jesus tradition and elsewhere in the New Testament."[6] Felder concludes that the Bible may not be the most suitable rule for traditional family values because it is not limited to a monolithic, static view of family life that assumes the nuclear family model as the categorical norm but affirms both the extended family and kinships not based on blood relations.

City of Refuge is an example of the changing attitudes, values, and practices that result as God's Word seeks expression in diverse cultural settings.

The congregation finds affirmation of diversity in contemporary family system theories which recognize that family bonds may be created by biological relatedness, by legal commitments such as marriage or adoption, or by choice. Family structures can include the family of origin, the nuclear family, the extended or multigenerational family, the single-parent family, the blended family, unmarried couples, and foster families. Although nuclear or married-couple households compose an estimated 57 percent of U.S. households and prevail as the norm, viewing the family solely in terms of this traditional model can minimize the significance of family life's changing dynamics and needs, and the possibilities for family ministry.[7] Pastor Flunder is aware of the danger of literally and rigidly applying the Bible to the vastly different context of contemporary society. Uncritical biblical hermeneutics that does not account for the historical, social, and cultural background of the text is particularly problematic when dealing with human sexuality. Her congregants have suffered from prejudicial moral and ethical values fostered by a fundamentalist interpretation of the Bible and a belief in its absolute authority.

Pastor Flunder welcomes the historical-critical reinterpretation that has given rise to new questions about the texts which are commonly cited as condemning and prohibiting homosexuality.[8] Since the concept of homosexuality as a biologically based sexual orientation grew out of scientific developments of the nineteenth century, the texts are viewed with the awareness that in antiquity same-sex or homogenital acts held a different meaning. There was no specific understanding of homosexual relationships. The concern was not with homosexuality itself but with homosexual and heterosexual practices that violated other moral requirements.

This new perspective on the five primary texts influences City of Refuge's biblical interpretation and instruction. The narrative of Genesis 19:1–11, which has traditionally been the basis of the belief that Sodom was punished for male homogenital activity, is viewed as a violation of the social norms of hospitality as well as criticism of the humiliating practice of subjecting men to a passive sexual role like a female. Leviticus 18:22 and 20:13, which are often taken to prohibit male homogenital acts as an abomination, are understood as portions of The Holiness Code, which lists practices from which Israelites were to refrain in order to distinguish themselves from Gentiles and to maintain the integrity of their religious identity. Romans 1:18–32, on which is based the claim that same-sex acts are unnatural and the only passage that can be taken to refer to lesbian sex, is regarded as not singling out homogenital sex for moral or ethical condemnation but expressing disapproval of social practices in Gentile culture, particularly idolatry. 1 Corinthians 6:9–10 and 1 Timothy 1:9–10 are viewed as being concerned not with same-sex acts in and of themselves but with abusive and exploitative acts such as male prostitution and pederasty. Pastor Flunder concurs that in both heterosexual and gay/lesbian relationships, the expectation is for ". . . mutual respect, caring and responsible sharing— in a loaded word, love. The violation of these, but not sex in general, is what the Bible condemns."[9]

It has been noted that African Americans are increasingly embracing

fundamentalist ideology.[10] By and large, the African American community continues to condemn homosexuality as an abomination and to
perceive HIV/AIDS as God's punishment for sexual sins. This prevailing
conservatism precludes receptiveness to the reconstruction of family
structures and values by gay, lesbian, and bisexual persons.

The raw pain of exclusion is evident in the writings of gay, lesbian,
and bisexual African Americans. Author Cheryl Clarke asserts:

> Because the insular, privatized nuclear family is upheld as the
> model of Western family stability, all other forms—for example,
> the extended family, the female-headed family, the lesbian fam-
> ily—are devalued. . . . Homosexuality is viewed as a threat to the
> continued existence of the heterosexual family, because homosex-
> ual unions do not, in and of themselves, produce offspring—as if
> one's only function within a family, within a relationship, or in sex
> were to produce offspring. Black family lifestyles and homosexual
> lifestyles are not antithetical. Most black lesbians and gay men grew
> up in families and are still critically involved with their families.
> Many black lesbians and gay men are raising children. Why must
> the black family be so strictly viewed as the result of a heterosex-
> ual dyad?[11]

For City of Refuge this is a valid question given that literature on the
black family, while acknowledging the historical importance of the extended family, assumes the nuclear heterosexual model is the norm and
the only primary shift that is recognized is the increasing number of
families headed by single mothers.[12] Gay, lesbian, and bisexual family
patterns are not usually addressed and generally such relationships are
regarded as pathological.

The reduction of their personhood to sexual identity and of sexual
identity to sexual activity devoid of emotional intimacy—coupled with
the close identification of consanguinity and marriage to procreation—
has created the myth that gay, lesbian, and bisexual persons are incapable of procreation, parenting, and establishing kinship ties.[13] Since
their domestic partnerships are rarely legitimated in civil law, they do
not have the legal sanction, social privileges, or rights of heterosexual
spouses. The tendency to locate gay, lesbian, and bisexual relationships
outside the normative definitions of family fuels the belief that gay, lesbian, and bisexual persons are a menace to family and society.

City of Refuge challenges the view that homosexuality is detrimental
to traditional family values. The need to do so is noted by pastoral minister Louis Kavar who, in a study of the shifting dynamics of family

systems and the realities of extended families of choice within the context of the HIV/AIDS health crisis, writes:

> Many people in American society have been taught to embody what are sometimes referred to as traditional family values. The politicization of traditional family values equates these values with the life of the nuclear family. In addition to this political strategy, most theories of family dynamics and the majority of pastoral training have focussed on the nuclear family and view other family units as somehow hurting or broken. The underlying assumption at work in the political use of family values, many family system theories, and an abundance of pastoral practice is that family wholeness and unity are based on the nuclear family.
>
> In truth, the intimate connections among people which form the experience of family and family values such as honesty, integrity, and commitment have little to do with biological relatedness. . . . Because the life-giving experience expected within families is not limited to biological relatedness, it is important to conceptually "re-member" families in order to recognize, respect, and support the commitment and special relationships among people.[14]

The meaning of family and the importance given to the relational bonds that can be identified as family are social and ideological constructs shaped by individual experience, sociocultural context, and changes in historical and social conditions. The family is not a monolithic institution but varies according to the needs of its members. African Americans have defined and experienced family in diverse ways, including informal adoption and extended kinship structures. The gay/lesbian/bisexual community has since the 1980s become more vocal in demanding recognition of its family structures, ethics, and values as well as their basis in mutuality, concern, and relational justice.[15] Two dimensions of disputation as a theme are reflected in City of Refuge. It is a pastoral community that nurtures those who have been hurt and rejected by disputation in church and society about their sexuality. It is also a prophetic voice that engages in disputation with church and society over the issue of gay/lesbian/bisexual households and of gay, lesbian, and bisexual persons parenting their biological children or choosing to parent children as couples through adoption, artificial insemination, or surrogate arrangements. African American lesbian feminist writer Audre Lorde postulates that gays and lesbians of color, as members of a community under siege, know that raising children ". . . is one way of participating in the future, in social change."[16]

In order to strengthen congregants' family life, City of Refuge has to redress some adverse effects on the family structure. A common problem is g/l/b/t's who feel compelled by social norms to hide their sexuality by entering into relationships with the opposite sex, marrying, and having children. If their sexual orientation is disclosed, they risk losing their children in custody battles and the degradation of publicly revealing the intimate details of their sex lives.[17] Gay fathers voice the opinion that societal taboos against them are often stronger than those against lesbian mothers, and that they sometimes receive little support from their communities.[18] Irreconcilable differences, the breakup of family units, and a traumatic impact upon children are tragic results. Other trends with implications for pastoral and family ministry are the breakdown in family and personal relationships created by the fear of gay, lesbian, and bisexual persons of revealing their sexual identity; by the inability of family members to accept their sexuality; and by the assumption of parents that their moral failing as parents caused their child's homosexuality. Assisting gay, lesbian, and bisexual persons to integrate and balance their male and female qualities within their relationships is another pastoral care issue.[19]

New perspectives on family ministry are emerging as psychological and theological approaches to homosexuality change.[20] An older approach in psychotherapy views homosexuality as a disease to be treated by either a change to heterosexuality or sexual abstinence. This is undergirded theologically by the belief that homosexuality is a sin because it deviates from the heterosexual order of nature created by God and that repentance is necessary for salvation. A newer psychological approach that is modeled by City of Refuge accepts homosexuality as a valid sexual orientation and seeks to assist gay, lesbian, and bisexual persons in integrating their sexuality into a healthy life. The theological corollary is the acceptance of homosexuality as part of the wholeness of human sexuality and the affirmation of the gay/lesbian/bisexual experience.

Pastor Flunder is convinced that the theological position of the black church on gay/lesbian/bisexual rights has major consequences for its pastoral and family ministry. Black theologian James Cone attributes the black church's conservative tendency to an absence of the tools of social analysis.[21] He argues that its failure to understand the depth of human oppression in the black community makes it incapable of either comprehending the evil nature of patriarchy or fully addressing the interrelated "isms" that accompany it. An analysis of domination and oppression such as he calls for involves the critique and dismantling of

sociopolitical and ideological structures that hinder the exercise of individual freedom, and leads to developing strategies for transformation.
Theologies of liberation serve to remind communities of faith that they
should not selectively identify with struggles for freedom but be committed to the holistic liberation of all people.

The need to recognize and fight against heterosexism and homophobia as dimensions of oppression is being increasingly demanded, particularly by self-identified gays and lesbians who criticize the general
silence in African American Christian theology on issues of human sexuality.[22] The need for progressive theologians to examine the way in
which black churches participate in the persecution of gay, lesbian, and
bisexual persons is also articulated from outside theological circles.[23]
Churches are called upon to engage in the liberation and empowerment
of gay, lesbian, and bisexual persons, but also in the liberation of African
American Christians from their homophobic fears and prejudices. As
stated by black theologian Elias Farajaje-Jones:

> Some of us need to articulate theologies for the Black Church that
> teach that we are inclusive, not exclusive; that we are about life and
> not about death.[24]

Pastor Flunder finds an important historical perspective in historian
John Boswell's documentation of the shifting pattern of attitudes towards gays and lesbians in Western Christianity—from acceptance as
different but equal in the ancient world and the early Christian church,
to toleration as inferior in medieval society, to the condemnation shown
in modern times.[25] He argues that gay and lesbian people lost their position of influence and prominence in Christian society and became increasingly marginalized with the rise of new expressions of social
intolerance and hostility after 1250, the emergence of the medieval notion that homosexual activity was sinful because it was nonprocreative,
the more rigid expectation of celibacy as the alternative to Christian
marriage, and the modern belief that homosexual activity and the homosexual person are abnormal.

Given the rejection and oppression that they have experienced in organized religions, many gay, lesbian, and bisexual persons are faced
with the dilemma of how to integrate their spirituality and sexuality. The
main options they can exercise include trying to effect change within the
institutional church from outside, creating competing alternative structures, or attempting to change the structure and nature of the institution
from within.[26] City of Refuge has chosen the latter alternative because it

recognizes the profound influence that organized religion has on peo-ple's minds and lives, and feels a divine calling to share the inclusive message of Christ's love for all people and of freedom for the oppressed. The emergence of a gay liberation movement in the churches since the 1970s has empowered gay, lesbian, and bisexual persons to increasingly demand full acceptance as members of the community of faith with the same rights and responsibilities others enjoy.

This appeal for full and equal rights resonates with the ideals for which this nation fought and on which it was founded: the Declaration of Independence's affirmation that all are created equal and are endowed by God with the inalienable right to life, liberty, and the pursuit of hap-piness; justice and liberty as guaranteed by the Constitution; and the freedoms protected by the Bill of Rights. Rejection of their claims is in-consistent with the principles that constitute the very essence of what is held to be American.

Some members of the African American gay, lesbian, and bisexual community have formed their own churches in reaction to the oppres-sion of sexual identity in the black church and the racial biases in white gay churches. Faced with the choice of downplaying either their homo-sexuality in the black community or their cultural identity in the white gay/lesbian/bisexual community, they have intentionally created their own community and culture in a step toward true pluralism and inclu-siveness. The call is issued to the church to put the Christian faith into practice and to make it possible for African American gay/lesbian Chris-tians to remain Christian by ". . . being 'catholic' by making the faith uni-versal enough to include Black gay Christians; being 'reformed' by making Black gay Christians themselves participate in the priesthood of all believers; and being 'evangelical' enough to sound like good news to Black lesbians and gays who have been outside the church."[27]

The black church has not yet adopted the reconciling congregation movement that has emerged in several predominantly white denomi-nations since 1978. Currently, some 644 welcoming communities in eight major denominations publicly affirm their ministry with the whole family of God and welcome gay, lesbian, and bisexual persons and their families into the community of faith.[28] City of Refuge found strong appeal in the U.C.C. Open and Affirming Program. In addition to support organizations such as the Coalition for Lesbian and Gay Concerns and the Parents and Friends of Lesbians and Gays, the de-nomination publishes an educational sexuality curriculum designed to help end the exclusion, misrepresentation, and discrimination that occur when churches are not open to diversity. Components of the family ministry offered by reconciling congregations include services of union, dedication of children, and congregational and ministerial support.

Traditional pastoral care in Christian ministry has drawn upon the total resources of the church as a caring community functioning to sustain, guide, heal, and reconcile persons in crisis, and the history of oppression experienced by African Americans has added to pastoral care the dimension of liberation in the black church.[29] Defined in this context, liberation entails not solely transforming socioeconomic and political structures but also freeing persons from internal and external conditions that inhibit them from realizing their full potential as self-actualizing human beings in wholesome relationship with God and other people. City of Refuge provides the biblical, theological, and ethical tools for members to experience such liberation.

Social scientist Robert Hill argues that the strength of a viable family unit is determined by its ability to meet the needs of its members and the demands made upon it by systems outside the family unit, as well as by the survival and maintenance of effective family networks.[30] The traits that contribute to this strength include concern for family unity, the ability for self-help, the ability to perform family roles flexibly, the ability to establish and maintain growth-producing relationships within and without the family, and the ability to provide for the family's physical, emotional, and spiritual needs. City of Refuge's family units demonstrate these traits. The family ministry is one that supports and empowers strong and healthy family life and relationships.

This case study affords the opportunity to explore the correlation between two of the major social institutions that shape values and play determinative roles in human lives: the family—the primary and possibly most important institution—and organized religion, the institution that instills foundational social values. Studies of the black family have pointed to extended kinship bonds and religious orientation as two of its characteristic strengths and to the black church as its greatest resource.[31] The black church has traditionally served as an extended family that has provided moral education, positive group identity, and a sense of personal self-worth. Examining the mutual relation of families and churches in the African American community, black theologian J. Deotis Roberts argues that the strengthening of families is a primary task of the black church and that its failure to minister appropriately and urgently to black families will not only affect the future of African Americans as a people but will hasten its own death.[32]

Liberating praxis has been a hallmark of the black church, which was born in oppression and suffering and which has assumed the prophetic role as a moral agent for social justice and change. The themes of survival and liberation have been woven into the black church tradition as it has participated in the struggle of African Americans to overcome racial domination and to pursue freedom and equality.[33]

Pastoral social psychologist Archie Smith, Jr., cautions that to achieve true human liberation a black Christian ethic must involve disciplined reflection and analysis as well as direct action, and that the black church must become self-conscious and self-critical in order to retain its moral vision and leadership.[34]

City of Refuge offers a mirror for such reflection. In light of its moral conviction that God cares for the oppressed and honors the inherent dignity and worth of all people, the black church needs to examine how it has participated in the oppression of gay, lesbian, and bisexual persons. As it has affirmed the humanity of African Americans, the black church is called upon to honestly confront its homophobia so that it can accept the personhood of gays, lesbians, and bisexuals as God's creation. As it has served as God's household for African American Christians, the black church should strive to create communal kinship and solidarity that embraces those who are alienated and discriminated against because of their sexual identity. As it has fought against racist social structures, the black church must seek to transform dehumanizing social relations that victimize persons because of their sexuality. As it has nurtured the broken, wounded, and excluded in its community, the black church is summoned to expand its notion of family ministry to encompass the emerging realities and needs of gay, lesbian, and bisexual relationships.

City of Refuge's teaching and practice are responses to God's demand for social and sexual justice. It challenges the black church to remember that the Christian community and its ministry should be one of inclusivity, mutuality, and acceptance. It is a paradigm for a reconciling ministry that makes God's grace and love known, lives out the gospel of liberation and healing, and transforms humanity. The congregational life and family ministry of City of Refuge Community Church indeed exemplify Pastor Flunder's maxim: "God is expecting the church to do the unexpected for the undeserving so they may see the unbelievable."

NOTES

1. Resolution 91-GS-67, *Minutes, Eighteenth General Synod* (Cleveland: United Church of Christ, 1991), 71.

2. Resolution 93-GS-79, *Minutes, Nineteenth General Synod* (Cleveland: United Church of Christ, 1993), 76–77.

3. Chauncy Bailey, "Allen Temple takes a stand on AIDS," *The Oakland Tribune,* 2 December 1994, sec. A, p. 13.

4. *The Oakland Tribune,* 2 December 1994, sec. A, p. 8.

5. David Michaels and Carol Levine, "Estimates of the Number of Motherless Youth Orphaned by AIDS in the United States," *Journal of the American Medical Association* 268:24 (December 23–30, 1992): 3456–61; and Carol Levine, "Orphans of the HIV epidemic: unmet needs in six US cities," *Aids Care* 7:Supplement 1 (1995): S57–62.

6. Cain Hope Felder, *Troubling Biblical Waters: Race, Class, and Family* (Maryknoll, N.Y.: Orbis Books, 1993), 157.

7. J. C. Wynn, *Family Therapy in Pastoral Ministry: Counseling for the Nineties* (San Francisco: HarperCollins, 1991), chap. 1.

8. For example, Derrick Sherwin Bailey, *Homosexuality and the Western Christian Tradition* (London: Longmans, Green & Co., 1955); L. William Countryman, *Dirt, Greed and Sex: Sexual Ethics in the New Testament and their Implications for Today* (Philadelphia: Fortress Press, 1988); Victor Paul Furnish, *The Moral Teaching of Paul* (Nashville: Abingdon Press, 1979); Daniel A. Helminiak, *What the Bible Really Says About Homosexuality* (San Francisco: Alamo Square Press, 1994); Robin Scroggs, *The New Testament And Homosexuality* (Philadelphia: Fortress Press, 1983).

9. Helminiak, *What the Bible Really Says,* 96.

10. Vincent L. Wimbush, "The Bible and African Americans: An Outline of an Interpretative History," in *Stony The Road We Trod: African American Biblical Interpretation,* ed. Cain Hope Felder (Minneapolis: Fortress Press, 1991), 81–97.

11. Cheryl Clarke, "The Failure to Transform: Homophobia in the Black Community," in *Home Girls: A Black Feminist Anthology,* ed. Barbara Smith (New York: Kitchen Table-Women of Color Press, 1983), 199–200.

12. Ranging, for example, from W.E.B. DuBois's pioneering work, *The Negro American Family* (Atlanta: Atlanta University Publications, 1908; reprint, New York: Negro Universities Press, 1969) to E. Franklin Frazier's classic, *The Negro Family in the United States* (Chicago: University of Chicago Press, 1939) to more recent studies such as Edward Billingsley, *Black Families in White America* (Englewood Cliffs, N.J.: Prentice-Hall, 1968); Robert Staples and Leanor Boulin Johnson, *Black Families at the Crossroads* (San Francisco: Jossey-Bass, 1993).

13. Kath Weston, *Families We Choose: Lesbians, Gays, Kinship* (New York: Columbia University Press, 1991).

14. Louis F. Kavar, *Families Re-Membered: Pastoral Support for Friends and Fam-*

ilies Living with HIV/AIDS (Gaithersburg, Md.: Chi Rho Press, 1993), 35–36.

15. Michael L. Stemmeler, " 'Family' in the Gay Nineties: The Explosion of a Concept," in *Spirituality and Community: Diversity in Lesbian and Gay Experience,* eds. J. Michael Clark and Michael L. Stemmeler (Las Colinas, Tex.: Monument Press, 1994), 182–83.

16. Audre Lorde, *A Burst of Light* (Ithaca, N.Y.: Firebrand Books: 1988), 42.

17. Diane Abbitt and Roberta Bennett, "On Being A Lesbian Mother," in *Positively Gay: New Approaches to Gay and Lesbian Life,* ed. Betty Berzon (Berkeley, Calif.: Celestial Arts, 1992), 94.

18. A. Billy S. Jones, "A Father's Need; A Parent's Desire," in *In The Life: A Black Gay Anthology,* ed. Joseph Beam (Boston: Alyson Publications, 1986), 143–51.

19. Horace L. Griffin, "Giving New Birth: Lesbians, Gays and 'The Family,' A Pastoral Care Perspective," *Journal of Pastoral Theology* 3 (summer 1993): 91.

20. Anita C. Hill and Leo Treadway, "Rituals of Healing: Ministry with and on Behalf of Gay and Lesbian People," in *Lift Every Voice: Constructing Christian Theologies from the Underside,* eds. Susan Brooks Thistlethwaite and Mary Potter Engel (San Francisco: HarperCollins, 1990), 234–39.

21. James H. Cone, *For My People: Black Theology and the Black Church* (Maryknoll, N.Y.: Orbis Books, 1984), 96.

22. See the chapters by Elias Farajaje-Jones and Renee Hill in *Black Theology: A Documentary History, Volume II, 1980–1992,* eds. James H. Cone and Gayraud S. Wilmore (Maryknoll, N.Y.: Orbis Books, 1993), 139–59 and 345–51.

23. bell hooks, *Talking Back: thinking feminist, thinking black* (Boston: South End Press, 1989), 122–23.

24. Elias Farajaje-Jones, "Breaking Silence: Toward An In-The-Life Theology," in *Black Theology,* eds. Cone and Wilmore, 143.

25. John Boswell, *Christianity, Social Tolerance, and Homosexuality* (Chicago: The University of Chicago Press, 1980); and "Homosexuality and Religious Life," in *Sexuality and the Sacred: Sources for Theological Reflection,* eds. James B. Nelson and Sandra P. Longfellow (Louisville, Ky.: Westminster/John Knox Press, 1994).

26. Hill and Treadway, "Rituals of Healing," 231.

27. James S. Tinney, "Why a Black Gay Church?," in *In The Life,* ed. Joseph Beam, 77.

28. *Open Hands: Resources for Ministries Affirming the Diversity of Humans* 11:3 (winter 1996): 2, 29. The denominations are the U.C.C., the United Methodist Church, the Presbyterian Church, the Lutheran Church, the Disciples of Christ, the Unitarian-Universalist Association, the Brethren/Mennonite Church, and the American Baptist Church.

29. Edward P. Wimberly, *Pastoral Care in the Black Church* (Nashville, Abingdon Press, 1979), 18, 74.

30. Robert B. Hill, *The Strengths of Black Families* (New York: Emerson Hall Publishers, 1971), 3.

31. For example, Nancy Boyd Franklin, "Five key factors in the treatment of Black families," *Journal of Psychotherapy and the Family* 6:1–2 (1989): 53–69; Hill, "The Strengths of Black Families"; C. Eric Lincoln, "The Black Family, The Black Church and the Transformation of Values," *Religion in Life* 47:4 (winter 1978): 486–96; Michael R. Lyles and James H. Carter, "Myths and strengths of the Black family: A historical and sociological contribution to family therapy," *Journal of the National Medical Association* 74:11 (November 1982): 1119–23.

32. J. Deotis Roberts, *Roots of a Black Future: Family and Church* (Philadelphia: Westminster Press, 1980), 132.

33. Gayraud S. Wilmore, *Black Religion and Black Radicalism: An Interpretation of the Religious History of Afro-American People,* 2d ed. (Maryknoll, New York: Orbis Books, 1986), 220–41.

34. Archie Smith, Jr., *The Relational Self: Ethics & Therapy from a Black Church Perspective* (Nashville: Abingdon Press, 1982), 126–33.

6

The Fourth Presbyterian Church of Chicago

One Congregation's Response to the Challenges of Family Life in Urban America

LOIS LIVEZEY

Introduction
Public Church/Private Faith:
The Church Culture of Family Ministries at Fourth

A half-dozen parents, mostly mothers, of young children watch a film and discuss their own experience of a "family meeting"—sharing their efforts, frustrations, moments when "it worked"—clearly eager to try on the ideas and try out the suggestions and the process. The text for the parenting class is STEP (Systematic Training for Effective Parenting). In STEP, the family is seen as a democratic institution. Family formation rests on the assumption that humans are essentially social beings, motivated by the desire to belong. Family and world are inextricably linked: citizenship is developed within the family as a transferable skill from family to the public realm. Responsibility is key: "In a democracy, each person must behave responsibly. If we are to develop responsible adults, we must begin in the home by developing responsible children."[1]

An evening vespers service celebrating the confirmation of several youth exudes commitment to mission. An announcement at the beginning indicates that one-third of the offering will go to the church's ministries at Cabrini Green, a public housing project one mile west of the church. The confirmands share their faith stories. One youth speaks of recognizing his own family as a metaphor for the vulnerable world's relationship to God. The pastoral emphasis on service is clear: Jesus has chosen you; now you go out and serve him. The pastor, John Buchanan, speaks about what commissioning means: To be disciples, To be a light in the city, To reflect the love of Jesus in family, church, and community.

Fourthcomers is the "young adult" group of Fourth Presbyterian Church, primarily for people between the ages of twenty-one and thirty-five. On January 23, 1994, one of the Fourthcomer members, Lou Carlozo, gives a talk on obsessive/compulsive disorder. The group receives the talk with enthusiasm, and the ensuing question-and-answer session is lively. The conversation keeps drifting from gambling as compulsive behavior to whether the city of Chicago should legalize gambling.[2]

The family ministries of The Fourth Presbyterian Church of Chicago must be understood within the spiritual and conceptual framework of "public church." "We are a light in the city reflecting the inclusive love of God." So begins the mission statement of Fourth Presbyterian Church, as it seeks to catch the spirit of the church's historic identity, congregational practice, and theological foundation. In fact, of course, the congregational culture and family ministries of Fourth represent a complex weaving of public church and private faith. The appeal to the faith of the individual is grounded in God's gift of conscience, imagination, capacity for action, and the call to discipleship. It is grounded, too, in the congregation's commitment to faith as a private matter in a society that values preeminently freedom of choice and voluntary association.[3] This public-private vision is evident in the preaching on Sunday morning, in the educational and community-building activities of the church, and in the "protocol for public policy advocacy" recently adopted by the Session of the Church, discussed below.

The defining characteristics of Fourth Presbyterian Church are often noted in the literature on the public church as well.[4]

A Sense of Place

Fourth Church is a space of gathering and of going forth, a space for celebration and for service. The Fourth Presbyterian Church of Chicago is a *public* church by virtue of its sense of place. It is graced—and challenged—by the significance of its location and the sort of centrality, visibility, and accessibility such a location affords. Fourth was established at its location in 1914 in a neighborhood of rooming houses for young singles coming to work in the city and newly built homes of the wealthy.[5]

It now stands on North Michigan Avenue, across from the John Hancock Building, between Water Tower Place and Bloomingdale's. It anchors the transition from the shopping mecca of the "Magnificent Mile" to the lakefront residences of the "Gold Coast." Fourth is a lure to press and politicians as well as visitors from around the world. Indeed, the Sunday morning worship service is estimated to be one-third visitors.

The immediate context is consummate consumer culture—but there is more. The "neighborhood" of the near north side of Chicago is defined historically to include "the Gold Coast and the Slum," the most affluent residential area in Chicago and, now, Cabrini Green, a public housing project.[6] The church has spent thirty years bridging these "two nations, separate and unequal"—as the 1968 Kerner Report described the relations between black and white in this country. The tutoring program, rehab projects, and parenting and child care programs at Cabrini Green form the core of Fourth's outreach to and partnerships with the poor.

The geography of Fourth Presbyterian Church shapes other ministry activities. Fourth is within the central business area, which, unlike most cities, remains the employment hub of the metropolitan area (seven hundred thousand jobs). It is also within walking distance of one of the city's largest, most prestigious hospital complexes, Northwestern Memorial Hospital, and a short commute to several others, including public Cook County Hospital.

Worship as public space: The Sunday morning worship service takes place in a beautiful English gothic sanctuary. At 11 A.M., this twelve-hundred-seat cathedral-sanctuary is full. The service is high-quality, formal *and* participatory, albeit in set ways: hymn-singing, responsive Bible reading (Psalm), confession of sin, and affirmation of faith. There are no spontaneous "joys and concerns," no "Amen!"s. The space of worship is itself an integral and significant dimension of the worship service. Its beauty sets the context of worship. The bulletin for morning worship always includes a photographic detail of the art and architecture of the church on the cover, an explanatory paragraph about the cover photo, and a paragraph about the music for the service. Newcomers to the church are invited to tour the building after the service, and a brochure for a self-guided tour is available.[7]

Mission as public space: In 1994, Fourth Presbyterian Church began a $12 million building renovation project eight years in the planning. In the midst of the construction, the church's preoccupation with space was palpable. Inevitably, the talk of space led to talk of mission. In the Annual Report (1994), Pastor John M. Buchanan wrote: "Old spaces are becoming new spaces to serve us and our city as we faithfully follow Jesus Christ, Lord of the Church." Fourth Church also reiterated its commitment to shared space, multi-use spaces that increase the access of diverse publics, especially children: church school, day (nursery) school, child center, and tutoring program.

Sitting in a Sunday morning worship service, I think of the woman who poured very expensive ointment over Jesus' head. The disciples complained about her priorities, but she set the Christian Church on its historic commitment to live in the tension of preserving extravagant beauty and urging sacrificial service. ·

Identity[8]

Two elements of Fourth Church's identity are its history, the story that shapes its current self-identification as public church, and its people. We will come to know some of the people better in the stories that follow. But some demographic information helps locate the church's perspective and "style."

Fourth Presbyterian Church was formed from the merger of two Presbyterian churches, North and Westminster, in February 1871. The former North Church building was renovated and reopened with a celebrative service on October 8, 1871—and destroyed within hours in the Great Chicago Fire. The church was rebuilt in a new location (Rush and Superior) in 1874, and almost immediately its popular preacher and pastor, David Swing, became embroiled in a heresy trial that set congregation, presbytery, and synod in conflict. Whatever one's evaluation of Swing's theology, the moment is symbolic, I think, of a tradition of preaching at Fourth that reaches beyond "the converted" to a wider community of seekers.

In the mid-1880s, Fourth Church turned to respond to the needs of its changing neighborhood in a way that would come to define the church's "sense of self" in subsequent generations. During the pastorate of Elam Davies (1961–84), especially, the social mission of the church expanded and became increasingly professionalized. Thus, the church's identity as "a light in the city" is built up over a history of evangelical and service-oriented outreach to the community: neighborhood, city, and world.[9] As of the annual report of 1994, Fourth Church's membership was 3,859 (with 286 received into membership in that year and an overall increase in membership of 101 from the previous year). Church membership is about half-married, half-single; two-thirds female, one-third male. The median age is 46 years; the modal age is 35 (i.e., half the membership is over 35 and half is under 35). James Wellman's survey data confirm the Gold Coast culture of its members: median per capita income is $50,000–$74,999 (1993 dollars). Nearly all members have college degrees, and 70 percent (of the sample) have postgraduate education. Most members of the church are employed full-time. Nearly 97 percent identify themselves as white. A substantial number of members live on the near north side of Chicago, the neighborhood of the church; others commute to church regularly from Chicago suburbs (chiefly north: Evanston/Winnetka and west: Oak Park/Hinsdale), as well as the south side of Chicago and Indiana. There are 536 out-of-state members. But the neighborhood character of Fourth Church churchgoing is implicit in Wellman's study of travel times to church, which distinguishes among more and less active church members: more active, 11–15 minutes; less active, 16–20 minutes.[10]

Mission

A public church is defined by mission, its care for neighbor and stranger, its engagement with the powers (service and advocacy). Church members testify to the importance of mission in their increasing involvement in the church.[11]

Fourth Church's social ministries are many: the Tutoring Program, the Center for Whole Life, Cabrini Alive! and other programs provide educational opportunities, social service, and advocacy for the families of Cabrini Green. Other professionally staffed Fourth Church-based institutions include the Center for Older Adults (COA); the Lorene Replogle Counseling Center; and the Elam Davies Social Service Center (The Door), which provides emergency basic life needs, referral information, and community meals at Fourth on Sunday evenings. Mission activities include, also, the PACE tutoring program at Cook County Jail, cooking for homeless shelters and other involvements in hunger and housing programs, hospital volunteering, a myriad of benevolence activities, and ad hoc responses to need throughout the wider church and worldwide community.

The mission orientation of Fourth Church is expressed in the words of one member of the staff: "nothing at Fourth Church is 'for members only.'" The counseling services, social services, arts festivals, and various programs for older adults and children—even the church's education and fellowship programs—serve the church community *and* reach out to serve the wider community.

The new protocol on advocacy exemplifies the confluence of public church and private faith that defines mission at Fourth Church. This statement affirms the role of the church in public policy advocacy. It also sets parameters for church-based public policy advocacy, namely, public issues that emerge from the actual outreach ministries of Fourth Church or the actions of the General Assembly of the Presbyterian Church (USA). Institutional and personal experience with communities of need is key. The rationale is insightful: "Through direct services provided to individuals and groups in the community, Fourth Church learns first-hand of the needs and obstacles faced by those who are poor or otherwise disadvantaged." Thus, in view of the distance between Fourth Church membership and poverty, this engagement-based learning gives credibility to the public policy advocacy of Fourth Church on child poverty issues.

The protocol also focuses the advocacy energies of Fourth on educating members about public policy issues and encouraging members to communicate with public officials, as "individual Christians, not as representatives of Fourth Church." The church may only rarely act corporately on a public issue, but it expects churchgoers at Fourth to witness to their faith through involvement in public life.

Partnership

Fourth Church's ministry and mission are characterized by cooperation and collaboration. Many of its family-impact ministries are partnerships with other communities and institutions: with Chicago Presbytery (The Center for Whole Life at Cabrini Green); with other downtown churches (the Career Transitions Network); with community institutions such as Northwestern Memorial Hospital on wellness programs at the Center for Older Adults; and with neighborhood coalitions to improve the quality of life in the area's public schools and housing or to sponsor a forum on casino gambling in Chicago.

The Theology of It All

The integral relation of witness and worship at Fourth Presbyterian Church is expressed in the articulation of a theology for the public church. It is a richly textured, multifaceted symbolic universe, but there are some consistent themes.[12]

Grace, the gracious and sovereign love of God, is the first and last word in the theological orientation of Fourth Church. Every worship service emphasizes God's love and inclusiveness, from the Call to Worship through Communion. The stories of Jesus are stories of inclusion, stories of challenging the boundaries of the status quo. Recounting

Jesus' encounter with the scribes and Pharisees over the woman caught in adultery (John 8:1–11), the preacher says: "Church is where the stones start to drop from our hands as we learn compassion instead of condemnation, grace not judgment."[13]

Like inclusiveness, *responsibility and risk* are basic themes with variations: the commandment of neighbor-love, Jesus' definition of greatness as service, Paul on heroism as sacrifice, father-love as vulnerability.[14] Interestingly, the call to responsibility is grounded, not in sin and guilt, but in the image of God in us, human capacity rather than human depravity.[15] Individuals and the church community are urged to become involved, to contribute to the common good, to care for the city, to call institutions to account. Typically, there is a sermonic "go forth." Being faithful means taking risks.

Scripture is a starting point for cultural analysis and critique, including the critique of church tradition and its interpretation of scripture. But scripture is not the only bearer of the Word and its meaning in life. The preaching, teaching, counseling, and other activities of the church reflect the literary world of this congregation, which is "at home" in contemporary poetic, practical, and scientific literature. The Church's ethos is one of critical respect for biblical and modern wisdom alike.

The power of the preaching at Fourth is, in part, its connection to the *experience* of the people in the pew. For all its institutional sensibility, the ultimate appeal is to the hearts and minds of the congregation; it is an invitation to the imagination. The pastor articulates and challenges the congregation's "cultural identity," which is primarily a class identity, that of a high-culture, civic-minded economic elite, acculturated early to consumerism; this is a people of privilege. Cultural criticism is connected to specifics within the congregation's experience rather than a systemic critical analysis of the "dominant culture."

The Challenge: Fourth Church and the Modern Family Debate

Fourth Church appears to be increasing its attention to family issues, e.g., inauguration of the Center for Whole Life at Cabrini Green in 1993 and the Children's Center (full-day care) in 1995, a recently initiated "annual" intentional marriage seminar, and first meetings of a young married couples group and a grandparents network in 1995. John Buchanan confessed he was preaching his "first" fatherhood-focused

Father's Day sermon ever in 1995. "Visions of the Family" was the theme of the annual Festival of the Arts in 1996.

Clearly, the church is responding to the restructuring of family life: changing rules, roles, and relations between women and men; the changing paid work structure of families; increasing divorce and single parenting; gay men and lesbian claims to family status; delegitimation of sexual and domestic abuse. It is responding, also, to the complex dynamics of economic restructuring, which means increasing mobility for some, immobility for others (Cabrini Green), and economic instability and insecurity for many. The rapidly changing world of family and work, the "flexibility" required, and the unpredictability experienced shows up programmatically in forums on family-work issues, employment resources for church members at Fourth, and computers for the tutoring program now looking to prepare for the new era of knowledge workers.

The church is oriented to meeting needs, developing support networks, and encouraging conversation in a new situation rather than formulating definitions of "family"—or even definitive guidance. This problem-centered approach is of a piece with the focus on the actual impact of these changes on the experience of members of the congregation and the "neighborhood" as expressed in their voiced needs and interests. How these problems and principles get expressed concretely is interesting.

Mobility and Its Impact on Families

The mobility of families in church and society in urban America is a significant theme in the preaching and the activities of the church. This mobility is viewed ambiguously.

On the one hand, mobility is the fruit of change and choice. The sermon, "Oh, the Places You Will Go" (with Joshua 1 and Dr. Seuss as basic texts), affirms the reality of this congregation: a people on the move, experiencing a variety of life changes. The sermon also affirms the potentially spiritual significance of this mobility: change, and the world of choices that come with it, is not just a given; it's a calling. The challenge to go forth is analogous to a faith journey, the risk-taking of discipleship. The preacher even suggests that the refusal to move, that is, to change might be unfaithfulness.[16] The paradoxical outcome of this theological orientation is this: Fourth Presbyterian Church is significantly defined by the stability and solidity that its space represents. Yet, the theology of Fourth is grounded in a sense of faith as a journey. Abraham and Joshua are more appealing than Solomon, even in the midst of Fourth Church's own (re)building of the temple. The modern context is dominated by realities and mythologies of change, which Fourth mostly embraces as challenges and opportunities for growth, discovery and mission.[17]

On the other hand, mobility also means nuclear families and "families of one" who are without the connections of family networks, without the needed resources of love, support, nurture, and growth. These needs evoke loneliness and fear. Even divorce and single parenting are recognized for their ambiguity. They may reflect good and moral choices; at least they may be preferable to continuing destructive conflict (in the case of divorce). They may also have a negative impact on children and the potential for irresponsibility. In a Mother's Day sermon (1994), "Whose Family Values?" Rev. Buchanan recalls for the congregation that the Bible has no word for "nuclear family"—only for "household." One aspect of his analysis of the modern "crisis" of the family is the nuclear family living far away from relatives.[18] Listening, it struck me how well this analysis connects with the congregation's experience: great mobility and transition, many singles in the congregation. The costs of mobility can be felt in an adult education discussion on caring for aging parents, the grandparents network, and the Center for Older Adults.[19]

The ministries of Fourth Church are increasingly but not exclusively family-oriented. Thus, focusing only on the specifically family-related ministries of Fourth Presbyterian Church would obscure the way in which its fellowship and mission-oriented organization of activities relativizes the family—and obscure, too, the ways in which families flourish and community is built in the midst of activities that are not family-focused. Let me elaborate briefly, with three points.

For one thing, there is no litmus test, no categories of "appropriate" family forms at Fourth Presbyterian Church. The reality is diversity, respect for diversity, and pastoral care for the challenges that diversity brings. Increasing divorce and single parenting are viewed with a sense of ambiguity, problematic primarily by virtue of their negative impact on the children. The issue of homosexuality is treated mostly with public silence (with the exception of the discussion occasioned by the denominational controversy over ordination). Respect is basic.

A story related by the director of the Lorene Replogle Counseling Center illustrates Fourth's approach to the plurality of family forms. A series on "intentional marriage" had been designed for a small group of married couples. It dealt with the impact of family of origin, communication skills, conflict management, and intimacy. Nonmarried and gay/lesbian couples and singles not in intimate relationships asked, "Can we come, too?" This led in turn to a "Relationship Seminar" with the same content but not limited to married couples. This approach responded to the variety of family forms within the church and yet acknowledged the distinctiveness of marriage.[20]

Second, the "purpose" of families does not seem to be disaggregated from the basic understandings of the nature, purpose, and virtue of individuals and communities. These purposes and values, if not distinctive of family life, are essential to the well-being and moral development of family members. Thus, families—and the church—have a significant role and responsibility in the care, nurture, and formation of children, youth, and adults.

Finally, there are lots of family-oriented activities and, yet, the truth of the matter is that Fourth Church (like the Bible) is not primarily about defining and defending the family but about proclaiming the grace of God and nurturing discipleship. And, while the church may be a "village" for some of its members and a network of friendships for many, it is not constituted as a village, nor as a family. It is more like the norm, the ideal, of city life described by Parker J. Palmer and Iris Marion Young—"the being together of strangers": "In the city persons and groups interact within spaces and institutions they all experience themselves as belonging to, but without those interactions dissolving into unity or commonness."[21] Parker Palmer explicitly calls on the congregation to be the place where this norm of public life is practiced.[22]

Family Ministries at Fourth:
Moral Formation, Civil Discourse, and Social Capital

The sheer abundance of ministries of Fourth Presbyterian Church evokes a narrative more like an album of snapshots than a comprehensive analysis. To guide us, let me offer a schematic characterization of family ministries at Fourth. Its engagement with issues of family life exemplifies three perspectives on family ministry in a public church: church as community of *moral formation,* especially formation for mission; church as community of theological, moral, and *civil discourse* on issues of public significance; and church as community of care and community-building, within and without—in other words, with attention to strategies of "*social capital.*"

Spiritual and Moral Formation

Larry Rasmussen and Stanley Hauerwas, contemporary Christian ethicists, discuss the responsibility of the church for spiritual and moral formation essential to Christian life.[23] But it is Susan Okin, speaking of the family as "a school for justice," who makes the connection between the spheres of private and public and thus articulates a rationale of Fourth Church's engagement in the formational process.

> Almost every person in our society starts life in a family of some sort or other. . . . While its forms are varied, the family in which a child is raised, especially in the earliest years, is clearly a crucial place for early moral development and for the formation of our basic attitudes toward others. It is, potentially, a place where we can *learn to be just.* It is especially important for the development of a sense of justice that grows from sharing the experiences of others and becoming aware of the points of view of others who are different in some respects from ourselves, but with whom we clearly have some interests in common.[24]

Likewise, at Fourth Presbyterian Church, family values are not separable from the larger commitment to values for individuals and communities of self-understanding, cooperation, and growth. Within this framework, in church school and nursery school programs, in the Center for Whole Life and the Center for Older Adults, Fourth Church provides a spiritual foundation for family life and child development (with help from their friends in the social sciences) and nurtures children and adults into responsible citizenship—or, at least, service-oriented mission. The explicit connection between these formational activities and family ministries is made in the parenting class, albeit in a secular idiom. The theological articulation of this orientation to formation is to be found in the church school (for children and youth) and in worship.

Education as Spiritual Formation

Sitting in the midst of the children, I reflected on a child's culture at Fourth. The children I met are worldly wise enough in a third-grade church school class to raise the issue of wasting paper when the handouts are not double-sided; "caring and sharing" enough in a sixth/ seventh-grade church school class to make teddy bears (with the help of the sewing/knitting group of the Center for Older Adults) and to make the children-to-children connection by taking them to children in Cook County Hospital; culturally conditioned enough to compete with one another for "the best parts" in the Pentecost play and to worry about the fat content of their snacks; and self-confident enough to raise hands whenever questions are asked. Church-school classes learn about God and Jesus Christ, the Bible, and what it means to be a community of faith through a lectionary-based curriculum, *Celebrate;* each class does a mission project; and each class participates in worship after church school.

The nursery school (Day School), unlike the church school, includes children of diverse religious backgrounds and does not use an explicitly Christian curriculum. Yet, the structure of the school's self-directed and cooperative activities reflects, embodies, and educates toward some basic values: It seeks to develop a sense of self. This means getting to know yourself, making choices, and learning how to express feelings, needs, and problems. Several of the activities encourage the kids to pay attention to classmates' sense of self—for example, joining in the "Happy Birthday" singing for a nursery-school classmate with wishes for the things *she* likes and likes to do. It seeks to develop cooperation and trust among the children and among their parents.

In 1994, Chicago Presbytery, Fourth Presbyterian Church, and Cabrini Green residents established a center specifically to deal with family issues in Cabrini Green. The Center for Whole Life emphasizes building a positive—and productive—"sense of self," both for the children and for their parents (themselves often adolescents), which, with love, enables the growth of children into responsible, caring adults. The cooperation theme is directed toward engaging the whole community in this effort, as in the vision of a group of grandparents and elders in the community who are encouraged to become mentors. Both of these programs seek to embody the basic commitments and values of Fourth Church in new contexts.

Worship as Spiritual Formation

Theological and spiritual formation in this church community takes place in and through the variety of worshiping occasions of the congregation's life. In addition to the Sunday morning and evening vespers services, worship services include Children's Chapel every Sunday after church school held in a special chapel and led, in turns, by the various church-school classes. The monthly family service is a specific occasion for families to worship together; this service is held in Blair Chapel at 10

A.M., before the 11 o'clock service in the sanctuary. All Fourth Church services follow the Presbyterian order of worship, which embodies and communicates the Reformed tradition and its basic theological orientation. The formational role of the order of worship should not be underestimated.

The Sunday worship bulletin welcomes children and gives parents options (welcome to keep the child with you, information on child care). However, one rarely notices children in the Sunday morning service. The Palm Sunday entry of children into the sanctuary, waving palms and singing, is very much an "in-and-out" affair. Sunday morning worship in the sanctuary is for the spiritual and moral formation of adults.

Family experience and issues are, however, significant elements of Fourth Church preaching. In a recent year, sermon titles included "Homecoming," "Jesus Had a Mother," "The Children," "Whose Family Values?" and "Fatherhood: Human and Divine"—just to mention the obvious ones. Family-theme sermons center in the theological principles of grace and responsibility. They might acknowledge the Bible's realism about families (the Bible is a tale of disastrous family dynamics) or cite current biblical scholarship against patriarchal versions of the Christian tradition. Typically, Buchanan contrasts these traditions with Jesus' countercultural treatment of children and women, the poor and the ill— the excluded ones, who are the unlikely centerpiece of Jesus' ministry of inclusion, healing, and confrontation with the authorities. The modern urban impact on these excluded ones, especially on the children of the poor, is the most unambiguous evil of city life from the perspective of Fourth Church, as articulated in sermons and institutionalized in the substantial church-based programs for children and older adults.

The Tutoring Program

Formation is a complex matter—and more transactional and mutual than we sometimes acknowledge. The Tutoring Program exemplifies another perspective on the formational activities of Fourth Church. This program, in which 470 students and tutors participate, is the most visible outcome of the bridge-building between Fourth Presbyterian Church and Cabrini Green. It is publicly acknowledged[25] and passionately supported within the church, which recently raised twenty-eight thousand dollars for the program from the sale of Christmas cards drawn and written by Tutoring Program students. Acknowledging the destructive reality of racism, poverty, and violence, the program seeks to make a difference in individual lives. Indeed, it seems to make a difference on both sides of the color line. The testimony of the tutors is that the experience is transformative for them. The impact on the tutors (who are mostly *not* members of Fourth Presbyterian Church) is not the point of the program. But it is consistent with the intent of the church, which preaches that the way of discipleship is the way of service and seeks to establish opportunities for service for the wider community of seekers. For the students, significant relationships are formed,[26] and a recent study showed measurable academic growth among the group of students tested.

Civil Discourse: "Can We Talk?"

One hallmark of a public church is public discourse: the serious discussion of issues of common concern, characterized by the presentation of alternative points of view, respect for the diversity of perspectives represented, a call for revaluation of assumptions, and confidence in the moral power of communities in conversation. Fourth Presbyterian Church hosts many events of this nature. The orientation to discourse is pervasive within the educational and fellowship life of the church. There are many diverse opportunities for discussion, both within the church and in wider networks (according to age, interest, family/work situation, etc.), some ad hoc and some regularly scheduled for specific constituencies.[27] This means that when Fourth Church takes up family issues, it does so acknowledging the complexities and ambiguities of the issues, eschewing either/or solutions, emphasizing respect for diversity of perspectives, and taking care not to demean choices or stigmatize persons categorically.

The church-school classes for children and youth readily link church and world and foster the willingness of children to be open to different points of view as well as to express their own. In one third-grade Sunday school class, the topic for the day was *jobs:* What do your parents do? What would you like to do? They could and did answer both questions (often mentioning what their mothers did). The vocational (relation of work and faith) question—how can you use your jobs to help the church—evoked a lively and creative discussion of how their envisioned jobs become "first fruits" brought to God and to the church. The morning's class ended with a question and a preview lesson about Pentecost (being celebrated the next week). In this lesson, the coming of the Holy Spirit enables people who speak different languages to understand and communicate with each other.

Presbyterian Women in Fourth Church offers a discussion-support group for mothers with young children (MOMS), Bible study and prayer groups, and a books-by-women discussion group, as well as a tradition of benevolence activities. In recent years, PWFC has initiated a series of programs on the balancing of family and work as well as gender issues in the workplace. "Can We Talk? A Conference on Gender Issues in the '90s" included speakers and workshops on work, family, and interpersonal relationships. "Anger in the Workplace: A Workshop for Women" was conducted in 1994 by the Lorene Replogle Counseling Center. These and the regular discussion-oriented professional women's breakfasts reflect the concerns of many professional women, single and married, in the congregation. In 1995, the annual Women in the '90s event focused on family: "Family Values: A Global Perspective." The panel explored family values through the eyes of the world's religions. The speakers were women, living in the Chicago area, who spoke on the spiritual foundations of family values from the perspective of their religions (Buddhist, Christian, Jewish, Muslim, Sikh). It was a fascinating, learning occasion. It struck me as true to Fourth Church: responsive to a major public issue but in such a way as to broaden the parameters of the discussion and to initiate relationships with some new neighbors.

Social Capital

> "It takes a whole village to raise one child" (African proverb).
> By analogy with notions of physical and human capital—tools and training that enhance individual productivity—"social capital" refers to features of social organization such as networks, norms, and social trust that facilitate coordination and cooperation for mutual benefit.[28]

In the public discussion of family life, "social capital" expresses the findings of current research that "the crucial difference between functional and dysfunctional families lies not in the form of the family but in the quality of support networks outside the family."[29]

Networking is "doin' what comes naturally"

Networking at Fourth comes in many forms. A woman engaged me in conversation, expressing her delight with the newly formed Grandparents Network. Her children and grandchildren live on the West Coast, which means only occasional visits. She grew up with grandparents nearby and actively involved. She now finds it difficult to know how to be a good grandparent from a distance, how to relate to the grandchildren well.

I met with a group of single parents;[30] some women were adoptive single parents, others were single parents by virtue of divorce. The group had never met together as single parents, although they mostly knew one another and one (mother of a teen-ager) was clearly both model and mentor for others in the room. They shared the typical struggles and joys of being single parents. They expressed a positive sense of self and family well-being, but also acknowledged their sensitivity to being stereotyped. "I tell them, 'I'm a lawyer,' one said, 'to establish my competence.'" They recognized the difference poverty makes, the difference between the single mothers of Fourth and those of Cabrini Green (mentioning specifically the latter's lack of control over their lives as well as lack of resources). Reflecting on the role of the church in their lives, they spoke of their experiences of getting involved in "Family Camp" and other ways in which the church offered networks of support in their lives as well as religious and moral education for their children. One called Fourth her "village." Another emphasized the sustaining importance of her individual faith, which Fourth Church nourishes. I discovered that single parents at Fourth are involved in a myriad of church-related activities; their primary identity and participation in the church are not as single parents. Yet, as we talked, the group—gathered together around this common experience of single parenting—generated hopes, ideas, synergy, and plans for articulating needs, developing more adequate networks of mutual support, and structuring opportunities within the church (e.g., "big brother" programs as resources for their young sons).

The Employment Support Group is Fourth Presbyterian Church's contribution to the church-based Career Transitions Network of Downtown Chicago. The group is not restricted to Fourth Church members, but all were Fourth Church members at the meeting I attended. One person had been laid off after many years with the company; unable to find work, he had just decided to go into business for himself. Another, also a long-term employee with a well-established firm, was five days into unemployment (unexpected) and already actively networking. What she spoke about, however, was the opportunity to take stock vocationally. The meeting was upbeat. There was a lot of energy in the room, lots of sharing of ideas, contacts, and resources. The networking culture of Fourth Church members came to life in the midst of anxiety and a reflective eye on the wider context. Their shared experience led to a discussion of the destructive character of the "good jobs" (escalating work load, "on call" expectations, competitive ethos significant family-impact issues).

Fourth Church's response to perceived crisis and expressed interest is evident in increasing attention to family issues and care in developing languages and strategies of inclusion in family events. Sometimes, this response is ad hoc, experimental. There seems to be an openness to trying an educational event here, a new fellowship group there, as interest is expressed. Large-scale successes are not a prerequisite of new opportunities for sharing, learning, and socializing. A few people gathered together seems typical for many special-purpose classes and groups.

Networking is the professionalization of support networks: Center for Older Adults (COA)

The mission or service-oriented programs of Fourth give lots of attention to families, especially "families of one" as Jan Strong, director of The Center for Older Adults (COA), calls them. These people may be without relatives, or their relatives live far away, or they or their relatives may be unable to cope and meet their needs. Making and keeping the connections is difficult for these people.

At Fourth, well-established, ongoing needs such as these lead to the professional organization of service and caregiving institutions and a mixed structure of professional and lay leadership. One example of the professionalization approach to networking is COA. The programs of COA include members of the church as well as a constituency from the wider community—Protestant, Catholic, and Jewish; COA membership is about four hundred. They come together for many purposes: wellness, education, mission, and social programs. Like other Fourth programs, COA promotes self-understanding, respect, and responsibility; commitment to lifelong growth and change; and attention to and cooperation with others. It balances its wide range of activities with an extensive care network and a pastoral one-to-one role. "We take each individual very seriously," Jan notes, and provide a context of trust.

Conclusion:
Reflecting on the "Creative Tensions" of Family Formation and Democratic Publics at Fourth Presbyterian Church

Fourth Presbyterian Church stands in the mainstream of modern American culture and mainline American Protestant Church culture.

The leadership criticizes certain assumptions and destructive effects of modern society, within a framework of accepting its basic principles and structures. The public church ethos means that it understands itself to be a community of citizens rather than a community of "resident aliens."[31] The countercultural theme is not world-alienated but world-affirming; discipleship is not withdrawal into a Christian community but gathering for worship and nurture and dispersing to serve God and transform self and world alike. Discipleship at Fourth Church takes its power—and the gift of human capacity—for granted. It emphasizes responsible action.

The family-related ministries of Fourth Presbyterian Church invite further reflection in three broad areas: the challenges to democratic family formation in a public church; the prerequisites of effective public discourse on family issues; and the impact of the "creative tension" between public church and private faith on the service and advocacy ministries of Fourth Church with families at Cabrini Green.

Formation

Finally, I come back to where I began: the parenting class and its theme of the family as a model and mentor for democratic citizenship. On the face of it, teaching democratic parenting practices seems especially apt for a church committed to the flourishing of a democratic, just, and caring public life. Moreover, the significance of this issue cannot be overstated in view of the current cultural debate about family values and changing gender roles and expectations. The rhetoric among Christians on family life—seeking order amidst chaos—has shown a penchant for authoritarian solutions: hierarchical families and punitive laws. In *Brave New Families,* Judith Stacey asks: "Why do many people of both genders recoil from the prospect of a fully democratic family regime?"[32]

Fourth Presbyterian Church contributes to a more constructive discussion in three ways. One important contribution of Fourth Church is its *affirmation* of democracy in family life. The modern shift from authoritarian to democratic families—characterized by mutuality, equality, participatory decision-making, respect for diversity, and dialogue— seems to be greeted as an unambiguous good at Fourth Presbyterian Church: true to Jesus and good for family relations, child development, and the future of the public realm.

Yet democratic family formation is a challenge. It is a challenge for the formational ministries of Fourth Church to teach the values of co-operation and self-respect in an individualistic, competitive, and bureaucratic culture that becomes the lens through which children and adults alike view these values. Their culturally cued reading of these values is a barrier to church-based character formation. It is a challenge to model and mentor communal forms of empowerment in a social context shaped by expectations of individual achievement and the privacy and adequacy of nuclear families. There are cultural constraints.

The second contribution of public churches to democratic publics is the church's *practice*. What sort of connection is made among children and youth growing up in Fourth Presbyterian Church between this democratic model of family life and their responsibility in the wider world as disciple and citizen? Structure and vision are important. The vision of a Presbyterian church is discernment of the will of God in the faith community gathered together as in the Council of Jerusalem (Acts 15). Its structure, its polity, is representative democracy.

One challenge at Fourth is professionalization. The size of the membership and the scale of its activity has led to a large professional staff. Many theorists argue that bureaucratization means depoliticization, the transferring of decision-making from the realm of public discourse and action to administration. Yet, Fourth Church seems also to create spaces of initiation and participation, practices that prepare for citizenship.[33] Connections do happen. The confirmation class makes the connections—although the question of the confirmation class is always: what next?

Finally, Fourth Church contributes its capacity to articulate *a theologically grounded vision and rationale* for democratic practice. Interestingly, STEP is *not* religiously oriented; its values are not grounded explicitly in Christian faith. Nor did the discussion include any reference to the Christian basis of these parenting strategies.[34] Moreover, theological resources abound: the preaching of Fourth Church, social witness policy documents of the Presbyterian Church (USA), and historical literature on the relation between the Reformed emphasis on covenant-relation and responsibility and democratic forms of life together.[35] The dilemma for a public church is the tension between the specificity of its Christian foundations and its commitment to communication and dialogue in the public realm. The difficulty, then, is how to establish the theological grounds for a democratic pro-family orientation that the interpreters of the "culture wars" view as basically secular.

Discourse

The power of a community of moral discourse is its respect for diversity of perspective and purpose, its invitation to imagination and new possibilities, and its commitment to discussion in the midst of conflict and to discernment. At Fourth, these circles of conversation about family life are many, not just one.

The challenge for the discursive commitments of Fourth Church lies in the requirement to insist on respect for diversity of perspective and purpose *and* to acknowledge the inequalities of power and the injustices of social structures that, in turn, structure the conversation itself. In my experience, there is not much talk about inequalities of power at Fourth. Speaking out on family issues will require attention to the unspoken assumptions about the "good family." And this, in turn, will require dealing with issues that arise by virtue of differences of culture and power, differences with respect to freedom of choice and access to well-being due to the differences of class as well as race. These differences, for example, for single parents at Fourth Church and at Cabrini Green, call for *both contextualized analysis and, in addition, the search for grounds of solidarity* in the discussion of family strategies of Fourth Church. Presently, these groups seem to have little in common and little connection.

The other challenge to Fourth Presbyterian Church's search for effective public discourse has to do with perception and language. The Center for Whole Life, the family empowerment and childhood development center at Cabrini Green, describes its mission, Fourth Church's mission, in terms of meeting needs.[36] Indeed, Fourth Church—responsive, collaborative, and committed to service and mission—typically uses the language of meeting needs in its statements of purpose related to outreach activities. This is understandable: needs are real and, in devastated communities, easy to see. Furthermore, an orientation to helping others directs one's gaze to the points where help is needed. But as John L. McKnight and John P. Kretzmann have argued, a needs-driven analysis sees only the problems and leads to a response that makes people consumers of services rather than producers of solutions; ignores the importance of building relationships; and settles for a survival strategy rather than social change and community development. At the heart of the matter is, of course, the question of power.[37] Interpreting a community in terms of its needs obscures both the realities of power in that community and the limits of power of the serving community. Fourth

Church's involvement in the Center for Whole Life is more thickly textured. But the needs-analysis orientation persists. Interestingly, this needs approach actually stands in some tension with the theology of Fourth Church, which, as I noted above, focuses on human capacity rather than deficiency.

Social Capital

The changes at Cabrini Green, the end of welfare for the poor "as we know it," and the restructuring of the workforce constitute a "needs" argument for the importance of reevaluating Fourth Church's social outreach ministries with families. The shift of authority (but not taxing capacity) from federal to state government and the shift of governmental support requirements from welfare to workfare—without substantial attention to prospects for work for the people impacted by these changes—are going to mean unmet needs that challenge the capacities of the nonprofit sector, including the churches. For Fourth Presbyterian Church, this will require some serious strategizing about mission priorities.

But it is not just a matter of prioritizing. This situation refocuses attention on partnerships and advocacy—and the requisites for fundamental social change. Fourth Church's approach to advocacy is clear: the purpose is social change; the method is primarily individual involvement. Social capital is caught in the crossfire between public church and private faith.

Some will be skeptical about the capacity of churches like Fourth to engage in the social changes requisite to a just and caring society. Given the American church's accommodation to "religion as a private matter" and the class identity of Fourth Church, the question is inescapable: Can faith so deeply rooted in privacy and so deeply shaped by privilege stand against the socially structured sins of urban life?

Others will remind us that "new occasions teach new duties." *Work* becomes both a pressing matter for the residents of Cabrini Green and an opportunity for Fourth Church to draw on its talents and relationships to develop prospects for work, perhaps through public-private (profit and nonprofit) ventures in strengthening work accessibility for Cabrini Green residents.[38] *Advocacy* becomes newly significant. The church's experience with family issues in its many programs of care and education, as well as the increasing role of state government in family matters, suggest that family and family-impact work issues constitute a legitimate focus of advocacy for social change, corporately articulated and institutionalized.

New occasions teach new duties—and new delights. That's a fitting closure for our story. It catches the spirit of Fourth Presbyterian Church's continuing journey with family ministries.

NOTES

1. Don Dinkmeyer and Gary D. McKay, *The Parent's Handbook* (Circle Pines, Minn.: American Guidance Services, 1989), 7.
2. I would like to acknowledge my gratitude to The Fourth Presbyterian Church of Chicago for their willingness to entertain this study and for the generous gifts of time and conversation on the parts of many. I especially thank John M. Buchanan, David Donovan, Tereatha Akbar, Karen Maurer, Fred Milligan, Kevin Olson, Sara Pfaff, Thomas Schemper, Victoria Snow, Janet Strong, John Wilkinson, and the single parents, church-school teachers, young people, and adult participants in the classes and community events I attended. My conversations with you—and observations of your conversations with one another—are the bedrock of this essay. I acknowledge, too, that my participation in the life of Fourth Presbyterian Church, albeit limited, has been a time of real delight as well as learning. I'm doubtless a partial observer in both senses of the word. Finally, while I did most of the field research for this study of Fourth Presbyterian Church, my colleagues in the Religion in Urban America Program at the University of Illinois at Chicago (RUAP), Lowell W. Livezey, Matthew Price, Reece Pendleton, and Iraida Rodriquez, also observed some events. I thank them and other RUAP colleagues, David Daniels, Janise Hurtig, and Elfriede Wedam, for introducing me into the world of congregational studies and for their discussion of this material.
3. James K. Wellman, Jr., "Boundaries of Taste: A Gold Coast Church and Cabrini Green," unpublished paper for discussion on February 19, 1994, at the meeting of the Chicago Area Group for the Study of Religious Communities.
4. Robert N. Bellah, "How to Understand the Church in an Individualistic Society," in *Christianity and Civil Society,* ed. Rodney L. Petersen (Maryknoll N.Y., Orbis Books, 1995); James W. Fowler, *Weaving the New Creation: Stages of Faith and the Public Church* (San Francisco: Harper Collins), 1991; Martin E. Marty, *The Public Church* (New York: Crossroad, 1981); Martin E. Marty, "Public and Private: Congregation as Meeting Place," in *American Congregations,* vol. 2, eds. James P. Wind and James W. Lewis (Chicago: The University of Chicago, 1994); William M. Sullivan, *Reconstructing Public Philosophy* (Berkeley, Calif.: University of California Press, 1982).
5. Marilee Munger Scroggs, *A Light in the City: The Fourth Presbyterian Church*

of Chicago (Chicago: The Fourth Presbyterian Church of Chicago, 1990), 75–76.

6. See Harvey Warren Zorbaugh, *The Gold Coast and the Slum: A Sociological Study of Chicago's Near North Side* (Chicago: The University of Chicago Press, 1929). Also: Albert Hunter, "The Gold Coast and the Slum Revisited," *Urban Life: A Journal of Ethnographic Research* 11/4 (January 1983): 461–76.

7. It might be thought that "place" is not a family issue. I learned otherwise from a lifetime member of the church. Rachel told me about her mother, who had become disabled and unable to attend Sunday worship at Fourth because the sanctuary was not wheelchair accessible. The building reconstruction included wheelchair accessibility to the sanctuary, and Rachel expressed her delight with being able to attend church with her mother once again.

8. In the *Handbook for Congregational Studies,* "identity" is defined as *"that persistent set of beliefs, values, patterns, symbols, stories and style that make a congregation distinctively itself"* (italics in original). Jackson W. Carroll, Carl S. Dudley, and William McKinney, eds., *Handbook for Congregational Studies* (Nashville: Abingdon Press, 1991), 12. We will turn to the distinctively religious dimensions of the church identity later.

9. Scroggs, *A Light in the City,* especially chaps. 2–4 and 8. The story of service is "awesome" and wonderfully told by Marilee Munger Scroggs.

10. Wellman, "Boundaries of Taste," 24–25. The survey, done on a random sample basis, was sent to every third parishioner between the ages of twenty and fifty in spring 1993. The sample return was about 31 percent.

11. Ibid., 25.

12. In this effort to thematize the theology of Fourth Church, I have drawn primarily on sermons whose issues and/or stories are about families.

13. John M. Buchanan, pastor, "Sex, Scripture, and the Presbyterian Church," sermon delivered June 16, 1991. Buchanan preached this sermon on the Sunday following the General Assembly of the Presbyterian Church (USA) decision not to adopt either the majority or the minority report on human sexuality.

14. John M. Buchanan, "Oh, the Places You Will Go!" sermon delivered October 24, 1993; "Who Wants to Be Number One?" sermon delivered September 24, 1994; "To Be a Hero," sermon delivered October 9, 1994; "Fatherhood: Human and Divine," sermon delivered June 18, 1995.

15. John M. Buchanan, "In the Image of God," sermon delivered September 18, 1994.

16. John M. Buchanan, "Oh, the Places You Will Go!"

17. See Marty, *The Public Church,* chap. 2, on the preeminence of *choice* ("freedom *of* choice linked with freedom *for* choice," 33) in a world of change, also the contrasting lures of "all-at-once" conversion and faith journey spirituality among the baby boomers, "the generation of seekers" (in Wade Clark Roof's terms). Clearly, many participants in Fourth Church are journeying seekers.

18. John M. Buchanan, "Whose Family Values?" sermon delivered May 8, 1994.

19. Shortly after I began observing at Fourth, noticing the way mobility issues came up in sermons, education programs, and conversation, I happened to read the first of the take-home issues for grades 5–6 in the *Celebrate* curriculum used by the church. It was an imaginative story about Jesus as a child, when Joseph decided to return from Egypt to Israel now that Herod was dead and Jesus no longer in danger (no mention of a family decision). The story is basically about how Joseph helped Jesus to prepare to leave the only home he had known. How apt for a church with a highly mobile constituency. *Celebrate* curriculum: "LIFESIGNS," Grades 5–6, winter 1993–94, unit 4, session 4, December 19, 1993. The story is called "At Home." P.S. Interestingly, the whole series of stories in this unit were father-son stories: Jesus and Joseph. I wonder about their impact on single parents.

20. The "family ethics questionnaire" distributed to the counseling staff of the Lorene Replogle Counseling Center offers another clue to Fourth's acceptance of a plurality of family forms. One has to be cautious here, because, while the Center is a ministry of Fourth Church, its counseling staff are not (mostly) members of Fourth Presbyterian Church—although the majority of the respondents to the questionnaire are active members of local congregations. On the issue of family forms, almost all of the respondents (sixteen) were willing to call a wide range of intimate relations "a family" (married, cohabiting, heterosexual, "bonded and committed" homosexual, with or without children, single parent and child). One respondent counted as "family" only those with children. Asked whether some family forms are "intrinsically more health-promoting for children than others," twelve (of sixteen) answered "no," at least not categorically.

21. Iris Marion Young, *Justice and the Politics of Difference* (Princeton N.J.: Princeton University Press, 1990), 237. This whole section on city life as "a normative ideal" (pp. 236–41) is particularly apt in thinking about Fourth Presbyterian Church and its character as public church in the city.

22. Parker J. Palmer, *The Company of Strangers* (New York: Crossroad, 1981).

23. Bruce C. Birch and Larry L. Rasmussen, *Bible and Ethics in the Christian Life* (Minneapolis: Augsburg, 1989); Larry L. Rasmussen, *Moral Fragments and Moral Community* (Minneapolis: Fortress Press, 1993); Stanley Hauerwas, *Dispatches from the Front* (Durham N.C.: Duke University Press, 1994), especially chap. 11: "The Church and the Mentally Handicapped."

24. Susan Moeller Okin, *Justice, Gender, and the Family* (New York: Basic Books, 1989), 18.

25. A Bob Greene article in the *Chicago Tribune* brought more responses of interest in being a tutor than Fourth could handle.

26. Tereatha Akbar, director of the Tutoring and Educational Outreach Programs, in speaking of the church's efforts to recruit more African American tutors, acknowledged the constraints of race in this situation.

Given black children's assumptions that "all whites are rich," the white tutor/black student factor may undercut the mentoring potential in these relationships.

27. In these respects, Fourth Church is very conventional in its boundary setting, e.g., the church school is mostly organized according to age groups.

28. Robert D. Putnam, "Bowling Alone: America's Declining Social Capital," *Journal of Democracy* 6/1 (January 1995): 67.

29. Stephanie Coontz, *The Way We Never Were: American Families and the Nostalgia Trap* (New York: Basic Books, 1992), 230. Coontz tells a wonderful story on herself to illustrate the difference between American parenting, with its preoccupation with parents' exclusive responsibility for their own children, and other "social capital" models. She was visiting Hawaiian-Filipino friends in Hawaii. She was "keeping an eye" on her child and tending to his needs—until she gradually realized that she was the only person getting up to attend to her child: "The other parents were *not* keeping an eye on their kids. Instead, each adult kept an eye on the *floor* around his or her chair"—and tended to any child who came into that space (p. 210).

30. The group were single mothers. A couple of single-parent fathers were unable to be at the meeting.

31. Stanley Hauerwas and William H. Willimon, *Resident Aliens* (Nashville: Abingdon Press, 1990).

32. Judith Stacey, *Brave New Families* (New York: Basic Books, 1990), 258.

33. See Sidney Verba, Kay Lehman Schlozman, and Henry E. Brady, *Voice and Equality: Civic Voluntarism in American Politics* (Cambridge, Mass.: Harvard University Press, 1995), on the significance of church participation for political participation.

34. I should add that, in this, it does not differ from a more evangelical church in the area, which uses the Myers-Briggs temperament material in its premarital classes. The use of contemporary social, psychological, and management science literature seems common to urban churches of diverse theological stances.

35. See Robin W. Lovin, "Covenantal Relationships and Political Legitimacy," *The Journal of Religion* 60/1 (January 1980): 1–16; A. D. Lindsay, *The Essentials of Democracy* (London: Oxford, 1929); Michael Walzer, *The Revolution of the Saints: A Study in the Origins of Radical Politics* (New York: Atheneum Publishers, 1968); and Jay Fliegelman, *Prodigals and Pilgrims: The American Revolution against Patriarchal Authority, 1750–1800* (Cambridge: Cambridge University Press, 1982).

36. See the statement-of-purpose insert in the bulletin for the dedication ceremony of The Center for Whole Life: "Here we try to address the needs of the children by addressing the needs and enlisting the cooperation of the whole community. On August 15, 1993, this program embarked upon its mission of attending to the spiritual, moral, social and physical needs of this part of the Cabrini Green community."

37. John P. Kretzmann and John L. McKnight, *Building Communities from the*

Inside Out: A Path toward Finding and Mobilizing a Community's Assets
(Evanston, Ill.: Center for Urban Affairs and Policy Research, Northwestern University, 1993).

38. See William Julius Wilson, "Work," *The New York Times Magazine,* Sunday,
    August 18, 1996. John Wilkinson, associate pastor for mission, has
    also expressed interest in developing work-related connections between
    Cabrini Green and Fourth Church.

7

"I Don't Mean to Offend, but I Won't Pretend"

Experiences of Family Life for Gay Men within an African American Church

D. MARK WILSON

One evening, while studying the experiences and definitions of family life at the Eastside Baptist Church, I had the pleasure of meeting with several gay men of the church in a focus group interview.[1] "I don't mean to offend, but I won't pretend" was the comment made by one of the men of this African American congregation, and according to our discussion, this comment seemed to summarize not only their experiences with the family life of the congregation, but their relations and interactions with the entire congregation as well. "I don't mean to offend, but I won't pretend" might sound, at first, like a great contradiction. However, this statement characterizes not a contradiction, but a story of faith and struggle faced by the gay members of the Eastside Baptist Church as they live with the realities of racism and homophobia, yet nevertheless persevere to find meaning for life and social support in Eastside's family ministry. The purpose of this essay is to investigate Eastside's definition of family, to describe Eastside's ministries to families, and to understand better the story of one population within Eastside's family life: gay men, who worship, fellowship, and offer their service on the margins between "not offending" their family culture and "not pretending" to be something other than gay.

The Historic Family Ministry of Eastside Baptist Church

Eastside Baptist is a historic and prominent African American congregation on the West Coast, organized in the early 1900s, when African Americans migrated to the West from the South following World War I. In comparison to other African American congregations on the West Coast, Eastside ranks as one of the largest black churches, with a membership of some five thousand people on role—although active membership is about half this number. Eastside has a progressive family ministry that functions as an extended family, not only to members of the congregation, but to those living in the community as well.

Given the void that racism and historical disempowerment have left upon the African American family and community, Eastside's ministry has stepped in to fill the gap, especially as government programs and social agencies have stepped out. Through its Economic Development Corporation and through collaborative efforts with community-based organizations, the progressive ministry at Eastside has created for families and for the surrounding neighborhood community a substance abuse counseling center, a housing development for senior citizens, apartment housing for persons living with HIV/AIDS, a Family Life Center to house programs targeted at empowering neighborhood families, and a credit union functioning as a community bank, where families are empowered economically to secure affordable loans for purchasing property. Moreover, the church has computer and job training classes for adults and houses a math and science program for youth, which has received great attention from the local city media.

At Eastside, a variety of African American families are empowered both spiritually and socioeconomically, as they worship on Sunday and throughout the week in Bible Study and Prayer Meeting, and as they are encouraged to participate with the community in the social programs created for them. From my observations at Sunday morning worship, and from talking with members and leaders of the church, I learned that the variety of families include single-parent families headed by women, two-parent families, blended families led by men and women in their second and sometimes third marriages, families where the grandparents are the main providers, interracial families, families with adopted and foster children, and homeless families who occasionally stroll into service and who are fed weekly in Eastside's food program. In the words of Eastside's senior pastor, who is both a spiritual leader and a prophetic community activist, the church, like many African American churches, not only ministers to families, but is the family for the people of faith who attend and for the community itself. A popular African proverb says, "It takes a village to raise a child." Similarly, Eastside's ministry may be viewed as the entire family village, supporting and empowering all of the members of the village with the faith to know God and the economic power to create opportunity.

The Interview

In context of this great spiritual institution, which also functions as the center of the village (i.e., its membership and surrounding neighborhood community), I conducted a focus group interview with a subgroup of the church family: eight men who were daring and proud enough to share their experiences of being gay and part of the African American church family. The interview was taped, and their comments were categorized and clustered around themes that emerged during our discussion. These comments and themes constitute the data upon which this paper is based.

I had hoped also to meet with lesbian women from the church. A staff minister referred me to a lesbian couple who later decided not to be part of the interview. When I asked the gay men whom I interviewed if they knew of any lesbian women who might share their experiences, the men commented that there were women in the congregation whom they felt or might have heard were lesbian; however, they had no real contact or relationship with them and felt it would be intrusive to approach them about being a part of my study. Therefore, I acknowledge that this study might have included richer data had the stories of lesbian women in the congregation also been included. One day when churches and communities of faith no longer perpetuate fear and shame for gays and lesbians in the family of faith, perhaps then gay men and lesbian women in the church will find the full pride to end their silence about their experience of family and their journey of faith in God.

Although the focus group lacked gender diversity, the dialogue with the eight men nevertheless was rich, and it gave the participants the opportunity to break their silence and to share stories of church and family life often not spoken and definitely not written about in theological literature on the African American church.[2]

Instead of gathering at the church, they requested to meet in a more private setting where they could share more discreetly and speak more openly about their experiences of family life at their congregation. Together we met in the office of one of the participants, and—after ripping open several bags of potato and tortilla chips, opening cans of french onion and bean dip, and sipping on soft drinks and juices that were provided to create a relaxed, party-like atmosphere—we settled down into a lively and meaningful discussion.

Many of these men had been friends for years, and in the tradition of extended family in the African American church and community, the older gay men of the group had been mentors and father figures for some of the younger gay men in the group. Yet even with their close familiarity and friendships with one another, they commented that this was the first time that they ever had a serious conversation with each other about their faith and their sexual orientation.

Most of the men in the focus group had professional occupations as doctors, social workers, psychologists, and the like. One of the men was a college student and another was in transition seeking a stable job. In terms of education and family background, most of the men had attended college, some had done graduate work, and most of them had family roots in the South. Either they had relocated to the West Coast with their parents during the great migration of African Americans in the post-war 1940s, or they had moved to the West Coast for employment following college. Those born on the West Coast also had families that had migrated from the South. It was clear through our dialogue that their education had given them the language to understand their sexuality and to voice their experience. Through our discussion it was also clear that their occupational achievements had made them familiar with their professional rights not to be discriminated against as gay men—whether they exercised these rights or not.

Findings

What really stood out in our discussion was the impact that southern cultural understandings had upon their experience of church and family life at Eastside. They tended to connect what they knew about the South, either through personal or familial experience, to how they viewed their faith and their life in the church. Several men who had lived in Atlanta, Georgia, maintained that the church was the entire life of the community and the center of their families. As one of the men put it:

> At night my mother taught us the Sunday school lesson and gave us religious instruction at home. On Sunday our family was in church all day long. Early in the morning we went to Sunday school, then we sat for two hours or more in morning worship, and if we had a three o'clock program we came back in the afternoon for more worship. Every week we would have to come back at night for BTU (Baptist Training Union), and then have night service for two hours more.[3]

As I listened to their experiences, I could not help but remember my own experience of church and family growing up in the African American community. My mother grew up in rural Mississippi, where African Americans created out of segregation communal networks of family to help, strengthen, and inspire one another. She carried this understanding of family to the West Coast, as she found strength as a single parent to raise all six of her children. Like these men, my brothers in the interview, my five siblings and I found ourselves in church, morning, noon, night, and sometimes at midnight listening to the last choir sing after a three-hour musical. These type of religious experiences have kept many young men and women growing up in African American families from falling into traps that might have put us on the streets and locked up in jail had we not had the spiritual conviction to know who and whose we were!

When asked what attracted them to join Eastside, several comments suggested that their membership and inclusion with Eastside was due to two things: their rich experience of religion in their Southern families and Eastside's progressive extended family and social ministry that they feel is inclusive and affirming of everyone, even themselves as gay. The following comments seemed to suggest this:

Experience of Religion and Family in Their Southern Heritage

Church in the African American community back home was something that you grew up with. Church is life and we were in church all day, from Sunday school to BTU (other brothers gave high fives to one another to affirm what was spoken). I could not think of being without it, and Eastside was just like my church in Atlanta.

Growing up in the South there were churches everywhere. Sometimes we went to the Baptist church, sometimes the Methodist church, even sometimes the Kingdom Hall. The church was always a very prominent part of our [his family's] life. There was so much violence, alcoholism, and substance abuse around us. My mother was always constantly giving us vivid examples of what-you-don't-want-to-do kinda thing. The church could not help but to have a major impact upon you. I could hear my mother pray early in the morning around five o'clock and hear her anguish. And basically out of growing up black and poor in the South—you know the Jim Crow Laws, my parents getting off the street when a white man walked by, or watching white men abuse my mother verbally in a store, and I may have been six, seven, or eight—and it left an impression I'll never forget. Sunday school taught us the Bible, about right and wrong, and suddenly I was taught that you always pray and have respect, for self, for the elders. There was a lot of the extended-family kind of thing.

When my grandmother died, I felt I never missed her because her relatives built the church, and the older members befriended me, wrote letters to me, and gave me an incredible educational experience. So I had a lot of family background. I had a lot of knowledge about the black churches in my county because I spent summers with my grandmother and drove her around to all the different churches when I was a teenager. That was something so special for her and I, and how I was admired in the church.

The people in my Sunday school class at Eastside are much older people, and they are very knowledgeable. And particularly growing up in the South and being removed from my primary family, it's important for me to have that adult-young person relationship. I feel at this point in my life I can reach back and help. In some ways in a big church it's like a small-church mentality.

When I first came here I felt so welcomed and everyone treated me like family. I am far from my home in Tennessee, but the people here are from the South and have those southern ways. They open their heart to you. There's one woman in the choir she's just like a mother to me. I could tell her that I was gay, but that's not the most important thing to me. People can say they accept you and still not be there when you need them. What's important to me at this church is not what they say about gay people. Sometimes some preachers have said, "God made Adam and Eve and not Adam and Steve" from the pulpit. That bothers some people but it doesn't bother me. I don't live my life for the preacher, and don't have anything to prove to him. In the choir and in my Sunday school class is where I feel real love. We are like family. We call each other on the phone and help each other out. I feel I could tell my church mother anything.

Eastside's Social and Inclusive
Extended Family Ministry

I feel intellectually satisfied at Eastside. They bring a balance between the spiritual and the intellectual. I was invited to Eastside and was impressed by how they promoted education. The pastor said, "All those who graduated from a black college, stand up!" All ministries are welcomed and offered at the church. I left my church and was really uplifted here.

The church is very inclusive. In the pastoral prayer, a name of someone in bereavement will be called out. Choir members are like extended family. There's something different about that southern hospitality.

At Eastside I understand the family to be very inclusive. Eastside has the reputation in the community of being bourgeois, but every class is here. Poor and professional people are not singled out. You see everybody working together. We have an AIDS ministry. It's inclusive.

Family can be a group of people of the same age, family can be friends. When I came, I was immediately accepted. One lady in the choir calls me her son. My Sunday school class is a family. When you don't have family around, you make family.

Whoever lives together, that's a family. One time a single man who adopted two boys was asked to stand. The pastor kept saying, "This is a family." When the pastor said it, the church accepted it.

There's lots of support for single parents and foster parents. A lot of recognition. It's a huge church, people develop linkages and friendships. People adopted me. There was one woman who heard about my sexual orientation, and there was a wonderful change in our relationship. I was invited over for dinner.

We can laugh and joke with each other as gay men in the church. We are like family to each other. We have a secret world as gay men, and I can just be myself. We just have our space sectioned off. A space where we can laugh.

There was so much going on at Eastside, so much to do and to be active in, everybody seemed to be welcomed and included, and my mother would be proud that I'm active in the church. I was attracted there [Eastside] because as I became an adult I was very much aware of the social and political environment of the community. The church is able to reach out to its people and its masses. The church has knowledge about the diversity, the pain, the agony, or whatever of the community. Eastside really embodies that in many levels.

One thing I liked the first time I came to Eastside was that this church is involved in the community. There's something for everyone to do. It just doesn't stay in the four walls of the building. The church is involved in politics and in helping people. The pastor teaches this, and that's the kind of church I am interested in being a part of.

I just like the energy, the serious-mindedness of people who are members of the church, and again I think there is a general openness about life, that life is not perfect but we will keep on trying and praying, because we do this as a large group kind of thing.

These comments highlight the extent to which Eastside as a church functions as an alternative family in creating networks of social support for its members. The experiences of these African American gay men are like the experience of their foreparents, former slaves who found in their religious community a means to preserve kinship ties and elements of family life that slavery attempted to destroy.

Literary Connections

The church as an alternative family since slavery has been well documented in the early works of African American sociologists. E. Franklin Frazier's study, *The Negro Church in America,* maintained that the church was the primary institution through which African Americans were assimilated into understanding of family and marriage from the dominant American culture.[4] According to Frazier, the black church was itself "a nation within a nation" emulating the values and mores of the white majority culture. While W.E.B. DuBois's 1898 classic work, *The Philadelphia Negro,* also pointed to the important role and impact of the church upon the African American family, DuBois disagreed with Frazier's concept of assimilation, and argued that the church as the center of African American life was the institution that preserved African traditions of family.[5] According to DuBois, the church as an institution predated the family and did not assimilate African Americans into definitions of family and marriage created by the dominant white culture. Rather than objects of assimilation, African Americans were subjects of their own reality and utilized the church to create alternative family definitions that modeled African society and offered both spiritual and sociopolitical support:

> As a social group the Negro church may be said to have antedated the Negro family on American soil; as such it has preserved, on the one hand, many functions of tribal organization, and on the other hand, many family functions. Its tribal functions are shown in its religious activity, its social authority and general guiding and coordinating work; its family functions are shown by the fact that the church is a centre of social life and intercourse; acts as newspaper and intelligence bureau, is the centre of amusements—indeed, is the world in which the Negro moves and acts.[6]

Eastside's family ministry indeed appears to be like DuBois's church. It is a community center where African Americans create family culture, and at the same time it provides a sacred space for African Americans to "move and act" in areas of life where racial inequality has prevented their social and political mobility. In denominational debates about sexual orientation, I have often heard more conservative voices (and sometimes liberal ones) ask why gay men don't just leave traditional congregations and join congregations where gays and lesbians are welcomed and affirmed. In the religious experiences of these men there is an answer to this question. The extended family culture that is offered to heterosexual members of Eastside is also offered to them. First, the church offers to them a way to preserve their cultural heritage as African Americans and their family traditions as it offered to their enslaved ancestors who likewise preserved their African heritage through religious practices. The family culture is not foreign to them; it has been and continues to be their extended family and home. Why should they leave home and journey to another congregation that may welcome lesbians and gays, but that might not have any appreciation for their cultural heritage and family experience within the African American church? Eastside functions as their extended family, where they find affirmation to continue familiar traditions of family from their African American southern heritage. Second, on some level, Eastside affirms their sexual orientation, particularly due to what they identify as an openness from the leaders and members of the congregation. According to their comments, they are either affirmed in smaller units of family they create in the Sunday school or choir, or they are fully recognized and accepted as they network and create safe space and family with other gay friends. In those spaces, they can laugh and share their truth. Why should they leave their extended family in the church, particularly when the inclusive nature of the congregation has given to them such a warm welcome? Like other members who attend Eastside, they too find a family of faith in which they can share their gifts in serving and making life better in their community.

The Story Continues

Affirmation, spiritual and social support, and extended family may be what these men find in Eastside's ministry; however, as our conversation continued, other stories and experiences emerged from their voices, stories that highlighted the difficulties and ambiguities in their experience, stories about "offending" and "pretending."

As I pushed them to clarify their comments that had to do with sexuality, and directly asked whether or not they as a group of gay men felt included in Eastside's theology of family, it was then that our discussion began to change. Some of them said that Eastside and its leadership are very open and welcome diversity, and that "being out" as gay men was not an issue for them, since they came to church solely for worshiping God and serving the community. Those who expressed this view maintained that friendships and safe places which affirmed them as gay men outside the church made them less concerned with whether or not they were accepted within the church family. Other members of the group, particularly the younger men, expressed that being affirmed as gay men at the church was important for them. They maintained that Eastside was not always a nurturing extended family, but sometimes a family in which they struggle. They struggle with whether or not they should be vocal and help to transform a church family that means so much to them, and with whether or not they have any biblical or theological grounds to claim their right as gay men to be a part of the family.

During this period of sharing, a statement emerged from one of the members of the group that seemed to provide common ground. While sharing their diverse experiences of being included or excluded in the church family as gay men, one of the brothers seemed to experience a moment of revelation and stated, "Wait a minute, I don't mean to offend, but I won't pretend!" The rest of the brothers nodded their heads and spoke words of agreement as if he had summarized for them exactly how they felt about being included as gay men in the church family. I probed and pushed for further clarity, particularly since it seemed as if they had found some unified thought:

> Q.: "I don't mean to offend, but I won't pretend?" Can you say more?
> Respondent 1 (R1): What I mean is, in this society white people have more power. White men can "come out," say they are gay, and not be judged for their race. When I walk down the street in a gay neighborhood, I can't hide the fact I'm black, and that I still have to deal with race. It's an issue of pride and respect. I won't offend the community and the church which taught me pride. When I walk down the streets around the church and on my job, I see young black men who see me as one of the few positive, educated, black male role models in the community. I want them to look up to me. In our community we have to be unified and stand together, and I don't want to offend anybody. At the same time I won't pretend.
> R2: Yeah, it's an issue of pride and respect. I don't want to offend, but I won't pretend.

Q.: You won't pretend? What do you mean?

R1: I'm not going to walk into church and act like I'm not gay. I'm not going to pretend to be something else. I'm not going to pretend by dating a women to cover and hide my sexual orientation. I will bring my partner to church, walk in with him, and sit next to him. I won't be like some of the gay men at the church who pretend by acting like they date women and bring women to church with them. But, honey, we all know their "tea."[7]

This brief portion of our dialogue identified several obstacles that gay men in this African American church may have to negotiate. The first obstacle presented in this discussion is obviously the issue of race. Freedom and power in America have been highly skewed toward white men, whether they are in the heterosexual or gay community. The same barrier of racism that tends to limit the progress and socioeconomic mobility of African Americans and their families also presents a barrier for African American gay men to openly affirm themselves as black and gay. The second issue that appears to emerge here is the issue of taking communal and civic responsibility within the African American community. African American theologian Cheryl Sanders has described the African American church as the sacred place from which black Americans have attempted not only to critique and transform the larger social system of injustice and inequality, but where African Americans have also defined and take on their "civic responsibility" to develop and create a self-determined, independent African American community.[8] In this type of community, every member takes responsibility for lifting up the other, and gay men within this community of faith see it as their responsibility to use their gifts, talents, and knowledge as a means by which to lift up, encourage, and nurture younger African American men. The actions of African American gay men who take on such a responsibility critiques and disputes the notion among many in the African American political community that gay men are a threat to the survival of the black community and to civil rights.[9] Black gay men who have been blamed for the shortage of available black men to marry black women and to be fathers for black children are just as much responsible, concerned, and involved in nurturing children, strengthening black families, economically developing the community, and engaging in political struggle as are other men and women in their community.[10] The third concern of these gay men is with preserving the pride and respect they have for the African American church. While the black church, like other church and faith communities, has certainly played a major role in perpetuating homophobia and negative images of gays and lesbians, as has already been suggested, the African American church also has been a sacred center in which these men have found family support and affirmation. What sense would it make for one to find what one describes as support and affirmation in an institution and then suddenly offend that affirming institution by destroying it? How do gay men and lesbian women respect an institution, like the church, which has certainly been at the forefront of destroying them and at the same time take pride in the aspects of that institution that have nurtured and strengthened them? In the same regard, how do they hold onto their own self-pride and self-respect, lest their identity be lost in serving and perpetuating the needs of the larger faith community? For the gay men at Eastside, and perhaps in other similar faith communities, the answer is complexly this: "I don't mean to offend, but I won't pretend."

More Literary Connections

The experience of gay men within this congregation to not offend and not pretend highlights a struggle common for persons who face multiple discrimination and oppression. Angela Davis's work *Women, Race and Class,* for example, has shown that African American women have been reluctant to support fully the women's movement in the United States, due to racial discrimination they experienced from its white women leaders.[11] According to Davis, racial inequality within the women's movement led white women to organize with white men in blocking voting rights for African Americans, and caused African American women to be cautious and critical in supporting women's issues in labor and reproductive rights, lest such support work against them and members of their community. In this regard, African American women have been careful not to offend the beliefs and values of their own African American community, and at the same time have the task of not pretending that sexism within the African American community does not exist.

Isaac Julien and Kobena Mercer described well this multiple oppression for African American gay men in an article entitled, "True Confessions: A Discourse on Images of Black Male Sexuality."[12] Julien and Mercer argue that "the origins of the gay liberation movement" were dependent upon "black people's struggle." White gay men studied Martin Luther King, Jr., and the Civil Rights Movement became the prototype of the Gay Liberation Movement. They—as well as the women's movement, the peace movement, the ecology movement, and the antiestablishment movement—acquired their tactics for demanding justice from African Americans, yet they excluded the discussion of racism within the gay and lesbian community from their own liberation movement. In this regard, middle-class, white gay men created definitions of what it meant to be "out of the closet" without recognizing *the* different social locations which African American gays and lesbians—as well as other gays and lesbians of color, class, and with disabilities—were called to negotiate:

> Although gays derived inspiration from the symbols of black liberation, they failed to return the symbolic debt, as it were, by proceeding to ignore racism. The exclusion of race from the gay agenda was highlighted around the issue of coming out. As the London-based Gay Black Group has argued, the call by gay activists to reject the heterosexist norms of the nuclear family was totally ethnocentric as it ignored the fact that black lesbians and gay men *need* our families, which offer us support and protection from the racism we experience on the street, at school, from the police, and from the state. . . . *White gays have passed all this by because race is not an issue for them.*[13]

Julien and Mercer help shed some light upon the varied experiences and multiple discrimination of the brothers in my dialogue group. To be gay and worry about confronting homophobia is not enough. Confronting homophobia today is no guarantee that they will not have to confront racism or the destruction of their families and the incarceration of their younger brothers and sisters tomorrow. The church has provided for them some means of enduring and believing that these multiple discriminations can, by faith, be handled and faced. The church as an extended family has become for these men a haven of protection and a sacred space of spiritual power and familial support, as it has been in the historical lives of their foreparents and present-day sisters and brothers. This is their family and this is their home within a hostile world of racial inequality. Those who wish to live in community, who wish to find home with their family and heritage, and who seek not to be defined by the language and politics of a more dominant racial and social group struggle also to understand what sacrifice of self they must make to be in relationship with other members in their family. The pride and respect these African American gay brothers express in not wanting to offend their church family demonstrates their sacrifice to aid in the spiritual and social empowerment that strengthens their community.

Julien and Mercer, at the same time, let neither the gay men of East-side nor other African American gay men and lesbian women off the hook, and shed light upon what "not pretending" might mean:

> Our families are contradictory spaces: Sometimes we cannot afford to live without the support of our brothers and sisters, mothers and fathers, yet we also need to challenge the homophobic attitudes we encounter in our communities.[14]

While "not offending" and "not pretending" seem to highlight the multiple discrimination and challenge for the gay men at Eastside, these two concepts also characterize what Julien and Mercer identify as "contradictory spaces." On the one hand, not offending the church family by which one has been protected and empowered is valued, particularly since the church has been the spiritual foundation upon which many in the African American community have been able to stand and rise up out of severe oppression. "Not offending" is a statement of pride and respect that many of us in the African American community must have for our families, our churches, our institutions, and our traditions if we are to transform the social injustices that continue to economically undermine us. Yet it is not the intent of these men to take "not offending" their extended family to the point of inauthenticity. While "I don't want to offend" is a statement of pride and respect for their church, family, or community, "I will not pretend" expresses the respect these gay men must have for themselves. "I will not pretend" is a statement of pride. It is—in Julien and Mercer terms—their challenge to somehow confront homophobia wherever they encounter it, particularly in the African American church and community. "I will not pretend" expresses the effort of gay men at Eastside to hold onto their pride, a pride to be as authentic as they possibly can be and to challenge, in their own way, the homophobia that might be perpetuated within their extended church family. It is their effort to demand from the church family that they so respect, the same respect that is due to them.

The Scale of "Not Offending" and "Not Pretending"

"Not offending" and "not pretending" provide for us a scale upon which to measure the varied experiences of these gay men, who represent a sub-culture within the church family at Eastside. John Fortunato's work, *Em-*

bracing the Exile: Healing Journeys of Gay Christians, presents a model to help those involved in pastoral care understand behavioral patterns of gay men.[15] Fortunato learned from his own faith journey "coming out" as a gay clergyperson, and from the stories of gay men for whom he has cared as a pastoral counselor, that gay men will often live with their sexual orientation in three ways: ignore or avoid it, suffer through it, or fight to preserve and protect it. Ignoring or avoiding it, suffering through it, or fighting to preserve and protect it seem to be subthemes that underlie the scale of "not offending" and "not pretending" (Diagram 1).

Diagram 1.
The Varied Experiences of Gay Men at Eastside Baptist Church
on the Scale of "Not Offending" to "Not Pretending"

Action

Not Offending		**Not Pretending**	
as avoidance and denial	as suffering in silence	as suffering and trusting the process	as fighting and confronting homophobia

(Extreme)<——<——<—— (Mean) ——>——>——>(Extreme)

On one extreme of the scale, several comments seem to suggest that "not offending" the church family can lead to the ignoring, avoiding, and denying of their sexual identity:

"Not offending"—as a method to ignore, avoid, or deny sexual identity

> I don't tell people I'm gay; in the black community it is a different issue.
> I'm not walking around with "gay" attached to my forehead.
> I'm not there to tell everyone I'm gay.
> I have no desire to come out.

On the other end of the scale, "not pretending" might lead to their fighting and confronting homophobia in the church family and might lead them to a place of being open and "out." Several comments seemed to suggest this:

"Not Pretending"—a method of fighting and confronting homophobia

> I don't tell people I'm gay, but I don't hide the obvious.
> We can laugh and joke with our gay friends. We have a secret world. We just have our space sectioned off where we can laugh.

I have no problem walking arm in arm into church with my partner.

I'm not going to deny who I am.

I've been called everything, but I won't stoop down to their level. If I let them control me, I'm lowering myself to get down to their level.

I have talked with him (the pastor) about members in his ministry who could be hurt. When I heard someone from the pulpit say, "God made Adam and Eve, not Adam and Steve," I said, "That's it." I brought together the pastor and several pastors from other churches who made those kind of statements and told them that there were members in their ministry who could be hurt by what they said. I work with the AIDS ministry, and there are gay men at the church with AIDS who feel that they don't have a pastor to talk to. I told the ministers that I could help them, but I couldn't be their pastor. Our pastor was the only one to change.

The pastor is a generous person. If you accused him of homophobia he would cry. He has been accused before and cried. (To another member of the group) You should go to him and confront him.

"Suffering through it" might be perceived as a mean between the extremes of "not offending" and "not pretending." In this regard, some of the members of this focus group are willing to "not offend" as they suffer in silence and in distrust of their church family. The following comments seemed to express this:

"Not offending"—as a method of suffering in silence and in distrust of the church family

I don't feel included. One day the pastor saw me with another gay member. Since that time he has thrown me much shade (African American gay colloquial expression which means that the pastor has been ignoring him). Prior to this time, when he saw me with female friends I was always recognized and asked to stand up in church. I've lost lots of respect. That's why you don't see me in church that much anymore.

I get mixed feelings and hear mixed messages. I hear a lot about being open and that everybody's welcome, but I just don't trust it when I also heard preachers call it sin and say "God made Adam and Eve and not Adam and Steve." (Shaking his head with a quiet and fearful expression on his face) I mind my own business and sing with my friends in the choir.

I'm supportive of being gay in private settings. I'm not at this point in my life. I'm not into offending other people. I know that being gay has its limits.

I take off my gay personality when I come to church.

While for some, "suffering" may lead to silence and distrust, according to other comments, suffering might encourage others not to pretend, and to trust in the diversity and inclusive family theology they have found at Eastside, particularly from the church's leadership:

"Not Pretending"—a method of suffering and trusting in the evolving process and the open message of diversity from the leadership at the church

> The leadership recognizes that there are gay people. The leadership recognizes all individuals. I think people recognize me and my partner as partners. That's why I continue to participate in church.
>
> I've been in the church long enough to see evolution and change. I remember the Adam and Eve stuff, and all of a sudden it stopped. I don't know if anyone told the pastor about it, but no one says it anymore. It's like someone tells all the ministers before they go into the pulpit not to say it. The reason I think it stopped was because the ministers were confronted, and I remember the pastor talking on the issue.
>
> When you get older you process what you hear. You hear things at the church and process it differently. When I would hear, "God made Adam and Eve, not Adam and Steve," I would say that the person who said that has a personal problem. There is an intellectual side of the church which teaches us that we have to weed out what's not the right message.

These statements highlight the diversity of experiences of gay men who are members of the Eastside church family. Understanding the diversity of experiences of African American gay men has been encouraged by African American gay writers. In the work of African American gay writer and poet Essex Hemphill, who died in 1996 from AIDS, perhaps this diversity is best expressed:

> Much of the beauty of the black gay community is its diversity of expression and coping. Some of us vogue, some are butch, some give buppie, some give girl, some give fever; diva is an aspiration, darling is friend, and there are the boys who will be boys and the men who will be men no matter how the pants fall.
>
> It would be impossible to say there is one type of black gay male for all seasons. We haven't yet, nor do we need to, be clones.[16]

The comments from the focus-group members express that their experiences with the extended family culture at Eastside are diverse and numerous, perhaps as numerous as the sand upon the sea. As they move upon a scale from "not offending" to "not pretending," they, and perhaps others who live with a multitude of "contradictory spaces," experience not one but various behavioral patterns within the extended family of the church. Sometimes they experience exclusion within the family as they ignore, avoid, and deny their reality. Sometimes they experience affirmation and acceptance in the church family, as they affirm themselves; create alternative networks with each other; and confront, push, and challenge leaders who can make a difference. Whether they act not to offend or not to pretend within their church family, the reality is that either decision involves some extent of suffering. Fortunato's aforementioned work points to this ongoing reality of suffering in the lives of gay men and lesbian women, particularly those who are part of the Christian church family. In a sense, suffering and struggle are ethics of life for gays and lesbians, just as much as they are for all who face bigotry and discrimination and for all who seek to find a new and resurrected faith through the bearing of a cross. A gay member of the focus group may have worked not to offend the congregation, yet that does not mean that he won't in some way still be confronted by homophobic comments from the pulpit. A gay member of the focus group may work not to pretend and indeed confront homophobic members in the congregation, yet that does not guarantee that every one confronted will understand his experience and change. With either decision comes some interaction with suffering that may be connected to homophobia, which is nurtured, developed, and perpetuated in the larger culture and society and is, therefore, brought and institutionalized into the church.

Fortunato recommends to gay and lesbian Christians, and to others who face similar forms of oppression within and outside the church family, that they like other human beings must fight for change, but always should embrace their full experience of being an "exile," and live and accept uncertainty as a part of life. Living and accepting uncertainty, however, does not mean being passive or silent about one's oppression. Embracing uncertainty does not mean sitting down in silence, giving over to defeat, and allowing social definition to limit one's freedom and human potential. For Fortunato and for these gay men living in the family culture of the African American church community, this embracing of uncertainty is the basis and foundation for eliminating the stress brought on by suffering, for finding true liberation from both social and self-imposed expectations, and for finding faith upon their journey and walk with God.

Critique

A central concern in Marxian analysis is the nature of "contradictory locations."[17] Contradictory locations describe the experiences of groups of people who live upon boundaries between different cultures, different classes, different social categories, and different social experiences of the world. This phenomenon has been described in Julien and Mercer's aforementioned work on "contradictory spaces." If we really thought about it we would see that most people live in such locations and spaces, sometimes struggling to integrate a variety of social experiences. Some struggle to integrate middle-class values with working-class ethics, some struggle to integrate generational biases with present-day knowledge, some struggle to integrate racial identity with gender identity, and in the church community some are like the Apostle Paul in trying to integrate traditional laws of exclusion with the Pentecostal spirit of inclusion. We are never in one category at one time, and often find ourselves struggling to understand the full range of our diverse experiences.

What has been demonstrated in the experiences of African American gay men attending Eastside Baptist Church is the diversity of their experience as they reflect upon what it means to be part of the church family. "Not offending" and "not pretending" have been presented as a scale upon which they describe the full range of experiences that they are challenged to integrate. Some of these experiences are contradictory, just as contradictory as speaking about not offending and not pretending in one sentence. But if faith, as Fortunato has argued, is in fact living with uncertainty and being at peace with contradiction as a part of life, then it can be concluded that on one level these men of Eastside have come to find the answer and the faith that works best for them, at this time.

There is some concern in the mind of this author about what might be the outcomes associated with what I have called the scale of "not offending" and "not pretending." My particular concern is with what outcomes might be associated with what has been characterized as avoidance, denial, and being silenced about one's identity in the case of not offending the congregation. This concern is not one of my own, but was the concern of the acclaimed African American gay scholar and filmmaker, Marlon Riggs—who died from AIDS in 1994 and for whom I was honored to preside over and eulogize at his memorial service. In his award-winning film, "Tongues Untied," which documented the struggle of African American gay men who painfully suffer, often in silence, from racism, classism, and homophobia, Riggs suggested that such silencing and denial could be quite detrimental not only to African American gay men, but to their community as well. This is best described in a rhythmic chant from the film:

> Anger, Unvented,
> Becomes Pain, Unspoken,
> Becomes Rage, Released,
> Becomes Violence
> Cha, Cha, Cha

Underlying the scale of "not offending" and "not pretending" there may be outcomes, as might perceived by Riggs, Fortunato, and Julien and Mercer, which are just as diverse as the experiences in which these gay men live (Diagram 2).

Diagram 2.
The Scale of "Not Offending" and "Not Pretending"
with Possible Associated Outcomes

Action

Not Offending		**Not Pretending**	
as avoidance and denial	as suffering in silence	as suffering and trusting the process	as fighting and confronting homophobia

(Extreme)<——<——<—— (Mean) ——>——>——>(Extreme)

| *Anger Unvented | *Pain Unspoken | *Faith | *Rage Released, *Transformation, *Violence |
| (Riggs) | (Riggs) | (Fortunato) | (Julien and Mercer) (Riggs) |

Outcome

"Not offending" the congregation may be an expression of respect and pride in the family culture of the African American church; however, at what point does "not offending" become the sort of outright denial, anger, and pain that Riggs and other African American gay men have surely faced and lived with on a daily basis? At what point does "not offending" further perpetuate the silencing, denial, and pain that they may face within their own family and church? Many families and churches function in this way, denying that oppression is real, that domestic violence actually happens, that homeless families actually sleep around the doors of the church, that more African American men are being incarcerated than being educated and that, in some cities, the rate of African American women being imprisoned is doubling that of African American men. There are churches and families who live in denial of these things, and deny more than often the right for gay men and lesbian women to live an open life without being called a sinner and a damnation in the eyes of God, and without living with the threat of being brutally bashed and attacked. Such denial has often led to anger that is carried out in one's community, and unspoken pain that often turns against self. Could there be in the experiences of these men, something left that is unspoken?

Further, what about the denial of these topics in literature on the black family and in theological writings on the African American church? Since the Black Power Movement in the late 1960s to early 1970s, and even more recently, African American theologians and preachers have been proud to call our theology an inclusive theology of liberation and our families inclusive extended families modeling the family culture of African society. Is the African American church and family truly inclusive if one portion of its family, like the gay men in this study, feel as if they offend the family just because of who they are? Are we really inclusive and liberating when some members of the church family are recognized and others not? Anyone who has been a part of the African American church community knows well the great contribution of gay men to the ministry of the church; however, few scholars, if any, have considered writing about them, given what Cornel West has called a "taboo" of discussing sexuality among African Americans.[18] Moreover, many of us in the African American church will only acknowledge their contributions behind closed doors—often behind the doors of the pastor's study.[19] To speak openly about these topics can lead to sanctioning from other clergy colleagues as Rev. Jeremiah Wright, Jr., of Chicago describes in a sermon entitled "Good News for Homosexuals":

> I have been the ministerial outcast among many of my colleagues for some fifteen years because I refuse to believe that my God loves only some of his world. My Bible does not say, "For God so loved some of the world—or *most* of the world—that he gave his only

begotten Son that any heterosexual who believes in him. . . ." My
Bible says *all* and *whosoever*—not those I like.

I refuse to limit my God, to lock God into my cultural understandings because culture is fickle. And culture is often wrong. . . .
I refuse to leave my brain at the door when I come into God's presence to worship or when I read God's Word. And because I refuse,
I have been the pariah of many of my clergy colleagues who somehow see me as defective or not quite saved because I won't join them
in their homophobic gay bashing and misquoting of Scripture.[20]

The denial and ambiguity in the theology and practice of the African
American church lead many gay and lesbian people to either keep silence and not value their role in the African American church and family, or to run to a predominantly white religious denomination, where
they are welcome and affirmed for being lesbian or gay, but not for being unapologetically black. While not pretending might lead to transforming leaders and members of the church, as has been suggested in
the early comments made by the men of my focus group, one outcome
to not pretending as suggested by Riggs may be released rage and violence that has been pent up inside of them, much like the rage and violence of their foreparents that led some of their foreparents toward an
"any-means-necessary" philosophy or method of liberation (refer to Diagram 2).[21]

Although the African American community is diverse, African Americans do not, and often cannot, hide their race whether they are in their
own church and family or in churches and families where they are not
the predominant ethnic group. We have only hid ourselves when we've
wanted to assimilate and lose our identity in the larger identity of the
dominant culture, or when our physical characteristics have permitted
us to pass for something other than black. If we have learned anything
from our struggle with racial inequality, we have learned the pain of being silent about our experience: the pain that causes us to wonder
whether or not our actions or behavior as a people are offending or caus-
ing us to pretend within the dominant culture. That pain has caused us
rage against ourselves and others, and to struggle with nonviolence in
the face of violent attacks. Silencing creates problems not only for us,
but also for others in our extended family. One of the outcomes to not
pretending may indeed be rage or violence. Yet with an eye of hope, not
pretending may lead to transformation and faith, as Diagram 2 also suggests. As Fortunato has maintained, there may be for us a greater "faith"

not in ourselves, our prejudices, our stereotypes, and belief, but a faith in a God whom we have professed in our churches to be a Creator of all sorts, kinds, colors, and sizes of people. Surely, if we as African Americans could find the faith through our religion and spirituality to demand freedom, acceptance, and justice in the larger American family, then surely those things should also be granted to other members of our extended village and family. After the historical struggles against slavery, dehumanization, and discrimination of our families in the African American community, it would be unfair for us to turn around and practice the same discrimination and denial of others within our family, or anywhere else. After what we've been through as a race and family of people, every member of the family should have an open voice and a fair hearing in our churches and community.

Concluding Thought

Recently I received a phone call from one of the members of the dialogue group. "Did you hear about it?" the voice on the other end of the line said. "Hear about what?" I responded. "Did you hear what happened to him? The word is out that it was probably suicide," he replied, referring to one of the men whom I had the pleasure of interviewing for this study. He was an intelligent, articulate, well-read physician who loved his church, his Sunday school class, his family, his wife, and his children. Although they were not absolutely sure, his African American gay friends believed that he might have tested positive for HIV, and therefore took his life. They were as amazed as I was. One would expect a physician like him, a man so knowledgeable about medical issues like HIV/AIDS, so dedicated to his church, and so helpful to this study (he has spoken to you through his many comments in this paper) to know what to do about his condition. That was my feeling, as well as the feeling of his friend from whom I received the phone call.

My stomach dropped as I sat down quietly on the couch in my living room. I felt somewhat sad that he would never get a chance to read this essay, and see what hope might come to those who would hear his story. Although sad, I was not totally shocked, particularly since I received word about another African American friend of mine who attempted suicide as he struggled to "come out" as a gay man and considered the impact that it would have upon his ministry as a pastor. Since then he has left his congregation to find some peace, solace, and counseling for himself.

In the African American church and family, we've often thought that suicide was something more frequently committed by whites or rich folk, and less frequently committed by black folk. Could we have been wrong, and perhaps still wrong, particularly when it comes to those in our families who suffer in silence with so many contradictory experiences? Although articulate and confident in sharing his story with me, this physician lived in silence within his family, his church, and among many of his friends. Could it be that his suicide was a result of identities that were, perhaps, just too contradictory: black, gay, physician, HIV-positive, father, and husband in a heterosexual marriage? Was his suicide a result of not wanting to offend anyone and to respect the pride of his family and church? Was there some fear perpetuated by the church, his family, or from his community that made him silent? Why was his anger unvented and his pain unspoken in the church that he felt was a great extended family? Why did he release his rage and share more of his struggle in the interview I conducted with him and the others?

While the data presented in this study highlight the pride and support that African American gays and lesbians might receive from a church family like Eastside, it also has highlighted the pain and despair that they might simultaneously encounter in the same church. Just as struggles around sexual orientation are more often than not the reason that teens commit suicide, "not offending," as has been presented here, might lead to the same deadly dilemma. I would recommend to researchers on the African American church, its theology, and pastoral care to black families that they consider seriously in their investigation the experiences of those who live in silence and in fear, not only externally through interaction with racism in the culture, but also internally within our own community. There are many sitting in churches and neighborhoods within the African American community who face just as much discrimination in the black community as they face outside the community. While the outcome of their experiences might not lead to suicide, as it did in the case of one of my participants, it might lead to a lot of destructive acting-out behavior that I have often seen in the gay and lesbian community. While silence has led some to suicide, others have been led to cocaine pipes; unclean needles; frequent, anonymous, unprotected sex; and bar doors that are open by 12:00 noon, in many cities, to receive those who drown out their struggle and deaden their minds through alcohol abuse. Since the doors of the African American church, and other churches as well, have been often closed to gay men and lesbian women who refuse to pretend, the doors of the clubs and bars are often a welcome relief. They have sometimes created for us safe locations and opportunities for finding new family and for staying alive. Believe me, bartenders in gay bars have sometimes been to me good pastors and listening friends. Sometimes that's a blessing and sometimes that's a curse. Oops! I think I just spill't my tea! "I don't mean to offend, but . . ."

NOTES

1. The name Eastside Baptist is a fictitious name that was used for the congregation in this study, particularly given the sensitivity surrounding topics of sexual orientation and to preserve the confidentiality of the participants in this study.

2. While literature on the black family points to the significant role of the church in providing social support for African American families, what seems to be missing from this literature, particularly in reference to African American gay men and lesbian women, is the extent to which others are included or excluded from the church's definition of family.

3. From taped interview #1.

4. E. Franklin Frazier, *The Negro Church in America* (New York: Schocken Books, 1974), 7–40. Similar to a strict Marxian interpretation of the role of the church in the state, Frazier saw the church as a mechanism of social control on behalf of the nation. For the Marxian discussion on the relationship between religion and the state and the role of religion as the "opium" of the people, see Karl Marx, "On the Jewish Question" in the critique of Hegel's *Philosophy of Right: Introduction;* and "Economic and Philosophic Manuscripts of 1844," in *Marx Engels Reader,* ed. Robert C. Tucker (New York: W. W. Norton, 1978), 54; 26–52; 53–65; 70–81. In Frazier's terms, the church in this regard functioned to control African Americans by forcing them to adapt the ideas of family from the ruling culture. Frazier argued that all African customs of family were destroyed during slavery; therefore, what African Americans know as family has come from their assimilation of the ideas and standards from white Americans: "The close association between whites and Negroes, often from childhood, enabled the slaves to take over the language, manners, and ideas of the masters. These close contacts were enjoyed by the slaves who worked in and about the master's house. On many plantations, the masters provided religious and moral instruction for the slaves. The moral supervision included, in some cases at least, the chaperonage of female slaves. It was through those channels that the white man's ideas and sentiments in regard to sex and family relations were communicated to the slaves."

5. W.E.B. DuBois, *The Philadelphia Negro* (New York: Schocken Books, 1967), 197–235. For further reading and more recent work on the

preservation of African family traditions in African American families, see Peter Paris, *The Spirituality of African Peoples: The Search for Common Moral Discourse,* (Minneapolis: Fortress Press, 1994), 25–26. According to Paris, African "moral understandings" are embedded in the African cosmological view of the spirit and the world. These moral understandings are expressed in four categorical realms shared by African peoples in the world: the realm of the spirit, the realm of tribal or ethnic group, the realm of the family, and the individual person who seeks to integrate these "overlapping" realms. From this cosmology derives the moral understanding of family for African American people.

6. DuBois, *The Philadelphia Negro,* 201. While Frazier's model has been said to be similar to a traditional Marxian framework of the church in society, DuBois's understanding is similar to a Weberian interpretation of social institutions in society. Unlike the traditional interpretation of Marx that religion is a state-controlled phenomenon, Weber held that religious values and subjective human motives and tradition create and have the ability to transform culture and society. See Max Weber, *The Protestant Ethic and the Spirit of Capitalism* (London: Unwin Publishers, 1987).

7. The word "tea" is a colloquial expression formed by African American women and used in the African American gay and lesbian community to describe a person's real story, or unrevealed truth. The term is used to describe some good gossip that might be heard at a "tea party." In context of our discussion it refers to a man they feel is pretending not to be gay, but the "tea party" gossip says something else. Colloquial expressions like this represent the language that is often used by African Americans, and others who face similar forms of oppression, to name and critique oppressive reality. See Charles Nero, "Towards a Black Gay Aesthetic," in *Brother to Brother: New Writings by Black Gay Men,* eds. Essex Hemphill and Joseph Beam (Boston: Alyson Press, 1991).

8. Cheryl Sanders, *Empowerment Ethics for a Liberated People* (Minneapolis: Fortress Press, 1995), 26–27.

9. For a good discussion on this topic, see Ron Simmons, "Some Thoughts on the Challenges Facing Black Gay Intellectuals" in *Brother to Brother,* eds. Hemphill and Beam 211–28. Simmons points to the homophobia in the black academic community, particularly in the writings of Afrocentric authors who maintain that homosexuality in the African American community is due to: "1) the emasculation of black men by white oppression, 2) the breakdown of the family structure and the loss of male role models, 3) a sinister plot perpetuated by diabolical racists who want to destroy the black race, and 4) immorality as defined in the biblical scriptures." History has yet to openly record the distancing of Martin Luther King, Jr., from one of his political organizers, Bayard Rustin. Rustin, who organized King's 1963 March on Washington, was an African American gay man, and was thought to be a threat to the Civil Rights Movement by other leaders, like Adam Clayton Powell. Powell forced King to drop Rustin from his execu-

tive committee by threatening to reveal some "shocking information" about King and Rustin. See Peter Paris, *Black Religious Leaders: Conflict in Unity* (Louisville, Ky.: Westminster/John Knox Press, 1991), 48–49 (Paris mentions this historical event, but does not go into detail about the nature of Rustin's sexual orientation—more evidence of a denial of these topics in black academia).

10. In black families, gay men are often the sons who take care of elderly parents, the brother who listens unconditionally to all his siblings, the uncle who secures the financial security and inspires the educational development of his nieces and nephews, and the best friend of black women who know more about them and their struggle than even their husbands, male partners, and heterosexual men care to know.

11. Angela Davis, *Women, Race and Class* (New York: Vintage Books, 1983), particularly chaps. 1–4.

12. Isaac Julien, and Kobena Mercer, "True Confessions: A Discourse on Images of Black Male Sexuality" in *Brother To Brother,* eds. Hemphill and Beam.

13. Ibid., 168

14. Ibid.

15. John Fortunato, *Embracing the Exile: Healing Journeys of Gay Christians* (New York: The Seabury Press, 1983), 87–95.

16. Essex Hemphill, in *Brother to Brother,* eds. Hemphill and Beam, xxx.

17. For a discussion on contradictory social spaces or "the boundary problem," see Frank Parkin, *Marxism and Class Theory: A Bourgeois Critique* (New York: Columbia University Press, 1979), chap. 2; Erik Olin Wright, *Classes* (Norfolk, Va.: Thetford Press, 1985), chap. 2.

18. Cornel West, "Black Sexuality: The Taboo Subject," in *Race Matters* (Boston: Beacon Press, 1993), see 89–90 for the dilemma for gays and lesbians in the African American community.

19. I cannot count the number of times in my ministry that I have heard other ministers talk about how great gay men are in the church and how viable they are in building up the music program and in increasing the giving at the church. Since my youth I have heard them say to one another, behind the closed door of the pastor's study, "Man, if you want to build a church, hire yourself a 'sissie' and make him play that organ. They can really build a choir." Many ministers know well that a lot of people come to church and contribute financially, not to hear them preach, but to hear the music of the choir, often led by a gay and sometimes a lesbian musician. For that reason, some African American ministers are cautious about condemning gay and lesbian people, lest they miss out on a good offering!

20. Jeremiah A. Wright, Jr., "Good News for Homosexuals" in *Good News!: Sermons of Hope for Today's Families* (Valley Forge, Pa.: Judson Press, 1995), 73–74.

21. For a discussion of the "any-means-necessary" methodology during the antebellum period see Sanders, *Empowerment Ethics,* 30–31. For a discussion

on this methodology particularly as conceived by Malcolm X and utilized in the Black Power Movement, see Paris, *Black Religious Leaders,* 183–222, and C. Eric Lincoln, *The Black Church Since Frazier* (New York: Schocken Books, 1974), 127.

8

Informal Care, Cooperative Programs, and Deliberate Process

The Family Ministries of a Church of Language Congregations

BARBARA MCGINNIS-GILLISPIE

> We are a church of many diverse peoples
>   who affirm our common humanity as children of the living God.
> We are united by our devotion to Jesus Christ.
> We are empowered by the Holy Spirit.
> . We are committed to work for reconciliation and unity among all
>   people
> Beginning in our community and extending throughout the world.[1]

At the Wednesday night service before a multiethnic all-church worship service, the interim pastor of four weeks spoke of the ongoing attention to the various languages spoken in the church. Then she said, "We are going to use several Greek words in the sermon since that's nobody's language." Several people in the group looked at each other and laughed, adding "except for Bill Kosmas." Bill, a first-generation Greek, is a longstanding, active member. As the interim pastor was just beginning to realize, the cultural diversity of North Shore Baptist Church is not always apparent. Differences in styles of communication carried over into discussions in English as a common language go unnoticed. The subtleties of culturally different theological views, though definitive in church decisions, are more difficult to discern than differences in language or styles of communication. The various positions become evident in meetings leading to decisions of strategy and program rather than in Sunday classes or Wednesday evening sessions where sharing experiences, beliefs, and values is encouraged.

The aim of this study has been, first, to get a panoramic photograph, a comprehensive cross-sectional snapshot, of North Shore's family ministries, their theological beliefs and attitudes about family and church, and the influence of families themselves on the life and decisions of the church. Second, the aim has been to do a practical theological evaluation of North Shore's mixture of informal family care and cooperatively implemented programs for families in multiethnic communities.

The study covered approximately one year (1994) in the life of North Shore. To give substance to the description and to understand decisions and developments, I conducted conversations and interviews and studied records covering the last five years. I have noted milestones of earlier history to clarify the sequence of and relationship among events and structures. The period of study ended with North Shore preparing for an interim period between senior pastors.

In studying the family ministries of North Shore Baptist Church I found, first, that their family ministries consist of a loosely woven "tent" of deliberate strategies, informal care, and cooperative programs rather than distinctly structured, specific programs. Second, I found that unity in diversity is the guiding theological principle for the church and that other theological tenets held generally by members of churches mutually and voluntarily associated as American Baptist Churches USA provided the framework for maintaining the coherence and stability of North Shore when controversy over homosexuality occurred. The third discovery was that ministry with families was both a reflection of and a means for acting out these principles. That is, within North Shore the family experiences, beliefs, and values people brought to decision-making and implementation of ministry were as important in determining the outcome of family ministries as was the appropriateness of programs and strategies to the needs of families with whom the church ministered.

In this report I will describe the primary events, decisions, and statements of church leaders that support these findings. Then, with a practical theological critique of findings I will argue briefly that North Shore's experience in ministries with families suggests that an approach which attends to informal care, strategies for inclusion, and cooperation in programming both within and beyond the church offers a model for family ministries appropriate for any multicultural church, particularly in an urban setting.

Unrelated to the decision to study its family ministries but at about the same time, I became a member of North Shore. Thus, my role as researcher was that of participant-observer. Being a member allowed me accepted access to congregational activities and informal discussions. Yet, being a new member also allowed me to observe meetings of the board and ministry committees as more of an outsider than I could be as my time of membership lengthened.

An Overview

The North Shore Baptist Church[2] was organized in 1905 in the Edgewater area of Chicago. "The charter roll included about 100 people from at least 38 different church backgrounds. . . . As early as 1924, the senior minister noted that 26 nationalities were represented in the congregation."[3] The church has approximately 675 members, most of whom belong to the founding English-speaking congregation.[4] Approximately 10 percent of this congregation are African and African American, approximately 65 percent are European American, and the others Asian, Asian American, and Hispanic. The Filipinos are organized as the Filipino Fellowship within the English-speaking congregation. In addition to the English-speaking congregation, there are Hispanic, Japanese, and Korean congregations. On Sunday mornings worship occurs in Japanese, Spanish, Korean, and English. Church-school classes are taught in Korean, Japanese, and English for adults and English for children and youth. The congregations are governed by the church's Official Board, which supervises, directs, and decides "all matters pertaining to or affecting the work and policy of the Church."[5] The "work . . . of the church" is grouped into seven ministries: educative, fellowship, missional, property, shepherding, stewardship, and worship. The congregations are free to conduct worship in their own manner, make their own internal rules, and do ministry consistent with the constitution and bylaws.

North Shore has an annual budget of approximately five hundred thousand dollars. The church supports in full-time positions a senior pastor, an associate minister of Christian education, a secretary, and two custodians. It also supports part-time two language pastors, a director of the Pastoral Counseling Center, a minister and associate minister of music, an organist, four choir section lead singers, and a financial secretary. The main building includes a sanctuary seating 800, a chapel seating 120, meeting rooms, offices, and a fellowship hall with an adjacent kitchen where meals for 300 can be prepared and served. The educational building includes offices, classrooms, snackery, and gymnasium. The church owns a parsonage and an additional house next to the church where the current custodians live with their families.

Members are active and many willingly assume responsibilities. They have a wide range of theological views, biblical knowledge, and methods of biblical interpretation. Though not fundamentalist or even unanimously conservative, they consider themselves evangelical Christians in that they see their purpose as "perpetuating the gospel . . . and extending the Kingdom of God throughout the world."[6] The church seeks to be socially inclusive while requiring for membership profession of faith in Jesus Christ as personal Savior and baptism by immersion or evidence of such in the past. North Shore maintains its typically Baptist local church autonomy but throughout its history has been both a leader in the agencies and structures of its denomination, American Baptist Churches USA, and active in ecumenical organizations.

Neighborhood and Surrounding Community

In 1993, as part of an eighteen-month long-range planning process, North Shore had a demographic study done[7] of the three-mile area surrounding the church. It revealed the total population to be only six thousand short of half a million (493,897). The average household income was $38,400 (92 percent of the national average). By 1998 the number of African Americans was expected to increase 4.2 percent; the number of Hispanics to decrease by 2 percent; and the number of Asians and other foreign nationals or first-generation Americans to decrease 1.3 percent. The total population is expected to decrease from 1993 to 1998 at approximately the same rate per year (0.2 percent) as from 1990 to 1993. In other words, about 885 persons leaving the area each year would not be replaced. Thus, North Shore as a community church could expect to see its membership change with a possible increase in African American members if it conducts the community outreach[8] proposed by the long-range planners. This had already become apparent in the youth programs.

Within one mile of the church there were almost twice as many single-person households as married-couple households. Only 27 percent were married-couple households compared to 55.1 percent nationally. Of households with children, 43 percent were single-parent households and 55.5 percent married-couple households. Only 63.5 percent of all people within one mile lived as families compared to 83.7 percent for the whole country. More than 20 percent of all adults were divorced or widowed. Of these two of every three were women. More than 43 percent of the adults had never married. Thus, whether or not new members were African Americans, they most likely would be unmarried and living in a nonfamily household or a family headed by a single person rather than a married couple. Approximately, 8 percent (35,500) of the people within three miles consider themselves Baptists; 18 percent (80,800) have no religious preference. These numbers are the basis for the urgency the church expressed for engaging in community outreach.

Congregation Life as Context for Ministry with Families: Informal Care

Members' theological views on family and on the church's relationship to families vary as widely as their cultural experiences. Examining the congregations of the church reveals only brief and veiled glimpses of the range of views and practices regarding relationships, values, and ethics. Furthermore, the relationship of each congregation to the church differs. The power of the congregation in church decisions varies widely. This section describes each congregation's family theology, informal strategies of ministry with families, and the interactions with the larger church as influenced by the different family cultures. The schedule of activities as well as the range of views for this multiethnic congregation is not only complex but can be confusing. The Sunday morning schedule is illustrative.[9]

English-Speaking Congregation[10]

The English-speaking congregation worships in the main sanctuary with Sunday school classes prior and a fellowship hour following at least once a month. Dinner and a "prayer-and-praise" service that usually includes Bible study are held on Wednesday evenings. As stated above, this congregation, the oldest, consists primarily of European Americans. African Americans are most active and visibly present in the Sunday school and youth programs. Africans from Cameroon, Zaire, Nigeria, and the Caribbean and Indians worship with the congregation, though who is member or visitor and who attends regularly or occasionally is not obvious. They do not seem to have a public, political voice within the church. The Asian and Hispanic members of this congregation are those who speak English and are likely to be younger or of second or later generations. They bring the views of their ethnic backgrounds to this congregation in varying degrees. While there are some families with children and a number of couples of all ages, as well as several multi-generational families, there is also a cohesive, long-standing group of mostly middle- to older-age singles and a significant number of widows.

The English-speaking congregation has few if any distinctive views or activities of its own as a language congregation. Rather, it carries the major responsibility and leadership for the work of the Official Board. For this congregation the theology of family is occasionally evident in the sermons preached, the weekly newsletter, the teaching and materials of Sunday school classes and Wednesday evening Bible studies, and in the discussions and decision-making processes of the ministries and Official Board. Among adults, however, little is said explicitly about family.

The Educative Ministry is carried out with children central and family understood primarily as those household units with minor children. As in Worship and Fellowship Ministries, programs and events are planned with attention to appropriateness of schedule, setting, and activities for all ages (an intergenerational focus). There is an underlying assumption that the family is important, that in spite of contemporary changes in structure, families still have the same functions and roles in society and church as they have had in the past. The senior pastor speaks of families in his sermon:

> Family is the *place* where the flame of faith begins to grow, where one is taught to be human. It is as though each person needs a label when she or he is born which says "some assembly required."[11]

He speaks of families' burdens in "The Morning Prayer":

> Families are facing tides of change, new challenges, complex questions to answer, supports besieged. Families are adrift on an angry sea. [Bring us to the] center point and solid place of Your Light and Truth. Deepen our trust in You, God. Root families in the good soil of Your Wisdom and in courage to stand fast for those things that are *eternal*: justice, forgiveness, and reconciliation. Give us wisdom to change our minds on hearing Your Truth. In the name of Christ, our Brother. Amen.[12]

The high value placed on family relationships is perhaps more evident in actions than words. Caregivers, spouses, parents, or children of those who are in trouble, ill, or incapacitated also receive cards or telephone calls and are named in midweek services to be included in prayer.

Filipino Fellowship within the English-Speaking Congregation[13]

While not worshipping as a separate congregation, the Filipinos are organized as a group, the Filipino Fellowship. The participants elect officers and sponsor several activities for Filipinos. Because their views on family and other issues were common to most of the Filipinos and af-fected the course of the church, I am including this description of their background and presence in the church.

Economic and political hardships in the Philippines led to an influx of Filipinos to the United States in the 1960s and 1970s. Many who came to the Chicago area are alumni of the Central Philippine Univer-sity, an American Baptist-supported school in Iloilo City. The current Filipino Fellowship grew out of a Sunday school class begun in 1974 as entry point for newly arrived immigrants. By 1990 approximately sev-enty Filipino families, only ten or so not related, had joined or were par-ticipating actively in the English-speaking congregation. In 1992 many families left the church (though members did not remove their names from the roll). The sources of dissatisfaction included the senior pastor's view that "people are neither Christian nor not Christian based on sex-ual orientation, that Christian commitment is on a different level"[14] and procedures and decisions of the Stewardship Ministry Committee con-cerning a lost bank deposit and the sale of the parsonage to the senior pastor. Five or six Filipino families remained active. These families span all ages. Despite attempts at reconciliation following the major with-drawal of Filipinos, an undercurrent of dissatisfaction persisted. The as-sociate minister of Christian education, a Filipino, resigned in July 1994 and the senior pastor resigned in October 1994.

The Filipinos of North Shore were converted from Roman Catholi-cism to Protestantism or from no faith commitment to Christianity by Baptist missionaries associated with Central Philippine University. In the Philippines wealth and education are highly valued. Within churches those with the most wealth and education dominate the gov-ernance of the church. The pastor is often paid poorly and thus lacks status. In American Baptist churches this pattern is not as strictly ob-served and is often reversed. Yet, Filipinos are very loyal to their church. As one member described it, "I toss back and forth. I say to myself, 'Do you really expect the church to meet your needs and your family's or should you continue to go and take what it does give since the church needs you to build it right now?'"

"Family" for Filipinos includes even second- and third-degree cousins. The obligation to stick together and to help family members is strong. At the same time, feuding within families, such as adult sibling rivalry for status or authority, is more likely to occur than feuding between families. Families in the Philippines are closely knit and authoritarian; what the father says, goes. In the absence of the father the "natural" leader in the group, the elder son or a son with education and social status, decides for the family. When families come here, husbands and wives relate more as partners, though how much depends greatly on the wife's ability to adapt to American culture. The Filipino families remaining at North Shore are more democratically oriented than those with strong ties to older generations still in the Philippines. In several families, children have a voice in family decisions. One family, for instance, joined North Shore because their children liked the Sunday school better than others they had visited. Though here permanently, many families still send money home to the Philippines and support a church there.

Hispanic Department[15]

The North Shore Spanish Baptist Church began as a Spanish Sunday school in 1957. After the Spanish church moved to its own building in 1960, a group returned to North Shore and formed the Hispanic Department. The Hispanics have called themselves the Hispanic Department to signify that they are working towards becoming a permanently integral part of North Shore rather than moving out as a separate church. The group has forty-eight members. Approximately twenty-five children attend Sunday school. They worship at 12:30 P.M. after Sunday school of five classes for children and one for adults. They meet for Bible study monthly in a home and have a community celebration meal monthly.

Worship is the center of their life and, according to the department's pastor, is "communitarian." That is, informal participation in singing, speaking, and praying is high and often includes concern for the political situations of family and friends in Central American countries. "Communitarian" also signifies that the collective body in cooperation with the pastor controls the flow and outcome of worship. A guitar and other Latino instruments are used when available; the piano is a last resort. Children and youth prefer Sunday school in English but worship in Spanish. The visitation committee is the one organized structure of the Hispanic Department and has succeeded in uniting members as a community of faith and in drawing in new people through telephone calls and visits. The people are from several Latin American countries but mainly from El Salvador. Many escaped war and came here to find work and safety. They earn little and send a large portion of it to family members in their native countries. Pastor Sanchez feels that part of his work is to help the people stay informed and involved so as to understand thoroughly political and social developments there. The Hispanic Department tries to be family for each other. Pastor Sanchez explained that to Hispanics this means sharing problems and joys, laughing and crying together. This, they believe, can happen without speaking the same language.

Japanese Congregation[16]

After World War II many Japanese evacuees came to Chicago. A small group of Japanese Christians approached the senior pastor at North Shore needing a place to worship. After agreeing that all members would be baptized, they became an organized congregation in 1954. In 1959 the congregation called Masaru Nambu, the current Japanese-language pastor. Approximately twenty attend worship on Sunday morning. Bible study is held prior to worship. Fellowship hour follows worship. During this time there is open exchange about family, politics, and many other topics. On the fourth Sunday, lunch follows worship, after which they have Bible study, testimony, and sharing of concerns and prayer. Besides organizing this meal, members of the congregation usher, read scripture, and sometimes make announcements during worship.

Though there are several couples, most members are elderly women who came as war brides. Their ages now are sixty-five to seventy; their children are grown and prosperous but do not live close. Emotional ties between most parents and their grown children are strong in spite of the distances. Of the war-bride families, ten to fifteen of the husbands attended irregularly but eventually not at all. The women have come more for psychological and emotional support and common understanding than from religious motivation. Most of the marriages ended in divorce, though not until the children were in their late teens or on their own. The differences in customs and values became too obvious without the children present as a common tie. While current members have no family here other than their grown children, they are related to extensive clans still living in Japan.

Except for Japanese nationals residing in the northwest suburbs temporarily here on business, there has been little influx of Japanese to the Midwest since the 1960s. The likelihood of new members is not great. According to Pastor Nambu, members of the congregation have "discussed the future and are willing to accept the reality. We believe that at a certain point in history a need has been met and we have done our job." The Japanese congregation is generally self-supporting in terms of resources for ministry. The pastor functions as a member of the church staff and attends meetings of the Official Board. He doesn't remember ever having a written agreement with the church or a written work description. Though the number of members decreases, the congregation has extended its ministry to the Japanese senior housing project, Japanese nursing home, and to those who have returned to Japan.

Korean Congregation[17]

In the late 1970s through the 1980s Cambodians and Koreans moved into the Argyle Street area near the church. In October 1991 North Shore's Official Board approved a proposal from Young Ran Park to hold weekday language classes in the church. In October 1993 the Official Board formalized the relationship between the church and the Koreans as a congregation. According to Ms. Park, the sixty to seventy participants range in age from infancy to late eighties but most are elderly. Besides Sunday morning worship, they meet for Sunday school prior to worship and for prayer on Tuesday evenings. She described the congregation as hard workers, but with little money and no friends or acquaintances whom they might invite to come with them. Besides teaching English as a Second Language four days a week, Ms. Park spends many hours counseling and resolving problems created by the language barrier. She said that Koreans are very sad and afraid in America. She spends many hours visiting people in their apartments, hospitals, and nursing homes. She also goes with many to welfare, public aid, and Social Security offices. Of her sixty language students only one has a car. She often provides transportation.

Ms. Park became a member of North Shore because of the inclusive views held by American Baptists (in general) and North Shore (in particular) regarding women. Koreans, especially older generations, are still greatly influenced by Confucian Family Law. Consequently, intergenerational conflict is frequent and common; for example, the older son is heir with all the attending privileges and authority in Korea; in the United States no such hierarchy exists. Therefore, the question of who is in charge in the family creates tension on a daily basis. In Korea women's work is viewed as inferior; women are looked down on in family and society. Even pastors deny women the right to be pastor. So, Ms. Park said, "I preach that Jesus is on woman's side; Jesus freed women— the poor and oppressed." Many Koreans who have come to the area close to North Shore recently are elderly, invited here by their children to live in the many senior apartments nearby. So, households are often couples or single persons; extended families are uncommon. Influx has decreased. Koreans, like the Japanese, now have money and wish to stay in Korea or, if here, wish to return and so see themselves here temporarily.[18]

Miscellany of Informal Care

The contribution to family ministry of the informal and semiformal care networks of each congregation and their Sunday school classes should not be underestimated. In addition to these, the English worship choir, the geographically centered joint Cluster Groups of the English-speaking congregation and Hispanic Department, the Crisis Calling Team of the church, the four women's circles, and other groups provide strong, extensive informal care systems for staying in touch and meeting financial, instrumental (such as transportation), and emotional needs of church members and others in their family contexts or lack thereof.

Institutional Structure as Context for Ministries with Families: Deliberate Process and Cooperative Programs

In theory each congregation is represented on the Official Board by its pastor and at least two deacons.[19] However, the English-speaking congregation acting sometimes jointly with the Hispanic Department and with input from the Japanese pastor shape church and extrachurch cooperative family ministries. My intention in this section is to present a comprehensive overview, a snapshot, and to give details only of exceptional strategies or programs with regard to ministry with families.

Deliberate Attention to Process

Acquaintance with the diverse hardships and separations experienced by families of the various congregations has heightened the church's awareness of the need to consider how they conduct their life together as well as to what they do. The revision of the constitution and bylaws in 1988 increased discussion and raised consciousness about distinguishing the English-speaking congregation as one of North Shore's congregations rather than the church itself. However, changes in practice have occurred slowly. The Official Board and the ministries now have active representatives from the Hispanic Department. The Educative Ministry is working to join the programs of the Hispanic Department and the English-speaking congregation.

Perhaps more than language, styles of relating and communication have inhibited interactions between the congregations. The openly expressive style of Hispanics is the basis for their view that sharing problems and joys can happen without speaking the same language. On the other hand, Asian styles of expression are often nonverbal and indirect. European Americans are likely to be direct about technical, practical, or economic matters, but reserved in expressing feelings.[20] These differences played a crucial role in the resignations of the associate minister and the senior pastor.

When the dispute over homosexuality arose, the associate minister was cast in a role of spokesperson with the senior pastor for the dissatisfied Filipinos. Shortly after they left, she submitted her resignation. The Official Board tabled it for a month and then refused to accept it. With mounting pressure from her family to not just resign her position but to also leave North Shore and the increasingly difficult relationship with the senior pastor, she continued for another year to carry out her ministry to which she was strongly committed. In that time, however, she failed to carry through several leadership commitments. Her indirect, nonverbal style of communication increasingly frustrated the senior pastor such that he asked the board to assign her a period of probation for insubordination. The board called for a two-month period of attempted reconciliation and appointed a reconciliation task force since the staff relations committee had failed to ease the tension between the pastor and the associate minister. The associate minister responded to this action by asking for a leave of absence, after which her resignation was accepted by the board. Had more members of the Official Board and other church leaders known how or been willing to navigate the communication dynamics, the dispute over homosexuality might have had a different outcome.

Several ministry committees have been working on language, scheduling, and structuring of events to include all peoples, forms of relationship, and lifestyles. For instance, in November the Worship Ministry chairperson began the meeting of her committee: "Christmas is a family time, of course." The committee then proceeded to plan a Christmas worship with representatives of all generations and lifestyles participating in leadership. In planning an all-church dinner to follow, the committee discussed the needs of different generations. A report on the stewardship campaign during worship illustrates efforts to acknowledge both family relatedness and singleness. Though it is more common to use the phrase "pledging units" or "households pledging," the chairperson of the Official Board announced, "The number of pledging families and individuals is. . . ."[21]

One African American mother had a Sunday morning open-door policy for all teens at her house. They could show up at their convenience. She would provide breakfast and see that they all arrived at church in time for Sunday school. Educative Ministry is working to include parents in more events by replacing unstructured care for elementary-age children with learning activities during congregational meetings as well as during worship. Though Educative Ministry had long ago sponsored picnics open to the whole church, North Shore held its first picnic to include all congregations on a Sunday in August following worship. Careful planning created occasions of interaction between families of the different language congregations and between generations.

In July Educative Ministry held vacation Bible school in the evening for the first time. They hoped to increase attendance since many children of working parents are in full-time summer day programs and to draw those who tend to do activities as families. Thirty-two children, a decided increase, attended, but there were fewer European Americans than expected.

Intrachurch Cooperative Programs[22] with Attention to Families

Significant portions of the work of the ministers (such as in bereavement, premarital counseling, and marriages) and the availability of the building facilities to such agencies as the YWCA, which administers a day-care program, provide invaluable ministries to families. Programs and activities that serve families in one way or another include Sunday church school classes (see various citations above); American Baptist Women's Ministries; vacation Bible school; programming for children (which provides at the same time care for children of English-speaking congregation during worship and Sunday school for Hispanic children); bus ministry for elderly; youth basketball team, after-school program, and Bible study targeted to reach gang members; sending twenty to thirty children and youth to the regional Baptist camp; a library with a section of approximately sixty-three books labeled "family"; and the Pastoral Counseling Center.

Several of these programs deserve to be highlighted. First, the American Baptist Women of North Shore collected twenty-five hundred dollars for mission in 1993–94—significant portions of which went to support cooperative efforts discussed below. Second, the church supports a counseling center with a part-time counselor and director who is an ordained Baptist minister and a clinical psychologist. In the last five years he has counseled in multiple sessions approximately fifty-five persons annually. Premarital counseling decreased from 11 percent in 1989 to zero in 1993. However, marriage counseling increased from 21 percent to 32 percent and family counseling increased from 5 percent to 14 percent.[23]

Finally, in 1993–94, approximately twenty to thirty males attended after-school tutoring classes, basketball sessions, and Bible study. They have been encouraged to attend Sunday school and worship. They also are asked to do fifty hours of "community service" such as painting in the church or removing graffiti from neighborhood buildings. Upon the resignation of the associate minister during summer 1994, a young man who had participated in the youth program was hired part-time to continue the basketball and after-school activities. He said that up to thirty boys and young men attend daily, that they are building "family" and learning how to get along. Family for him is "a group and a unit that we draw from." Important features of family for him as a leader are that God is a partner and role modeling takes priority over other methods of teaching/learning. He leads a Bible study one evening a week, but uses no supplementary materials and postpones until Sunday school any questions he cannot answer. Many of the participants attend Sunday school and worship but also attend other religious services on Sunday as well. Their families are not participants at North Shore and the director does not envision working with their families except incidentally. Many of the youth are being raised by single or divorced mothers.[24] Thus, he explained, he feels great responsibility for modeling a husband's relationship to his wife as well as respect for all women.

Extrachurch Involvement
in Cooperative Efforts

North Shore has supported several regional American Baptist institutions and programs with money, volunteers, goods, and publicity. Major ones are Central Baptist Children's Home and Family Services, Baptist Retirement Home, Cook County Jail Ministry, Refugee Families Resettlement program, and Family Matters.

The children's home and retirement home are long-standing denominational institutions that North Shore supports with funds, sponsorship of fund raisers, clothes, other supplies, and leadership to their boards and auxiliaries. The jail ministry provides Bible study, pastoral counseling, literacy training, evangelism, and family support. North Shore has participated in leading Bible study and evangelism, but also contributes to meeting the needs of families facing various deprivations because of the incarceration of their family member.

In the last year, working through the InterChurch Refugee and Immigration Ministries, North Shore cooperated with five other American Baptist churches to settle a Bosnian family of three. Immediately prior, North Shore took the lead and with the help of the same five churches settled a Vietnamese family of five. At the end of 1994 they were preparing to help settle up to twenty Cubans per month who were to be released from U.S. detention in Guantanamo because they have children, elderly, or disabled family members.

Family Matters, which North Shore began with three other American Baptist churches, is one of the cooperative programs that emphasizes the family as a unit. It seeks to provide "a healthy, positive oasis where families can come to work together, instead of being torn apart."[25] Family Matters began as a Latchkey Learning Program for ten children and their parents and now has multiple programs for children, youth, and parents with a high level of parent participation in children's programs. The lessons for participants in the programs are formed around the topics of positive thinking for enhancing self-esteem, creativity, and responsibility; making good choices and living with consequences; and nonviolent conflict resolution.

Besides the cooperative church efforts, North Shore participates in community programs that serve and advocate for families with financial support, board and committee representatives, and project volunteers. Such programs include Organization of the North East (O.N.E.); Care for Real, the local food pantry; Edgewater Community Council; Lakewood-Balmoral Residents' Council; and Uptown Chicago Commission.

As a member of the Organization of the North East, North Shore cooperates with fifty-nine community institutions. Churches, businesses, tenant associations, ethnic associations, and not-for-profit community services organizations work in partnership toward creating a successful, mixed-economic, multiethnic community. They recently have been working on locating, developing, and making available adequate low-income housing to those who need it.

Because North Shore engages in a vast array of informal and cooperative ministries with families, monitoring the quality and effectiveness of Christian ministry is essential. In the next (and last) section I will explore evaluatively several aspects of their family ministries.

A Diverse Peoples United as Children of the Living God: Correspondence of the Congregation's Family Theology to an Interpretation of Christian Witness

American Baptist churches, described by Roof and McKinney as "moderate mainline" Protestant churches, are located in the middle of a spectrum "between rampant individualism . . . and a more collectivist response"[26] on social issues, sometimes more conservative, sometimes more liberal.

> Informality, simple faith and piety, an optimistic and confident outlook, and a deep egalitarian spirit all found expression in these truly 'American' churches. . . . [American] Baptists would find a place in the mainstream culture as the "recognized democrats of the Protestant world." They are known for their strong emphasis upon individual conscience and religious freedom, and their congregations are among the most racially inclusive of any in the United States.[27]

According to North Shore's constitution,

> The vision of the Church shall be to articulate through deed and organizational structure that it is an inclusive community of faith which incorporates people who represent the ethnic and language pluralisms of the world and demonstrates that "[Christ] is our peace, who has made us both one, and has broken down the dividing wall of hostility. . . ." (Eph. 2:14 RSV)[28]

Certainly, this vision is consistent with the "moderate mainline" position of the denomination. Over the years North Shore has been a leading financial supporter of denominational endeavors. Its members have served on denominational boards, committees, and commissions that have shaped policy, articulated positions, and determined the direction of denominational mission. For example, Ralph H. Elliot, senior pastor of North Shore, 1977–89, chaired the Commission on Denominational Identity that completed work on a statement of vision, "The People Called American Baptist," in 1987. Consequently, the family theology that North Shore "articulates through deed and organized structure" can be found in the American Baptist policy statements[29] entitled "Family Life"[30] and "The Church Is Family."[31]

The statement on "Family Life" includes three sections: biblical-theological base, situation analysis, and policy. The first section delineates three "highly valued" themes from the Old Testament that "Baptists read . . . from the perspective of the New and especially in the light of Jesus' teachings"; "a vision of marriage as monogamous, life-long one-flesh union affirmed by Jesus as God's intention for marriage"; "a vision of the parent-child relationship as one of tender care, mutual responsibility, and mutual benefit"; and "a recognition that God creates new family bonds where none existed before." This first section ends as follows: "We affirm [the New Testament] vision of Christian family living in which Christ is the head of the household and all members are mutually responsible to one another and to Christ."[32] The situational analysis section argues in support of two conclusions: "Diversity of family patterns is normative for America"[33] and "New knowledge about family life is available."[34] The policy section includes ten points: (1–3) the three themes from the Old Testament, (4–5) affirmations of Christian families as agents of evangelism and the church as God's family, and commitments (6) "to providing programs of education and support," (7) "to advocacy for the rights of all families . . . ," (8) "to the necessities of life . . . ," (9) "to advocacy on behalf of families with special needs," and finally, (10) "to modeling in our congregations and denominational life a vision of an inclusive, intergenerational community, a family of God, in which the variety of family forms, the richness of ethnic traditions, and the gifts of all persons from newborns to the very old, are respected, enjoyed, and celebrated."[35]

The policy statement on "The Church Is Family" challenges churches to do four things as God's family for persons regardless of family structures: to become aware of the need to be inclusive in attitude and program, to assess and plan for specialized needs, to promote the use of intergenerational materials, and to include and plan for all groups in worship, education, and fellowship.

Taken together these two statements indicate that for most American Baptists, including members of North Shore, the church is neither a more excellent family for which family members must forsake their existing families nor a substitute for nonexistent families. The church may be God's family and its members may provide various supports for human families, but it is not a human family as such. Some persons are clearer than others about the distinctions. American Baptists like other Christians often use confusing rhetoric. Nonetheless, except in the youth programs, these distinctions are clear in North Shore's ministries with families. The church provides specific but temporary financial, instrumental, or emotional support where obligational and affectional ties have been broken, strained, or underdeveloped, or are nonexistent.

Because of its ethnic diversity, North Shore's family theology must also be examined in light of theologies articulated in the contexts from which people come to this church. Euro-American members, whose theology is directly rooted in European theology, have Americanized their particular blend of Calvinism, Arminianism, and Anabaptist theological tenets. Thus, their primary theological distinctives are baptism of believers, soul liberty, local church autonomy, separation of church and state, and inclusion of all who profess belief in Jesus as the Christ. Soul liberty means that every individual within the ongoing dialogue of the local church has the right and obligation to study, using the best available resources, and interpret Scripture for herself or himself and to have a relationship with God without determination or interference from any other person.[36]

Though the controversy over homosexuality was in content about family relationships, the Baptist distinctives shaped the final outcome. According to the records, leaders who had supported the pastor in the early stages of the dissension gradually began to withdraw support, expressing their dissatisfaction in silence and absences. From statements made in informal discussions after his resignation, the withdrawal of support appeared not to center on his views on homosexuality or his proposals for moving the church beyond the disagreement but on his inability to keep disagreeing members within the church and his inability to stop the push to get the church to vote on a statement on homosexuality that allowed for no variation of views on specific points. It seemed that for some long-time, influential members he was unable to guide the church in upholding the Baptist principles of soul liberty and inclusiveness and in breaking "down the dividing wall of hostility" in accordance with the vision statement of their constitution.

Many of those coming to North Shore from Asia, Africa, and Central or South America had already received an American Baptist version of Christianity but the gospel message had been shaped to fit their situations. Young Ran Park, North Shore's Korean pastor, has much in common with Korean feminists whose recently articulated theologies emphasize striving towards a world of harmony and peace[37] between the divisions of their country and between men and women. These dominant themes have a pattern and expression uniquely Korean.

The Latin American experience calls forth other theological themes. Latin American liberation theologian, George Pixley, an ordained American Baptist missionary in Nicaragua, writes of the events in Exodus to persuade nonpolitical believers that "Exodus is at once a religious and a political document."[38] When North Shore's Hispanic pastor participates in monitoring El Salvador's elections and keeps his congregation informed of events in their native countries, he shares this theological perspective.

Finally, Filipino theology as articulated by Eleazer Fernandez in *Toward a Theology of Struggle*[39] explains in part the differences in viewpoint of the Filipinos and those of the senior pastor and other church officers regarding stewardship matters and homosexuality. Fernandez distinguishes people's power from people power. People's power is the use of right principles and strong convictions by the people for the people. People power is the use of the power of the people against their interest for the benefit of the powerful.[40] "Shaping the new tomorrow means a concrete political praxis inspired by those who have been marginalized but who have arisen from their oppressed condition."[41] The goal is converting power without love to power with love that is politically viable.[42]

In Fernandez's words, shaping a better tomorrow requires struggle— resistance, suffering, and hope[43]—as the means to identity and subjecthood. The church is understood as "space, sign, and seed, in which a new sense of 'humanity' is affirmed and experienced, and liberative ways of thinking and dwelling are explored."[44] From such a background it is not unreasonable that Filipinos seeking identity and subjecthood through a church in the United States might view the necessary interactions as political praxis and struggle. North Shore's senior pastor, in part on the advice of a prominent community leader but one who knew nothing of professional ministry, adopted the tone and stance of authority (granted to him as chief executive officer by the church constitution) with those who called for a church vote to affirm a statement that declared homosexuality as such a sin. It was not his natural style and he carried it out awkwardly (perhaps to his credit). With support and pressure from Filipino friends and family members who were members of another church, the Filipinos reacted by escalating their struggle both behind the scenes and overtly with the senior pastor and church officers for power to influence policy decisions. Perhaps the interactions reminded them of negative personal experiences in their homeland that called for resistance to power and agitation for reform. After all, the church, Roman Catholic and then Protestant, in the Philippines has often represented people power not people's power. Their struggle then was with the church as well as the government. Whether appropriate or not and to what degree, if so, at North Shore now, struggle may well have been learned as the initial, intuitive, first response to any challenge.

The history and world views of these theologies are similar yet different and shape their positions on family. Korean theology is shaped by the struggle of women for change in family structure and practices. In the Philippines the extended family is itself a political unit—the individual has little or no political power. Thus, solidarity as a family in any struggle as a deeply held practice explains in part the Filipinos' stance in controversy at North Shore.

In Latin America a family's immediate struggle for physical survival often takes precedence over its participation in the larger fight for political power that will assure access to resources needed by families for their members. Thus, the interest Hispanics bring to North Shore is that of meeting the immediate survival needs of families in the church and community. This includes a strong interest, which the Filipinos share, in the moral and religious education of their children. For each ethnic group the role and importance of family are both influenced by and influence their larger world view. In the words of Pastor Nambu regarding family roles,

> We cannot perceive purpose and function of the family in a vacuum, although it may be quite possible to state [them] in highly idealistic and abstract ways. Culture, tradition, and norm of society in which families live and function always exert important and lasting influences in determining the roles of male and female in the family. A certain set of functions may be quite acceptable and families may be quite comfortably adjusted with it in one society, but in another society, such a set of functions for male and female may not be conceivable. Though there are differences between male and female resulting in different functions, these differences should not be used to determine either superiority or inferiority of either sex. Rather, these different kinds of functions should complement to each other for the purpose of fulfilling the ultimate goals

grants must make major changes in their lives (especially in the public spheres of work, school, and acquisition of goods) when they come to the United States. They seek to preserve those patterns of living that meant the most to them in the past and for which alternatives are most difficult to identify. The church, particularly one with a democratic polity such as North Shore, is a common place in which to seek support and reinforcement for such patterns. It should not be surprising when immigrants express even more vehement views regarding family forms and functions than formerly held in their native countries and which may appear rigid and exclusive. This is perhaps the best explanation for the Filipinos' drive to exclude gays and lesbians from church membership and to get North Shore to vote against admitting a church, many of whose members are openly homosexual, to the regional association of American Baptist churches.

Moral Fruitfulness of Ministries: Raising Children, Guiding Youth, and Learning How to Get Along

North Shore's Sunday school, vacation Bible school, and other children's programs depended heavily upon the Filipinos. Their children were most of the students and the adults were teachers and leaders. Since their withdrawal the church has not yet satisfactorily reestablished the Sunday school. Though members are active and take responsibility in many ways, this is now the weakest area of North Shore's ministry with families. Many church members have expressed concern, but few have volunteered to teach. For most it would be an addition to current church responsibilities. They see moral development as important, but cultural correctness (fear of offending); lack of confidence and training in methods of teaching (rather than lack of content knowledge); reluctance to commit to a long-term, weekly schedule; and lack of a common church policy regarding children's behavior and disciplinary needs are some of the obstacles to reconstructing the program. Church leaders have begun to plan flexible schedules for teaching and leading. They have scheduled studies to deepen understanding of each other's cultures and training in teaching and facilitating discussion. They want more education and leadership development—the topic is common in committee and church discussions. However, except for the few committed leaders of Educative Ministry, church members seem reluctant to begin rebuilding the educational programs for children and youth and to increase participation in studies for adults. Though knowing that it may be several years before a staff minister for leadership development and evangelism is called, many indicate a preference for waiting until then.

Adequacy of the Ministries to the Sociopolitical and Psychological Dynamics of the Persons Addressed by Those Ministries

The controversy over homosexuality, as indicated above, heightened awareness of North Shore to the need for continual work towards ever-deepening levels of understanding each other's cultural styles of relating and communicating. How and how well they do this is yet to be seen.

Community outreach is discussed often and agreed upon as a major component of North Shore's mission. They have long ministered to the elderly and single persons while providing Christian education and supports for families with children. Responding to the findings of the demographic study with the resources they have will require adjustments in focus, such as addressing the needs of the increasing number of African Americans moving into the area, a larger population of elderly, and the growing number of younger singles.

North Shore already has a foundation of basic programs for ministries with families on which to build. The various congregations and the weekday activities in the building present opportunities for increasing and refocusing ministry. Besides the Sunday school, after-school, basketball, and other youth programs, contacts could be made, for instance, through the bus ministry to senior sites and the YWCA day care. Ms. Park could use family-to-family assistance with members of the Korean congregation in their learning English and American social practices and in providing transportation. She feels that Korean children need more attention from the church because they must be both fully Korean at home, learning all the customs and traditions, and fully American at school and elsewhere. Korean children are very lonely because Koreans make contacts and relationships family-to-family rather than friend-to-friend. If their parents are not socially comfortable with English or if American parents are not accessible for building family-to-family or home-to-home ties, the connections between Korean children and others are not made. Korean families with children often have enough money for family activities; but, if both parents work, they lack energy and time.

Another program on which to build is the counseling center. The change in who uses the counseling center may provide an opportunity. According to the director, a gradual shift from North Shore members in counseling (52 percent in 1989 to 23 percent in 1993) to nonmembers (48 percent in 1989 to 77 percent in 1993) "may suggest that the Counseling Center has become more of a Missional ministry to the community than it is a Shepherding ministry to our own congregation."[46] Without violating the center's integrity or the counselor-counselee relationship, clients can be invited to move into additional involvement and possible membership in the church.

In this section two concrete areas have been described that offer potential for more effectively meeting the needs of people in the community. First, North Shore should adjust its focus of ministry in light of the population changes suggested by the demographic study. Second, they should cultivate to greater advantage the openings they already have available for witness and ministry with families. Reestablishing a comprehensive and holistic program of Christian education is a necessary task. The church will strengthen its ability to address the social and psychological needs of families as members increase their understanding of diverse theologies within the Christian witness and those that form the basis of American Baptist policy statements. It will also do so as members work to understand the cultural differences of each other's patterns of thinking and assumptions about social relationships.

Conclusions

North Shore offers a model of response to the world in that its ministries, particularly those directly and indirectly with families, reflect the complexity of the global microcosm both within and surrounding the church. As noted in the beginning section, the church has financial, spatial, and human resources. It uses many of these for ministry with families as units and with individual family members. It also ministers to families indirectly by focusing on particular problems or issues that families face. It has attempted to maintain a long-standing commitment to families even as forms and relationships are changing while also including those who are single. The attempt to blend these efforts has created a more complex and somewhat different set of dynamics than those of a church who has decided to either adopt an emphasis on families (with children) or, in the interest of inclusiveness, to ignore relationships and develop ministry for individuals. While especially appropriate for larger, urban churches, this model of ministries with families is also appropriate for smaller churches or those with few resources. Informal care requires few spatial or financial resources, and cooperative ministries are highly efficient ways to use scarce resources.

North Shore describes itself as "committed to working for reconciliation and unity among all people." The diverse views and expressions of family exert tremendous influence in their efforts to build relationships between individuals and among groups within their church, neighborhood, and wider community. Subtleties in understanding family structure, function, and "place" in social context create issues and tensions of organization. Organizational issues consume time and energy needed for ministries—not just ministries with families. Yet, working to resolve such issues within the American Baptist framework of soul liberty and inclusion of all who profess belief in Jesus as the Christ has made effective ministry possible. In spite of such setbacks as the dispute over homosexuality, the family ministries of North Shore Baptist Church continue as an informal and cooperatively constructed mosaic of reflecting and extending God's Love.

NOTES

1. 1993–1994 Book of Reports, North Shore Baptist Church, 2,7.
2. Throughout this article, "North Shore" and "the church" will be used where appropriate instead of "North Shore Baptist Church."
3. "A Profile of North Shore Baptist Church" compiled by the Pastoral Search Committee, 1990, 1.
4. From this point throughout the article "congregation" will refer to one or more of the language groups of the church; "church" will designate the whole of North Shore Baptist Church, i.e., the collection of congregations.
5. North Shore Baptist Church Constitution, Article VI.
6. Constitution, Article II.
7. They contracted with Church Information & Development Services, Inc., 151 Kalmus Drive, Suite A-104, Costa Mesa, CA 92626-5900.
8. The church described "community outreach" as meeting needs with evangelism, service provision, and advocacy.
9. The listing in the worship bulletin for the English congregation is of the present morning's events but not of next week's schedule. Many people—visitors and members alike—see it after most of the morning's activities have already taken place. Others do not see it at all. If there are changes in the schedule, they often are not noted in this list. For those who want to attend activities next week, information must be obtained from another source. Consequently, most information among members of each congregation is passed along orally. Some can barely tell what their own congre-

gation is doing, much less what the other congregations are doing. Unless accompanied by a member, visitors are almost entirely uninformed.

10. Information for this section was gathered through interviews with Senior Pastor Marcus Pomeroy, participant observation, informal conversations with many members, and "A Profile of North Shore Baptist Church," 1990.

11. Marcus C. Pomeroy, "Families and Faith," sermon delivered June 19, 1994.

12. Marcus C. Pomeroy, "The Morning Prayer," from the service of June 19, 1994.

13. Information for this section was taken from interviews with Manette Monteclaro, Rudolfo Mayol, and Mary Florence Abiera; conversations with others; participant observation; and "A Profile of North Shore Baptist Church," 1990.

14. From a taped interview with Senior Pastor Pomeroy on August 1, 1994, in which he also stated, "Homosexuality is a sexual orientation, it doesn't have anything to do with our relationship to God; homosexual marriages are appropriate as an attempt to bring faith and sexuality into responsible [living]." About the covenant service of a Baptist clergyman and his partner, the senior pastor said that he reported to the church "that he didn't have all the details worked out for himself as to appropriateness or inappropriateness, but he honored their effort."

15. Information for this section was gleaned from interviews with Pastor Carlos Sanchez, participant observation, and "A Profile of North Shore Baptist Church," 1990.

16. Information for this section came from interviews with Pastor Masaru Nambu and "A Profile of North Shore Baptist Church," 1990.

17. Information for this section was taken from an interview with Young Ran Park, minutes of the Official Board, and "A Profile of North Shore Baptist Church," 1990.

18. In addition to those just described, the church organized a Chinese Mission School in 1926 with members teaching English and the Bible to more than one hundred Chinese on a one-to-one basis until 1940. Later a Chinese Sunday school was started, which became the Chinese North Shore Baptist Church in 1959. This church moved into its own building in 1981. Currently, as Chicago Chinese Baptist Church, it maintains close ties with North Shore in that many people retain membership in both churches and North Shore's secretary is the sister-in-law of the Chinese church's first pastor.

19. Three members said independently that each congregation is entitled to two deacons serving on the Official Board. A formal statement of such is not in the constitution, bylaws, or the minutes (1988–present) of the Official Board.

20. In Pastor Nambu's words, "Asian expression is often through nonverbal, while American communication is verbal. Asian communication style is indirect in both verbal and physical while the American way is direct" (in

written answers to "Questions for Ministers of North Shore Baptist Church," 8–9). See Edward C. Stewart, *American Cultural Patterns: A Cross-Cultural Perspective* (Yarmouth, Maine: Intercultural Press, 1972, 1985) for a good description of the consequences for communication of cultural differences in patterns of thinking and assumptions about the self, world, activity, and social relations.

21. James Fong, November 6, 1994, Sunday worship service.

22. Intrachurch cooperative programs for North Shore are those in which people of more than one or all of the congregations work together.

23. "Report of the Pastoral Counseling Center for calendar year 1993," H. Rhea Gray, 1993–1994 Book of Reports, 15–17.

24. Information in this paragraph was drawn from interviews with Dorothy Lauderback and Ezelle Sherrod, participant observation, and conversations with Elizabeth Grapentine.

25. From promotional materials received from and telephone conversation with Kim DeLong.

26. Wade Clark Roof and William McKinney, *American Mainline Religion: Its Changing Shape and Future* (New Brunswick, N.J.: Rutgers University Press, 1987), 90.

27. Roof and McKinney, *American Mainline Religion*, 88.

28. Constitution, Article II.

29. An American Baptist Policy Statement represents the position of the American Baptist Churches on a broad issue. Each policy statement lays down the principles on which American Baptist resolutions and American Baptist program and/or action on the issue will be based. American Baptist Policy Statements are adopted by the General Board of the American Baptist Churches U.S.A.

30. The "Policy Statement on Family Life" is a seven-page document, first adopted in June 1984 and then modified in September 1992 to reflect changes in ethnic designations (e.g., from "Blacks" to "African Americans," from "Native Americans" to "American Indians").

31. The policy statement entitled "The Church Is Family" was adopted in June 1989.

32. "Policy Statement on Family Life," 2.

33. Ibid., 3.

34. Ibid., 4–5.

35. Ibid., 5–7.

36. Walter B. Shurden provides a recent compilation of statements of Baptist distinctives in *The Baptist Identity* (Macon, Ga: Smyth & Helwys, 1993).

37. Ahn Sang Nim, *We Dare To Dream: Doing Theology as Asian Women,* ed. Virginia Fabella and Sun Ai Lee Park (Maryknoll, N.Y.: Orbis Books, 1990), 128.

38. Thomas L. Schubeck, *Liberation Ethics: Sources, Models, and Norms* (Minneapolis: Fortress Press, 1993), 4–5.

39. Eleazar S. Fernandez, *Toward a Theology of Struggle* (Maryknoll, N.Y.: Orbis Books, 1994).
40. Fernandez, *Toward a Theology of Struggle* 57–58.
41. Ibid., 56.
42. Ibid., 57.
43. Ibid., 4.
44. Ibid., 5.
45. Masaru Nambu, a response to "Questions for Ministers of North Shore Baptist Church."
46. "Report of the Pastoral Counseling Center," 17.

9

Robinson Community AME Church

A Church's Response of Liberation and Healing to Its Community

DENISE SENTER

Like most major cities, Indianapolis, Indiana, faces the challenges, opportunities, and threats that affect the quality of daily living for many of its citizens. These challenges and threats are due to crime, inadequate housing, health concerns, drugs, and inadequate education. Shifts in the economy, education, and employment also hold tremendous power in the lives of families. These shifts impact individuals and families in ways that are particular to the political and technological times in which we find ourselves. Perhaps now, as never before, individuals and families sense that they are not in charge of the communities in which they work and live. What then is the task or place of the church? Who is the reconciling agent that brings individuals and families together to reclaim their investment in the hope and vitality of their lives?

In the city of Indianapolis one example of this reconciling agent comes in the form of the Robinson Community AME Church and its pastor, Rev. E. Anne Henning Byfield. Located on the central northside of the city, Robinson Community Church is situated within a neighborhood that is rich and complex in its diversity of people, needs, and influences.

The Nature of the Study

This study explores this congregation's understanding of itself as family, prophetic ministry, and community. To begin an investigation into this church's identity and family ministry, a series of personal interviews with congregational members and staff were conducted. In addition, information gleaned from observations of congregational meetings and worship services were utilized. The study is guided by six important questions: How does the church define itself for its particular community and context? How do members define "family" and how do they define the church's ministry in light of their self-understanding as family? What do members find important in responding to and supporting the congregation? How has the church's historical context shaped its present focus? What are the social, cultural, and economic contexts that shape the congregation's present and future foci? How is family defined through the theology and organization of the church?

For the purpose of investigating these six concerns, a qualitative analysis of Robinson Community Church's ministry—its sense of congregational and community identity and commitment—is viewed from the congregation's perspective. A sample of the congregation was selected for in-depth interviews. This sample included ministerial staff, husband-and-wife families, single-parent families, senior members, and single members. These members and families volunteered to become participants in this study.

I believe that one's locus of concern cannot be separated from one's context. In considering the six questions of this study, I believe that the context of the congregation's social, cultural, historical, and economic being must be addressed in order to come to an appropriate and critical view of the congregation as a whole. For this purpose, I have employed an interdisciplinary approach in this analysis. I am applying a narrative approach in which the understanding of the life story of a person within a family system and the history of a congregation are seen in analogy to hermeneutics of texts as they are developed by feminist and womanist theologians. A hermeneutically sensitive approach that incorporates the psychological, sociological, historical, and theological influences on Robinson Community AME Church reveals the rich complexities and uniqueness of this congregation's life.

In addition to a sensitivity for the contextual framework, I have listened carefully to common metaphors that provide significant self-identification and understanding for this congregation's view of family (as individual members and as a congregation as a whole). Metaphors that emerged in interviews—home, sanctuary, death, and Sabbath—were applied as a means to speak coherently about this congregation's self-identity. These metaphors gave meaning to how Robinson sees itself in its particular location, how it uses its space, and how dignity is recognized and shared. What emerges from these expressions is the congregation's understanding of community building, congregational empowerment, and liturgical witness.

As a final note, it is important to state the limitations of this study.

The process of determining the participants of the study was not "scientific" in that it did not employ a random means of obtaining individuals for interviews. Whenever a nonrandomized process is used, one has to be careful in making generalized statements regarding the larger group being considered. Those who volunteered may present views that may be biased in particular ways, or only present information that is deemed favorable to the ministry as a whole. However, due to the representative makeup of this congregation's sample, which included a good cross-section of the membership, I believe these concerns are minimized. The makeup of the interview groups, the experience of congregational meetings, and the worship experiences were appropriate to this study and yielded the means for an intensive investigation of the beliefs of Robinson Community AME Church and its particular response to the call of God to be co-creator and co-sustainer in the care of its members and community.

Robinson Community AME Church History

The history of Robinson Community is rooted in the African Methodist Episcopal Church tradition of liberation, independence, and community.[1] Robinson Community AME was begun in 1983 by three founding families: Bishop Hubert Nelson Robinson, then presiding bishop of the 4th Episcopal District, AME Church; Rev. Dr. William Sampson Nelson, presiding elder of the South District Indiana Annual Conference; and Rev. Charles and Mrs. Mary Beadles. Bishop Robinson desired to establish a church due to the lack of a major black church on the central north side of the city. It was his desire to meet the needs of the surrounding community, including those who were unchurched and those who desired an Afrocentric church for African Americans. While most AME churches are seated (have congregations or people committed to supporting them) prior to their construction, Bishop Robinson and the two other founding families began building without a dedicated (seated) congregation.

The new church began in the home of Rev. and Mrs. Beadles. Robinson Church began with a congregation of twenty-five adults and sixteen children. When Robinson Church moved out of the Beadles home, it met during the afternoons at Coppin Chapel AME Church, and moved to its present location on June 21, 1982. Blackburn and Associates, an architectural firm owned by an African American architect, built the Robinson building.

The name Robinson Community Church is born out of the dedication and work of Bishop Hubert Nelson Robinson. Bishop Robinson asked that "Community" be added to the name of the building as it reflected his vision of ministries for the church. On August 27, 1983, the Indiana Annual Conference at Bethel AME Church, Indianapolis, officially recognized Robinson Community AME Church.

Three male pastors were the leaders of the newly seated church from 1983 to 1989. In December 1989, Rev. E. Anne Henning Byfield was assigned as pastor. Prior to her assignment at Robinson, Rev. Byfield was successful as pastor of Bethel AME Church in Bloomington, Indiana, for ten years. As pastor of Robinson, Rev. Byfield is intrinsically connected with the community. She, her husband, Ansley, and their seventeen-year-old son, Michael, live in the neighborhood.

The members of this early Robinson Church were members of families that began the congregation, as well as residents of the neighborhood; many had never belonged to a church and were unfamiliar with church rituals, religious teaching, and services. Approximately 40–45 percent of the congregation had not been active church members in their adult lives. This presented a challenge for the ministry, as these members had no model for how to do the work of the church. Rev. Byfield was consciously aware that her work involved creating the model. As such, in 1993, with a congregation of approximately 250 adults, Rev. Byfield set forth a six-point Vision of the Church, outlining objectives and strategies for programs and activities involved in worshipping, teaching, empowerment, evangelizing, giving, and administrative functions. In accordance with this Vision, the purpose of the church was "to liberate, educate, consecrate and demonstrate."

Robinson Community affirms a black theology of worship that is born out of the black religious experience and the African Methodist Episcopal tradition. It continuously prepares itself for expanding its worship experiences, which are liturgically appropriate, charismatic, and participatory. The worship experience includes diversity in music, diversity in the types of evening worship services (teaching/musical/healing services), celebration of Kwaanza, services commensurating such annual observations as Black History Month, and special services honoring men, women, children, and senior citizens.

Robinson affirms a Bible-based teaching that leads to wholeness, empowerment, and liberation. Its vision for teaching includes the establishment of a coordinated Christian Education Department with a full adult curriculum. Goals include ongoing leadership training, creative and educational children's ministries, and churchwide participation in Christian education classes. Ongoing work and training continue in new members training, Sunday school, youth ministries, vacation Bible school, and Bible study.

As an empowering church, Robinson commits itself to "bringing people to the liberating, reconciling healing power of God." Programs and church-sponsored activities to service the needs of each other include outreach to single adults, men, women, and older adults; grief recovery programs; after-school programs; domestic violence recovery groups; Saturday school; community-based supports (Big Brothers/Big Sisters/Kaleidoscope); and voter registration. Other established outreach programs include substance abuse recovery as well as health education in HIV/AIDS, high blood pressure, diabetes, prostrate cancer, breast cancer, and nutrition. Violent death support groups have been pivotal in the assistance to youth and families of the church and community.

Robinson identifies its purpose to be a church that leads others to the saving knowledge of the Lord Jesus Christ and teaches them to become disciples. Robinson's programs and activities that comprise its evangelizing arm include visitors ministries, a church referral network, participating in targeted visitations to congregant members and members of the community, neighborhood canvassing, and printed materials about its ministry and the church.

Teaching and encouraging the membership in stewardship, sacrifice, targeted giving campaigns, tithing, finance planning, and the support of community ministries are important and integral parts of Robinson's giving vision. The church also focuses on the importance of being responsibly prepared administratively. Robinson is engaged in continuous training of its staff in being responsible managers for what God has given the church. The hiring of professional staff, hiring a full-time assistant to the pastor, leadership development, apprenticeship training, acquiring needed materials and equipment, and maintaining a sound building are examples of the administrative vision of the church.

Given the vast scope and objective of Robinson's vision, a long-range and strategic plan has been its outgrowth. Initially, when Rev. Byfield revealed her vision and model for achieving it to the congregation in 1994, the response of the membership was negative. The congregational impression and critique of her was that she was brash, too assertive, and a woman. Rev. Byfield acknowledges that she had a reputation for be-

ing outspoken and for challenging established patriarchal beliefs, traditions, and rituals based on gender issues. However, her nurturance and
persistence in creating wholistic and sometimes new models in the practice of leadership (preaching and teaching) soon resulted in trust building and membership growth. Rev. Byfield presented a model of how to
empower members to develop programs, classes, and groups based on
the needs of the members. In the past two years, members have grown
to learn how to take on more leadership in the development and maintenance of programs and outreach.[2] Three major concerns form the
foundation of Robinson's overall plan/vision: family preservation—e.g.,
teen parenting and building stronger family unity; stemming community chaos—e.g., intervening in illiteracy, homelessness, and estrange-
ment of the underprivileged due to victimization and deprivation,
increasing one's sense of stewardship for the earth, and making education a priority; and economic development—e.g., management and
investment of funds, personal and finance assistance, endowment development, entrepreneurial interests, and church financial development.

Robinson as "Family"

As a result of the re-visioning of their long-range plan, the members
of Robinson are conscious of lending support to each other, to become
interdependent as a family of members united by their faith. Members
of the Robinson Community AME Church have defined "family" as a
collection of individuals who may be children, single women and men,
single parents, or married couples (with or without children), who provide a sense of trust, stability, tradition, patience, and respect for difference among themselves. Within their definition of "family" there is an
emphasis on the provision of space for addressing the needs of members, whether there be common interests or differences. For Robinson
Community AME, family is an eclectic group of people gathered for the
purpose of growth and healing.

Robinson Community sees itself as representing a haven, sanctuary,
or place of safety for children and families. Robinson offers a place
where one is affirmed and, psychologically speaking, offered a nurturing "holding environment" so that one can grow spiritually, to become
empowered to live responsively and creatively. Approximately 75 percent of the congregation is age forty or under, with a large participation
of youth and children. Children are important members of Robinson

Community Church. Their presence is incorporated into the life and mission of the congregation. Children and youth at Robinson Community are provided with a loving, nurturing, and age-appropriate environment in which they learn about God's love for them, and how to love others. An accomplished and dedicated staff of teachers offer creative teaching methods, which include an African American curriculum. Robinson's goal in its ministry to children and youth is to supplement the family, and to lay a spiritual foundation for all teaching that will enable them to live fulfilling and liberating lives. Robinson offers Sunday school for young children to age seventeen. An Allen youth group offers youth ages twelve to seventeen life skills using biblical principles evoked through arts and crafts, activities, and field trips. The Young People's Department of the Mary I. Robinson Missionary Society teaches youth community and church work through mission principles and field work. Robinson also offers Boys 2 Men and Girls 2 Women groups (ages eight to seventeen for boys, and ages twelve to seventeen for girls) in which one-to-one mentors, group discussions, field trips, and recreation instill valuable rights-of-passage lessons, experiences, and rituals.

Theologian Ursula Pfafflin[3] speaks of the symbolic expression of "fruit of our labor" in the context of mothering and being able to provide "good enough"[4] connections between our own values, concrete behavior, and ways of relating with the ways of our children within their environment and context. She speaks of "a betrayal of the fruit of our labor" as a "discrepancy between my vision of connective, respectful, creative life for which I invest in their daily work as mother and a professional, and the concrete reality of disconnecting non-respectful, uncreative cultural and economic developments on which I have very little influence."[5] This "betrayal" is all too often the reality of children and youth who, now more than ever, face threats to their basic rights of survival. Robinson Community's children and youth have not all been spared this harsh reality.

During a period from 1993–95, the church experienced crisis and challenges in its membership. A young girl who had been a member of the congregation was murdered. Her death was a terrible shock for the congregation and ministerial staff. Parents reported to Rev. Byfield that their children were acting out. They began having problems at school. Parents began having problems with their children at home; few of the youth had a means of talking about their pain. Out of the pain and need of the youth to make sense of their companion's death, several grief support groups were initiated.

Given the threats to the survival of the community's young people through gang or random violence, substance abuse, sexually transmitted diseases, and self-inflicted death, the grief support groups began to attract persons from the wider community. The grief support ministry, known as Grief, Loss and Share groups, was initiated by Rev. Byfield and is presently sustained by professional congregant members. These groups support those who have experienced the death of a loved one or suffered a significant personal loss through divorce, prolonged sickness, or any kind of separation. Robinson seeks to bring restoration and support in the process of healing from such loss. Rev. Byfield and members of the church have gone to the sites of gang-related shootings or deaths in the neighborhood to offer prayer. As such, Robinson views itself as presenting a model for proclaiming and providing a paradigmatic experience of sanctuary. The church offers a practical theological experience of sanctuary as a place where God and his creation meet among and with each other. God's act with Jesus brought sanctuary with and among persons. Sanctuary is now how God can be among Robinson where its members are, rather than a place that is outside and above them. If death comes to the neighborhood, sanctuary and succor must be found where death is. The offering and the finding of sanctuary means offering and finding peace. New life emerges through mourning. From this practical theological standpoint, Robinson has learned to transcend death.

The ministerial life of Robinson Community AME Church utilizes the metaphors of death and resurrection as lived experiences within the church. Robinson has witnessed death in its membership, as well as in the growth of its membership. In fall 1990, membership stagnated to an average of forty-five to fifty people on Sundays. For nearly seven months, membership stayed consistently low. However, during this period, singles groups, family nights, and other support programs were initiated and continued. Through the effective nurturing and care of the needs of its members, Robinson has also witnessed a resurrection. Membership has grown from 250 members in 1995 to 500 members currently. In the past eighteen months, people from the surrounding neighborhood have been coming to church. The church budget has increased from $150,000 to over $273,000 in two years. Robinson has instituted a Commission on Social Action that serves a ministry and opportunity for the members of the congregation to take active parts in the various programs for community outreach. The size of the church membership, however, does not accurately reflect the impact of Robinson Church to the Indianapolis community at large.

Robinson Community defines itself as called to make a difference by serving the total needs of its members and people from all walks of life regardless of age, gender, national origin, race, economic background, or impairment. The membership of Robinson Community Church is predominately African American and is diverse in its economic and education makeup. Members range from those who have not completed high school to corporate executives and business owners. Its ecumenical outreach services welcome a diversity of participants in ethnic and religious experiences. Robinson annually hosts a Celebration of Hope ecumenical service, comprised of several Indianapolis churches. The aim of the service is to break down barriers and achieve a breakthrough of racial and denominational harmony. Rev. Byfield is assisted in her ministry by a dedicated ministerial and administrative support staff. The staff includes an assistant pastor, a church administrator, a staff minister, and several lay ministers. An active Board of Stewards and Board of Trustees oversee the spiritual development of the life of the church, the administrative life, and the needs of the physical building. The Commission on Public Relations provides information about the ministries of Robinson Community through printed materials and the media. A radio ministry on a local FM station is broadcast three times each week.

Interviews with church members, a local community program director who has worked with Robinson Community's outreach programs, and a local minister provide a consensus that Robinson's community outreach within Indianapolis is what impresses them about the church and its members. Robinson is well known for its community advocacy, its social justice, and practical liturgical witness. In several critical events in the civil life of Indianapolis, Robinson has presented itself as a leading model for the concern of social and economic justice, safety, health education, and ecumenical witness.[6]

In the northside neighborhoods located near Robinson Community Church, disenfranchisement, drugs, and poverty provide an ongoing assault and threat to many citizens. Despite the efforts of parents who are dedicated to being "good enough" mothers and fathers, violence, disease, drugs, abuse, and miseducation too often leave parents, families, and citizens feeling unable to control what happens in their home and environment. The dedication of Robinson Community to supplement the efforts of parents and families by offering a good-enough holding environment[7] is exemplified in the existence of the Village House.

The Ministry of Village House

Liberation is knowledge of self; it is a vocation to affirm who I am created to be. Furthermore, it is clear from divine revelation as witnessed in Scripture that authentic liberation of self is attainable only in the context of an oppressed community in the struggle of freedom.[8]

The Village House was born in March 1985 and is a response to the need for a safe haven (sanctuary) for children and adults. Village House is located in an old fire station (the symbolism of which can not be ignored) that has been leased to the church by the city of Indianapolis. During summer 1995, the surrounding neighborhoods were under siege by civil unrest as a result of an altercation between some members of the Indianapolis Police Department and a few unruly teens. This civil unrest threatened the racial harmony of the neighborhood. Black youths assaulted the property of their white neighbors. In response, Robinson Community opened its sanctuary to host a series of meetings with city leaders, community residents, police, and local organizations. These meetings provided space to identify what was needed for healing and what assistance could be offered by the city of Indianapolis. Most local institutions requested money. Robinson asked for an abandoned fire station in order to expand its community outreach. In a meeting with children and youth, who were residents of the surrounding neighborhoods, young people stated they needed better education, job opportunities, and safety and protection from assault, abuse, or harassment. Village House is a direct response to these expressed wishes of the youth.

In April 1996, Robinson Community AME Church received the keys to their new building. The Robinson Community Foundation organized the mission of Village House in accordance with the church's long-range vision. The twenty-five programs of Village House are formed under the principle of building a sharing, serving community.[9] In building a sharing community, Robinson offers a place for the sharing of resources and a place where other institutions can partner with the community. Some of its projects include food, clothing, and services for homeless children and families; a satellite health facility; satellite testing and services for HIV/AIDS; summer camp; 4H training and foster care; and special needs adoption services.

In building a serving community, Robinson Community offers (or plans to offer) after-school programs, the continuation of a Train to Work program, a computer literacy program, literacy programs for adults, life enhancement for senior citizens, a G.E.D. training program, an alternative school (fall 2000), a Performance Academy (spring 1998), and the ongoing Peacemaking Program for children in kindergarten through eighth grade, with the focus on children ages five through nine. This program focuses on teaching peacemaking and conflict management skills.

Under strategies for building a healing community, Village House offers housing for the support groups of the church (Domestic Violence; Violent Death; and Survivors of Incest, Rape and Molestation). Village House also provides space for the church's African American Life Enrichment program (done in collaboration with a local college and two other community service programs), the Boys 2 Men and Girls 2 Women groups, a drug intervention and education program, the Interdenominational Churches for Educational Excellence program, and the Youth Diversion program. Village House proposes to be a future site for a Teen Court. The Interdenominational Churches for Educational Excellence program is committed to encourage and sustain educational excellence among all students, in particular African American students. Activities include math and science support, writing workshops, and field trips.

Under the talented leadership of Director Teresa Thomas, Village House is an outreach for the healing of families within the community. "We can have activities and programs for children and youth, but they cannot fully heal unless the family heals. This is not to say that programs and activities don't help. They do, but the outreach must go to the whole family and community," states Ms. Thomas. Because some families and parents in the community struggle with drug addiction and their children often are impacted by drugs, Village House plans to establish a drug intervention program.

Ms. Thomas trains young people and adults in conflict management as part of the mission's Peace-Making Program. Ms. Thomas brings to Village House a wealth of knowledge and experience in youth programs and employment training. Her personality and style, particularly in working with members of the city's gangs, give her credibility and authenticity in her relationships with youth.

The aim of the Family Conflict Resolution training is to reduce family stressors that can escalate to produce emotional and/or physical domestic violence. Ms. Thomas stated, "Resolution to conflict is a learned behavior, so what we do is teach parents and children how to deal with conflicts. Much of what happens is combating beliefs, attitudes, and influences such as TV, rap music, gangs, peers, and even parents who engage in fighting." Both the Peace-Making and Conflict Resolution programs have curriculum developed by Ms. Thomas that address the personal, psychological, social, and spiritual aspects of peacemaking.

The Homeless Program is also focused on youth and is a unique program that addresses the particular interests and needs of children and youth who are without permanent residences. Some of these children come from addicted or abusive parents. Some youth may choose to be homeless because their residences are not safe. Other children and adolescents, because of their behavior, end up in Juvenile Services and become at risk of homelessness due to parents who have all but given up on them.

Robinson Community AME Church, through the services of Village House, offers a youth diversion program for ages eight through seventeen years. Youth who have one to five assault or drug charges are eligible to be referred to the Village House program by the juvenile court. Due to the existence and success of this program, schools, clergy, parents, and even the program participants make referrals. "The aim of the diversion program is to break the cycle of involvement with the justice system before they get into the adult system, which usually happens at the age of sixteen. There are instances when youth are referred because they are exhibiting behavior that places them at risk of getting involved with the juvenile system, but who have yet to be arrested," explains Ms. Thomas. She further explains that "youth in the program themselves learn to recognize the behaviors that get them into trouble and they want to involve their brothers, sisters, cousins, or friends." Each cycle of the program meets four hours a week (meeting twice a week for two hours per session) for a period of fifteen weeks. Several youth who have completed the program can identify when they begin to relapse into their former risky behavior and call Ms. Thomas to reconnect or ask if they can come back into the program.

One success story is of a young man who had a history of gang involvement; he was expelled from school and had a particular problem in getting along with white people. However, while he was a participant in the Village House program, he ceased from his gang activities and ceased selling drugs. Although he had some difficulties after leaving the program, he has since become an active member in church and no longer participates in his old patterns of behavior. According to Ms. Thomas, this young man's story is not unlike several of the youth who participate in the diversion program.

The Training to Work Program offers training to adults and youth on preemployment work maturity skills. The program also assists participants in finding employment. The aim of the program focuses on job retention skills that incorporate conflict resolution. Ms. Thomas uses the concepts of "winning and losing" to teach principles of managing good work habits and skills of conflict resolution. "If a person is driven by winning, then when they get on the job they will remember what it takes to manage a conflict well (win) and not get fired."

One of the most impressive examples of Robinson's commitment to families occurred in March 1997 during the spring break vacation from school. Robinson Community and Village House recognize that the spring break vacation offers gangs a peak opportunity to recruit new members. For a low-income family having to provide food or daycare, the increased need to provide food and childcare during school vacations can be overwhelming. In an effort to support families, Robinson Community offered Village House as a safe, supervised home for young people during spring break. The members of Robinson Community responded in a united effort by volunteering services for cooking, playing with children, fixing up the facility for the activities, providing assistance by filing papers, and assisting in parenting. For one recently relocated family, the witness provided by Village House during spring break confirmed their sense that Robinson Community Church was the church for them. Robinson Community's sense of unity and support for the different programs offered as sanctuary displays their concept of family and an understanding of what is required in the nurturing, building, and healing of the family—whether they be individual members, children, adolescents, couples, or senior citizens. The lived witness of Robinson Community reflects their belief that the heart of their work is family work.

Who Do You Say That I Am?

Rev. Anne Henning Byfield understands that the doing of theology and the understanding of who God is is related to the social, political, and economic realities in which people find themselves. Don Browning may describe the work of Robinson Community AME Church as a "self conscious community of moral discourse."[10] Jacquelyn Grant, an ordained elder in the AME Church and theologian, speaks of three arguments theologians (and pastors such as Rev. Byfield) may make about the concern of who Jesus is, in the context of a black perspective. These arguments are: "1) the human condition results from the conscious (or unconscious) ethical decisions of human beings, 2) the divine reality is on the side of the oppressed, poor, the outcast, the wretched, the downtrodden; and 3) therefore the gospel reveals that the primary intention of God in the incarnation is one of liberation."[11] Rev. Byfield's method of theology is self-described as "womanist" or "afro-centric liberation theology." Her task, and that of Robinson Community, is to critically look at traditions, and to revise and correct them according to the experiences and situations to which that tradition does not adequately speak.[12] Paul Tillich contended that there is a point where individual experience, traditional valuation, and personal commitment must decide what is theology.[13] As Grant speaks of the inseparability of racism/sexism/classism, Tillich spoke of the interrelatedness of love, power, and justice. Rev. Byfield's ministry and leadership as defined from an afrocentric/womanist/liberation context provides an appropriate hermeneutic exploration and interpretation with other womanist theologians who emphatically point to the need to reconstruct traditional Christian theology to include experiences of women, of women of color and other cultures—along with their literature, art, and myths—to reinterpret the understanding of God and develop a more wholistic theology.

Robinson Community AME Church and Rev. Byfield incorporate this understanding of theology into its training of staff, as well as in the educational programs of the church. Robinson has begun to involve itself in a faithful and ongoing process of "reflective and considered understanding of the Christian faith; an understanding that is self-critical and keeps checking itself as to its appropriateness to that which it seeks to understand."[14] Rev. Byfield and Robinson Community are faithful to the African Methodist Episcopal tradition while engaging in a hermeneutical process that reinterprets and corrects tradition. Clark Williamson and Ron Allen, in *The Teaching Minister,* suggest thinking of tradition as a verb, not a noun; as a process, not a thing: "When we pass on a tradition, which families do when they tell stories from the family history, we also incorporate people into a tradition. Not to be incorporated into a tradition is not to know who you are, to whom you are related, where you come from, or where you are going. To 'tradition' is to engage in a socio-historical process."[15]

Robinson Community exemplifies what Williamson and Allen call "living tradition." "Looking upon tradition as a socio-historical process enables us to see how it is as true to say that we have no intelligence without tradition as it is true to say that a tradition without intelligence is not worth having. Living tradition is tradition that is 'perpetually criticized and brought up to date under the supervision of . . . orthodoxy (orthodoxy means correct thinking, not correct thought)."[16] However, by what standards do Rev. Byfield and the members of Robinson Community Church reinterpret their faith? This author's interpretation of the interviews presented for this study suggest that Robinson's hermeneutical principles, the self-evident truths by which Robinson understands itself as a church and its work in the community, are found in "the prophetic and the constitutive" truths of the Christian faith. An explanation of what is defined as prophetic and constitutive is supplied by Williamson and Allen:

> The constitutive axiom re-presents to us God's special love for us, for each of us in this community and for this community, while the prophetic recalls to us God's love for all of God's creatures as well as God's commandment that we do justice to all of them. The constitutive promise of God's love and the prophetic command that we love and do justice are wrapped up with the overall theocentric emphasis in this way: The gospel, the good news, is that God is the God of a singular promise and a singular command: the promise of God's love offered freely graciously, to each and all and the command that we are to love God with all our selves and to love (do justice to) our neighbor as ourselves.[17]

A Prophetic and Historical Woman

The remarkable development of family ministry at Robinson Community Church demonstrates the creative power of leadership in renewing Christian tradition in response to community need. Rev. E. Anne Henning Byfield has been described by her colleagues in ministry as "a prophetic woman," "a powerful teacher," and "a woman of historical firsts." As described in a written reflection of Robinson Community, an Indianapolis ordained minister and member of a large Disciples congregation stated:

> I am much impressed with the ministry of Rev. Anne Henning Byfield. I find her to be an extraordinarily gifted individual, the least of her talents being that she is a woman. I feel she brings much to her office as pastor, but more strikingly as community advocate, supporter, and defender of basic dignities.

Shortly following the community disturbance on College Avenue a few years ago, who was it that I saw among the first to respond to the potential threat of violence which seemed to be precipitated by the massive police presence? She like her sister Deborah, the prophetess (Judges 4:4), was in the midst of the conflict, calling for the Community to respond in ways that would maintain the peace. At the same time, she was calling on the police not to overreact and incite the community or to bring them to violence. She warned them (the police) to remember and realize that while they had a duty to restore order, they also had the duty to protect the very citizens who were on the streets of our city.

When it comes to preaching, it's best to put aside traditional ideas concerning the effectiveness or ability of women in the ministry, because Byfield can stand her ground against the best of them (men and women). She is the consummate minister-preacher, if you will. Sometimes I think that ministers (male) often forget who it first was who brought the news to Jesus' disciples. She (Mary) had seen the Lord alive; by Jesus giving her the command, "Go tell the disciples," equals the same inner command that calls and places many men into ministry.

An interview with a woman who served as chairperson of several ecumenical services hosted by Robinson Community Church addresses the church's commitment to being a healing community. Debra Lampkins, chairperson and founder of the Women of Color Dialogue Conference, provided the following testimony:

My initial contact with Rev. Byfield was in 1994 when I was working with the Indiana Community AIDS Action Network (ICAAN) in putting together a conference for local clergy. Rev. Byfield was one of the ministers who would attend the conference planning meetings. She is one of the few African American ministers who have embraced those impacted by HIV/AIDS and their families. She tries to give them a sense of comfort and belonging. For the past three years Robinson has hosted The National Black Church Day of Prayer for the Healing of AIDS. This multicultural and interdenominational service occurs on the first Sunday in March. Rev. Byfield and Robinson Community Church have been asked to serve in some capacity with agencies such as the Indianapolis Damien Center, Indiana Cares, and the Indiana Community AIDS Action Network: agencies all serving and caring for individuals and families impacted by HIV/AIDS.

This has been important particularly since African Americans and people of color are the fastest growing victims of this disease.

In 1994 Robinson Community Church hosted the Women of Color Conference. This conference served to address the lack of dialogue or network between women concerning women's health. This conference was largely attended by African Americans, Hispanics, and a few Asians. Rev. Byfield was instrumental in getting the Hispanic community involved in the conference. Rev. Byfield deals honestly with issues. The location of her church is diverse, affluent, poor, black, white, and it is near other churches serving white and Hispanic communities.

Robinson is a church which enjoys being in the community. Rev. Byfield opens her doors to people who want to serve the community. It reaches beyond its walls to embrace the community.

Making history and being among the first are not sought-after accolades by Rev. Byfield. However, she has represented women and represented them in several significant contexts. When Rev. Byfield accepted her call to ministry, she had been an active member of her AME denomination and was working for AME legislation that called for the inclusiveness of youth and young people in its assemblies. She was ordained in 1980 in Marion, Indiana, and was the only person presented for ordination in her AME ordination process that year. In 1978, when Rev. Byfield was ordained a deacon, she insisted that a woman participate in the ceremony of the laying on of hands. This was the first time that a woman elder (Rev. Marion Jones, itinerate elder) had ever laid hands on anyone during an AME ordination.

In 1987, Rev. Byfield became the first black woman president of the Indiana Interreligious Commission on Human Equality. Also, in that same year, she was the first woman to preach to the Indiana AME Annual Conference, the first time in the tradition of the conference that a woman was invited to preach. In March 1990 Rev. Byfield was the first woman to preach the AME Mid-year Convocation—a districtwide meeting that includes the states of Michigan, Wisconsin, Minnesota, and Indiana in addition to Canadian provinces. In 1991 Rev. Byfield was the first woman delegate from Indiana to the AME General Conference. Prior to her call to preach, Rev. Byfield worked with the U.S. Department of Labor, where she managed equal opportunity programs—one of the first women in the area hired for the position.

Her ministry has not gone without deep pain, struggle, or questions. When she accepted her call to ministry, her family, while not directly opposing her, could not provide much aid in discussing models of women in the ministry. She worked with her family and others in dealing with biases of women as ministers. Beliefs such as "women are reactionary, less qualified, less prepared, and tend to be shallow" were dispelled by Rev. Byfield's example.

Rev. Byfield represents the third generation of ministers in her family. She has two brothers and a brother-in-law who are pastors (one brother is an AME bishop, assigned in South Africa). Both of her brothers and her brother-in-law are viewed by Rev. Byfield to be "exceptional in leadership and pastoring." She acknowledges that one brother was very vocal in encouraging her to develop a vision for the church. The other brother was helpful in church counseling, leadership style, and pragmatic strategies. Rev. Byfield speaks of the tremendous respect she has for the men of her family who have supported her.

Such was not always the case with her male ministerial colleagues. As described in an Indianapolis magazine article that featured a profile of Rev. Byfield's ministry, she was shunned at ecumenical events and often not invited or asked to speak if she did attend. Rev. Byfield makes the analogy of her treatment by some male pastors to that of racism. "Men could understand mistreatment. They could understand male gender bashing . . . but they couldn't understand how I could compare sexism to racism."[18]

As a "historical woman," Rev. Byfield creates new and appropriate models for women, children, and families in her preaching. She looks to historical women of the Bible and history to reinterpret the meaning of God's faithfulness, love, and healing in the lives of today's women, particularly women of color. The stories of women pioneers in ministry, such as Rebecca Cox Jackson and Jarena Lee, provide a model for dealing with the difficulties and personal challenges ministry can present. A natural storyteller, Rev. Byfield effectively employs the use of story to illuminate the meaning of the scriptures and its relevance to a current situation. She has her own style and does not try to copy a style to be popular. She does not imitate the style of many black preachers.

Several members of the Robinson Community AME Church compare Robinson to the early black churches. "When Blacks were denied access to inclusion in activities within the larger community, the church provided a place where black people could go and have some kind of power, dignity, respect, and acceptance," stated one member. Robinson provides an opportunity for members to be empowered by focusing on their strengths and then recruits people into activities and functions where they can use their strengths. As stated by one congregant, "Rev. Byfield balances the old and the new. The new is the development of programs which reach out to the community to address modern issues."

NOTES

1. See James Cone, *God of the Oppressed,* (Maryknoll, N.Y.: Orbis Books, 1975), 153. Liberation as the fight for justice has always been important in black religion. The AME church and Richard Allen, its first bishop, were vital in attaining freedom during and after slavery.

2. Through a series of studies and organizational planning, Robinson has undergone a re-visioning process. The years 1995 and 1996 brought about the culmination of Robinson's long-range strategic and spiritual plan. Named "The Vision 2000 and Beyond," the vision of Robinson is "Building lives, Building families, Building church and community." As its mission statement implies, Robinson is a church called by God through the Lord Jesus Christ, to Worship, Proclaim, Teach, Evangelize, Give (Stewardship) and Empower in Indianapolis, the nation and the world; and to make a difference by serving the total needs of its members and peoples from all walks of life.

3. Ursula Pfafflin, a prolific theologian, served as a professor of religion at Indianapolis Christian Theological, where she and I worked together to complete a comparative church study of two urban churches. This original study was to involve Robinson Community AME Church and Our Redeemer Lutheran Church. Her commitments in Germany preceded the completion of this project; however, her contributions were invaluable. As a professor at the CTS, Ursula is remembered and respected as one who represented a voice of the "other." She regularly called others to the recognition, values, and truths of those who are marginalized and/or underrepresented in dominant systems and cultures.

4. Donald Winnicott proposed the first complete two-person theory in psychoanalysis of how the actual interaction between mother and child facilitated the gradual unfolding of the infant's innate potential for growth and development. Winnicott noted, "if the child receives 'good enough' mothering that is both need-satisfying and comforting, the infant's desire for omnipotent control of and fusion with the mother can be gradually given up." See Samuel Slipp, M.D., *The Technique and Practice of Object Relations Family Therapy* (Northvale, N.J.: Jason Aronson, 1993), 41.

5. Ursula Pfafflin, "Betrayal of the Fruit of Our Labor: Influences of Global Economical, Environmental, and Cultural Development on Women, Men, and Children" (Dresden, Germany: Evangelische Fachhochschule fur Sozialarbeit).

6. See Theodore Walker, *Empower the People: Social Ethics for the African-American Church* (Maryknoll, N.Y.: Orbis Books, 1991). Walker speaks of the black church as one that has more power and influence than any other institution in the black community.

7. "Holding environment" is a psychological term often defined as a safe and trusting setting; one that has the ability to withstand hostile, defensive, or aggressive feelings or actions so that one (usually a child, or client) is facilitated in what is essential for healthy psychological growth.

8. Cone, *God of the Oppressed,* 147.
9. See Walker, *Empower the People.* Walker contends that the modern liberal approach to the social question is distinguished from the more conservative approach "by its conviction that public or governmental and other sectors in society should go beyond the conservative public policy agenda (e.g., protecting the right of individuals to do whatever they individually choose to do) so as to include efforts to ensure the social well-being of all members of society" (pp.36–37). See also Nicholas Cooper-Lewter and Henry H. Mitchell, "Soul Theology: The Heart of American Black Culture." The authors note that in black culture, belief in God's justice may be documented as easily in the street as in the church (31).
10. See Don S. Browning, *Religious Ethics and Pastoral Care* (Philadelphia: Fortress Press, 1983), 48. Also compare the discussion on liberal and conservative approaches in setting policy presented by Walker in *Empower the People* and the discussion presented in Don and Carol Browning, "Better Family Values: A New Paradigm for Family Policy Can Bridge the Partisan Gap," *Christianity Today,* February 6, 1995.
11. Jacquelyn Grant, *"White Women's Christ and Black Women's Jesus: Feminist Christology and Womanist Response* (Atlanta: Scholar Press, 1989).
12. Womanist and feminist theologians emphatically point to the need to reconstruct traditional Christian theology, to include experiences of women, of women of color and other cultures, along with their literature, art, and myths to reinterpret an understanding of God and develop a more wholistic theology. Jacquelyn Grant asserts that black women must do theology out of their tridimensional experience of racism/sexism/classism. See Grant, *White Women's Christ.*See also Katie Cannon, *Black Womanist Ethics* (Atlanta: Scholars Press, 1988). Cannon speaks to the necessity of a creative means of cultivating values and virtues relevant to the black community in response to traditions of racism, gender discrimination, and economic exploitation. She addresses the existential and historical contexts from which black women have emerged as moral agents, speaking to their moral wisdom and ethical behavior, which have not been promulgated in dominant ethics or history.
13. See Paul Tillich's discussion of "The Theological Circle," *Systematic Theology,* vol. I (Chicago: University of Chicago Press, 1951), 8.
14. Clark M. Williamson and Ronald J. Allen, *The Teaching Minister* (Louisville, Ky.: Westminster/John Knox Press, 1991).
15. Ibid., 73.
16. Ibid., 74.
17. Ibid., 77.
18. Kathleen Prata, "Women of Faith," *Indianapolis Woman Magazine,* December 1995.